Father Kolbe in Nagasaki

Father Kolbe in Nagasaki

Tomei Ozaki, OFM Conv.

Translated by Shinichiro Araki
Supervised by Kevin M Doak

Father Kolbe in Nagasaki was first published in 1983 by the Knights of the Immaculata in Nagasaki, Japan. The English translation is a book prepared for publication by the Franciscans of the Immaculate [marymediatrix.com], POB 3003, New Bedford, MA 02741-3003.

©Academy of the Immaculate 2021
All rights reserved

Cum Permissu Superiorum
August 14, 2021
Feast of Saint Maximilian Mary Kolbe

ISBN: 978-1-60114-078-4

Book and cover design and production:
Mary Flannery · flannerystudios@comcast.net

Academy of the Immaculate
New Bedford, MA
academyoftheimmaculate.com

CHAPTER 8
Establishing *Mugenzai no Sono*
(the Garden of the Immaculate) 81

CHAPTER 9
Caramels from Our Lady 91

CHAPTER 10
Garden Covered with Snow on the Fiftieth Year 101

CHAPTER 11
Some Petty Daily Incidents 111

CHAPTER 12
The Bearded "Gyoja"............................ 121

CHAPTER 13
The Goat Meat was Tough......................... 129

CHAPTER 14
The Map of India Buried in the Archives................ 139

CHAPTER 15
The Dream of a Friar Sinking in a Swamp............... 149

CHAPTER 16
A Lighthouse Shining on the Mountain 159

CHAPTER 17
The Scent of Holy Virtue in the Soup 169

Table of Contents

PREFACE 1
Friar Tomei Ozaki

INTRODUCTION 3
Professor Kevin M Doak

CHAPTER 1
The Day of Arrival in Nagasaki 11

CHAPTER 2
In and About Oura 21

CHAPTER 3
The Friars and a Visitor from Kyoto 31

CHAPTER 4
The Seminarians Depart 41

CHAPTER 5
An Encounter with Holy Poverty 51

CHAPTER 6
Every Day is Mary's Day 61

CHAPTER 7
An Incident in the First Winter 71

CHAPTER 28
The Promise of Heaven 279

AFTERWORD
Professor Shinichiro Araki 289

INTRODUCTION OF AUTHOR, TRANSLATOR, AND SUPERVISOR 291

CHAPTER 18
Winter in the Room of Flame-Colored Wooden Walls 179

CHAPTER 19
Discord Among the Friars 189

CHAPTER 20
The Cobble-Stone Streets of Rome 199

CHAPTER 21
The Sound of Army Boots in the Distance 209

CHAPTER 22
Summer in the Homeland. 219

CHAPTER 23
Father Kolbe's Letters to his Mother 229

CHAPTER 24
Leaving Everything to *The Knights*. 239

CHAPTER 25
Enduring Chest Pains 249

CHPATER 26
Boys in the Sea Breeze. 259

CHAPTER 27
Farewell to Japan. 269

Preface

Christianity was banned and severely persecuted for more than 250 years during the Tokugawa Shogunate. Nevertheless, some Catholics kept their faith, going underground during this harsh period. In 1865, a French missionary who had entered Japan after the relaxation of the Tokugawa's isolation policy 'discovered' hidden Catholics who had survived in Nagasaki. This discovery is said to have been a miracle in the history of the Church.

In 1930, sixty-five years later, Father Maximilian Kolbe arrived in Nagasaki as a Conventual Franciscan missionary. He started publishing *The Knights of the Immaculata* in Japanese and founded the friary of *Mugenzai no Sono* (Garden of the Immaculate Mary) in Nagasaki. He lived here for six years and left for Poland in 1936, five years before he was killed in Auschwitz.

I have been in the friary Father Kolbe founded for seventy-five years, ever since I was accepted into it at the age of seventeen. It was just after I was in the atomic blast on August 9, 1945. On a rainy day after I had wandered around in the atomic ruins alone, Brother Zeno Zebrowski wiped my face at the entrance of the friary and let me in. I lived there at first as an orphan, then as a friar, with a dozen Polish friars who had faithfully followed the example of Father Kolbe whose own behavior was always consistent with his words.

From these amiable friars, I heard various episodes of Father Kolbe whose life was full of hardship, suffering, joy, and sometimes laughter, and even anger. These human features of Father Kolbe that I learned from the Polish friars fascinated me and motivated me to write about his life in Nagasaki. Their reminiscences, which I wrote down in my notebook, became the source material for the book I published from the Knights of the Immaculata Publisher in Nagasaki in 1983.

It is more than I can dream of, if my humble description of Father Kolbe leads some readers to become interested in this saint who entirely devoted himself to the Immaculata.

I heartily thank Professor Shinichiro Araki of Nagasaki Junshin Catholic University for translating my book into English for this version.

A special word of thanks also to Professor Kevin M Doak of Georgetown University, who wrote a most suitable introduction to this book from a broad perspective and supervised the whole process of translation.

ON THE FEAST OF THE IMMACULATE CONCEPTION, 2020, NAGASAKI
Tomei Ozaki, OFM Conv.

Introduction to the English Edition

Saint Maximilian Kolbe is best known for offering his life in exchange for a condemned prisoner in the infamous Auschwitz (Oświęcim) concentration camp. He is less known for his deep, personal connection with Japan and the significant impact he has had on the history of Christianity in that country. Indeed, St. Maximilian Kolbe stands alongside St. Francis Xavier, S.J., who brought the Christian faith to Japan in 1549, as two of the most important saints in the history of Catholicism in Japan. Readers of this invaluable book by Friar Tomei Ozaki, OFM Conv., will discover the riches of St. Maximilian Kolbe's engagement with Japan during the six years from 1930-1936 when he lived and worked in Nagasaki. I cannot tell that story as well as Friar Ozaki, nor will I try to do so. Rather, in this brief introduction, I will offer a short history of St. Maximilian Kolbe's life before and after his time in Japan in order to present a comprehensive view of this great saint.

Maximilian was born Raymond Kolbe, the second son of Julius and Maria Dabrowska Kolbe, on January 8, 1894, in the town of Zduńska Wola, an important textile center in the Kingdom of Poland, at the time part of the Russian Empire. Julius was a weaver and of German ethnicity; Maria Dabrowska was an ethnic Pole. The Kolbe family soon moved from Zduńska Wola, eventually settling in Pabianice in 1897. It was in Pabianice where Raymond spent his childhood and where he received his First Communion at St. Matthew's Church on June 29, 1902. It was also at St. Matthew's Church where a formative event occurred shortly after Raymond's

First Communion. Scolded one day by his mother for his boyish behavior, Raymond prayed to the Madonna in St. Matthew's Church to tell him what would become of him. She appeared to him, holding two crowns, a red one (symbolizing martyrdom) and a white one (symbolizing perpetual virginity), and asked him which he would choose. He replied he wanted both. The Virgin smiled and then disappeared. But she never disappeared from Raymond's heart. From that day forward, Raymond Kolbe's spiritual life was deeply shaped by a fervent devotion to Our Lady, especially as the Immaculate One.

In 1907, Raymond and his older brother Francis entered the minor seminary of the Conventual Franciscans in Lwów and it was there where, three years later, he received the novitiate name by which he would become known throughout the world: Maximilian. In the meantime, his parents took a vow of perpetual chastity and lived apart, Maria moving to Lwów where she could be near her sons, and Julius moving to Krakow where he worked as a custodian at the Franciscan Monastery there. In 1912, Maximilian and his brother moved to Krakow to study at the Franciscan seminary, but in October, Maximilian was sent to Rome for advanced studies. Two years later, on November 1, 1914, Maximilian took perpetual vows and adopted the name Maria. Maximilian Maria Kolbe earned his first doctorate in philosophy from the Pontifical Gregorian University in 1915, and he continued his studies in theology at the Pontifical University of St. Bonaventure, more widely known as the Seraphicum. There, along with six fellow students at the Seraphicum, Maximilian Maria established the Knights of the Immaculata (Militia Immaculata, or M.I.) on October 16, 1917. Two characteristics of the Knights were clear from the beginning. First was their strong devotion to the Immaculata as the Mediatrix of All Graces. And part of that devotion was an emphasis on wearing and distributing the Miraculous Medal. The second characteristic was their opposition to Freemasonry. The Freemasons had just commemorated their 200th anniversary in 1917 with large demonstrations in the streets of Rome, even hoisting banners in Saint Peter's Square that read "Satan must reign in the Vatican and the Pope will be his slave." Through the organization of the Knights of the Immaculata, Maximilian Maria Kolbe was determined to resist Freemasonry and any other group or person who would attack the Church.

On April 28, 1918, Maximilian was ordained a priest by Cardinal Basilio Pompili in the Church of Sant'Andrea della Valle. One year later on July 22, 1919, he was awarded his second doctorate, this time in theology from the Seraphicum. He then left Rome, first to teach history at the Franciscan Seminary in Krakow and then to the Franciscan minor seminary in Lwów as novice master.

After only a few months in Lwów, Father Kolbe had developed signs of a serious health condition, one that would plague him for the rest of his life. He had tuberculosis. He was sent to the mountain resort of Zakopane to recover and spent eight months there from August 1920 to April 1921. Then he was sent to Nieszawa for further recuperation from May to November. In spite of the serious health problems Father Kolbe faced, he somehow found the energy to organize a new journal, the *Rycerz Niepokalanej* (*The Knights of the Immaculata*) that began publishing in January 1922 with a first run of 5,000 copies. In October of that year, he moved to the Franciscan friary in Grodno. The time in Grodno was a difficult period for Father Kolbe. There was strong disagreement in the monastery over his introduction of a printing press, struggles over the use of the proceeds from the journal, and the remote location was not ideal for proselytizing. After another eight months of recuperation in Zakopane from tuberculosis, Father Kolbe decided to look for a more appropriate location for his work.

In September 1927, Father Kolbe and a group of friars took possession of a plot of land given them by Prince Jan Drucki-Lubecki located forty kilometers outside Warsaw where they would establish a new monastery. Called "Niepokalanów" (The City of the Immaculata), it would grow to become the world's largest monastery by the outbreak of World War II, with 760 men and its own fire department. Yet, Father Kolbe was still not satisfied. He soon came up with the idea of taking his mission to Japan and establishing a Niepokalanów there and publishing a Japanese edition of the *Rycerz Niepokalanej*. It was an audacious idea. Father Kolbe knew no Japanese, had never been to Japan, and had very little knowledge of the country, its culture or conditions. His constant reply to those who raised such concerns was, "The Immaculata will take care of those things."

Why did Father Kolbe decide to go to Japan? There was a general reason and a specific reason. The general reason is that his religious Order was very much a part of the 1920s rediscovery of missionary zeal among Catholics. Father Alfonso Orlini, the Father General of the Conventual Franciscans, had just sent out a circular letter encouraging the friars to expand their missions abroad. They already had opened a mission in China in 1925 and added a mission in Zambia in 1929. The specific reason is that Father Kolbe had met four Japanese students on a train and had spoken with them and even given them Miraculous Medals. These Japanese students had impressed on Father Kolbe the need to spread the faith in their country where so few people were Christian. On February 26, 1930, Father Kolbe left Niepokalanów in the hands of his brother Father Alfons Kolbe, and he headed for Rome to get permission from his Father General to start a mission in Japan. Father General Orlini and Father Procurator of the Missions Antonio Rocchetti met with Father Kolbe and tried to dissuade him. At least, they argued, he should consider China instead. But Father Kolbe was persistent, confident that proselytizing in Japan was a mission that the Immaculata wanted him to undertake. So on March 7th, Father Kolbe left Marseilles on the freighter *Angers* for Japan, with friars Zeno Zebrowski, Hilary Lysakowski, Seweryn Dagis, and Zygmunt Krol. Out of respect for his superiors, Father Kolbe stopped briefly in Shanghai, where the Catholic millionaire Joseph Lu Bohong (aka Lo Pa Hong) pressed them to remain and to set up their publication center. Father Kolbe was not to be deterred. He left friars Seweryn and Zygmunt in China (they would soon join him in Japan) and sailed on to Nagasaki with friars Zeno and Hilary.

The story of Saint Maximilian Kolbe's life in Japan is best told by Friar Ozaki in the pages that follow. I will pick it up after 1936 when Father Kolbe was called back to Poland to attend the Provincial Chapter of the Conventual Franciscans. At the Chapter, he was appointed guardian of Niepokalanów and therefore was not permitted to return to Nagasaki. He would never again see his adopted homeland of Japan. These were the glory days of Niepokalanów. Under Father Kolbe's leadership it grew into a real city. In November of 1938, *Rycerz Niepokalanej* reached a publication run of one million copies, and before the year was out Niepokalanów Radio was also broadcasting. In May of 1939, Father Kolbe spent two weeks recuperating in Zakopane with Friar Pelagiusz; his mother Maria Dabrowska joined him for one week. These were surely the happiest days of Father Kolbe's life.

On September 1, 1939, Nazi Germany invaded Poland. Less than three weeks later, on September 19th, Father Kolbe and those who had remained with him at Niepokalanów (including a Korean-Japanese, Father Ludwig Kim) were arrested. With the exception of Father Kim (as a subject of Imperial Japan, he was seen as an ally of Nazi Germany) and a few others, Father Kolbe and fellow friars were sent to Lamsdorf prison, then to Amtitz and finally Schildberg (Ostrzeszów). The friars were released on December 8th and they returned to Niepokalanów. Within a few days, 3,500 displaced persons (including 1,500 Jews) had found refuge at Niepokalanów, with Father Kolbe doing whatever he could to care for them. On February 17, 1941, at 11:50 a.m., German officers came to Niepokalanów and arrested Father Kolbe, along with

Fathers Justyn Nazim, Pius Bartosik, Urban Cieslak and Antonin Bajewski. They were taken to the infamous Pawiak prison in Warsaw where overall approximately one-third of the general prison population was executed; the remainder was sent to extermination camps. Father Kolbe was among the latter. On May 28, 1941, he was transported along with over 300 other prisoners to Auschwitz (Oświęcim) where he was given the prisoner number 16670. Immediately upon arrival, Father Kolbe and the other prisoners were greeted with these words: "Jews may live no more than two weeks, priests may live no more than one month, and the rest of you have three months."

On July 29th, a prisoner from Block 14 (Father Kolbe's block) was found missing and presumed escaped (he was later found drowned in the camp latrine). Deputy Camp Commander Karl Fritzsch had announced that should any prisoner escape, ten prisoners from his cell block would be put in the starvation bunker as punishment. As the ten names were read out, one of them, Sergeant Francis Gajowniczek, cried out farewell to his wife and children. Thereupon, Father Kolbe stepped out of line and volunteered to take his place. When Fritzsch asked who he was, Father Kolbe merely replied he was a Catholic priest. With that, the trade was accepted, and Father Kolbe was marched off with the other nine men straight to the starvation bunker. For the next two weeks and two days, Father Kolbe encouraged the men in the starvation bunker with prayers and hymns. On August 14th, a man named Boch entered the bunker and gave Father Kolbe and three other surviving prisoners each an injection of carbolic acid. Father Kolbe had lived for over two weeks without food or water. Now his sufferings were over and he had gone home to be with the Lord.

After the war, Father Kolbe's story gradually became known to many. Rolf Hochhuth's controversial 1963 play *The Deputy* (translated into more than twenty languages) introduced many people around the world to the story of Maximilian Kolbe's self-sacrifice in Auschwitz. One of those was Ayako Sono, the Japanese Catholic novelist, who attended Kolbe's beatification in 1971, and then two years later published *Miracles*, her book about Kolbe. In 1979, her friend the Japanese Catholic novelist Shusaku Endo introduced the main features of Kolbe's life in his short story, "Japanese in Warsaw." And in 1982, Pope John Paul II canonized St. Maximilian Maria Kolbe, his Polish compatriot. But certainly one of the greatest testimonies to the influence of St. Maximilian Kolbe is the organization he started, *The Knights of the Immaculata*. There are now over three million Knights in forty-eight countries. And Seibo no Kishi, the press St. Maximilian Kolbe founded in Nagasaki in the 1930s, is still publishing today. Even as more and more people around the world are discovering this great saint, Friar Ozaki's book is a great reminder that the people of Japan have never forgotten their adopted son, St. Maximilian Maria Kolbe.

Kevin M Doak
GEORGETOWN UNIVERSITY (USA)

CHAPTER 1

The Day of Arrival in Nagasaki

On a spring day after it had rained, Father Maximilian Kolbe and other Knights of the Immaculata landed in Nagasaki and headed directly for Oura Cathedral.

The Rainy Skies of Nagasaki Suddenly Clear Up

In the Nagasaki Prefectural Library surrounded by lush green trees, I opened a file of old copies of the Nagasaki Shimbun newspaper.

April 24, 1930, was a memorable day for the Knights of the Immaculata. It was the day when the first Polish Knights, Father Kolbe and two others, set foot on the soil of Nagasaki. As I looked at the faded, reddish-brown newspaper photo, it seemed as if the bearded Franciscan friars were standing right in front of me. It was a Thursday.

The newspaper reads, "Rainy, then sunny." "London Naval Conference Ends." "Opening of the 58th Imperial Diet." "His Imperial Highness Prince Takamado Travels to Osaka." The large font draws the reader's attention to the headlines. There was an obituary for Father Yosuke Shimauchi of Nakamachi Church. What attracted my interest was the article which reported that the Hongouchi Reservoir filled up after a night of heavy rain following a long drought, and had to be drained of approximately thirty-five centimeters.

Four friars departed for Nagasaki with Father Kolbe.
(Father Kolbe in the middle, Brother Zeno on his left side seen from the front.)

There had been heavy rain and strong winds since the previous night. The passengers on the ship must have been tossed about by the turbulent sea.

Father Kolbe, Brother Zeno and Brother Hilary left China from Shanghai and arrived in Nagasaki the following day.

Father Kolbe arrived at Dejima Wharf, Nagasaki, on the Nagasaki-maru.

THE DAY OF ARRIVAL IN NAGASAKI

Although five friars had set out for Asia on the missionary trip, two of them got off the ship in Shanghai to settle there, and began learning Chinese. The other three left Shanghai for Nagasaki. They sailed on a 5,500-ton steamship that regularly ferried between China and Japan, a ship called "the Nagasaki-maru."

After twenty-six hours at sea, they entered the port of Nagasaki a little after 1:00 p.m.

The rain from the previous night had already stopped, the wind had calmed down a little, and the sky was cloudy.

As the ship entered the port of Nagasaki, it reduced its speed. On the port side, the passengers could see the white church on Kaminoshima (God's Island) and the Mitsubishi shipyard; and on the starboard side, the scenery changed quickly from the French-style building of the "Garden of Mary" orphanage, Oura Cathedral, and Kaisei Junior High School to the Dutch villas. The view of Nagasaki after rain was a fresh and splendid one.

Father Kolbe expressed his first impression in a pithy remark: "This is a beautiful place, with mountains, sea, and greenery" — Nippon, the land of martyrs that they had dreamt of. They must have been deeply moved.

It was after 3:00 p.m. when they arrived in Nagasaki.

Upon landing, they were interrogated by a government official of the Foreign Affairs Division and a police detective. This was because they had come from Poland in East Europe, a country that bordered on Russia. In those days the government authorities of Japan were extremely fearful of communism, and they were on guard against communists, whom they called "Reds," so it's possible that they were extensively interrogated. Brother Zeno did not forget the name of the police detective, Okatsu.

It is not surprising, however, because their connection with Detective Okatsu became much deeper in time to come. Later on, the Knights of the Immaculata settled in Nagasaki. When Japan rushed into the Second World War and looked to be losing the war, the minor seminary Father Kolbe had founded was closed and became an internment camp for enemy aliens. The police officer in charge at the time was the very same Detective Okatsu, who, then too, kept a close eye on the friars.

Brother Zeno told me once what the investigation was like when they landed: "Mr. Okatsu knew Russian. There were Russians in Oura and they had a church there. Detective Okatsu interrogated us. We were equipped with three cameras. Two of them were made in Germany, and the other was made in France. As Nagasaki was a restricted military zone, it was forbidden to take pictures; I was okay with that. Okatsu said nothing. There was a light rain that day. It seemed as if the skies were crying," said Brother Zeno, as he covered his blue eyes with his hands.

First, They Discovered Our Lady

When Father Kolbe came up with an idea of missionary work in Asia, he planned to establish three branches of the Knights of the Immaculata, one each in India, China, and Japan. He selected one friar for each branch: twenty-four-year-old Brother Hilary, twenty-one-year-old Brother Seweryn, and Brother Zygmunt, the youngest, only nineteen years of age. Thirty-two-year-old Brother Zeno was not among them at first.

With his plan in mind, Father Kolbe went to Rome and met with the Minister General of the Order of the Conventual Franciscans who ordered Father Kolbe to go to China and Japan, and to bring two friars to each country.

A telegram was sent to Poland, and the last one selected for the mission was the tough and brave friar, Brother Zeno, who later reflected that when Father Kolbe came to Japan, "he assigned the role of Martha to me and the role of Mary to Brother Hilary."

There were three ways of getting from Dejima Wharf where the ship left them to Oura Cathedral: in a rickshaw, by streetcar, or

Father Kolbe found the statue of Our Lady in front of Oura Cathedral just after he had arrived in Nagasaki.

on foot. Brother Zeno did not remember how they went to the cathedral. They may have ridden in a rickshaw which was common among foreigners; if they walked, it would have taken them thirty minutes.

A steep, stone-paved road leads up to Oura Cathedral, one of Japan's National Treasures. This uphill road must have been hard for Father Kolbe who suffered from lung disease. At the top of the hill, the view suddenly opens up and the white gothic-style, historical building of Oura Cathedral looms large! For a second, Father Kolbe's eyes fixed on the entrance to the cathedral, and then ran to the statue of the Immaculata.

"Oh!" he suddenly cried out in a low voice, turning around to the two friars. "Look! The Immaculata is welcoming us! As we found her right at the start, everything will go well for us in Japan." Father Kolbe smiled.

They had stayed in China for thirteen days. China had seemed the most promising country before their departure from Poland but, once there, they found the reality was not so good. They did everything they could think of, but they never got permission to publish *The Knights of the Immaculata*.

Father Kolbe's missionary method was quite unique. In the past, missionaries would go to unexplored territories and spread the word of God among uncivilized people. Father Kolbe's aim was different. Staying in big cities where people would gather and in the centers of culture, the friars would print and publish the magazine of the *Immaculata* in great numbers, and then distribute them to every home in the area. In this way, the Immaculata would lead all people to God. If enough magazines were published, half of the people on earth would come to know her. This was the bold dream of the thirty-six year old Father Kolbe.

Although the bishop of Shanghai gave his permission to open a branch of the Order and to disseminate the magazine, Father Kolbe could not get permission to publish it there. This was his first setback. The two friars who tried to settle in Shanghai would leave for Nagasaki four months later. In addition, the missionary district assigned to Father Kolbe's Order was in the interior of the country where there was no communication, neither by rail nor by water.

If that is the way things are going to be, then "I don't know what Japan will be like, what surprises the Immaculata is preparing for us there," Father Kolbe wrote from Shanghai.

And that is why they were so delighted when they found the Immaculata in Japan, right from the start! "We have come here for the Immaculata and she welcomed us. Now that we have found her, she will guide us. Let us offer her our youth and passion and follow the guidance of the Immaculata." Father Kolbe's heart beat brighter.

They entered the cathedral and prayed before the same Virgin Mary statue that witnessed the discovery of hidden Japanese Catholics over half a century earlier.

I would like to say in passing that there still remain Marian devotions deeply rooted among Catholics in Nagasaki which have been handed down from the earlier centuries of persecution.

Every Catholic church has a beautiful statue of the Virgin Mary where children, elderly people, and women gather in the evening to pray the Rosary. It was this Saint Mary, Mother of Mercy, who guarded the hidden Catholics during the period of harsh persecution. The discovery of the hidden Catholics, the increase in the number of Catholics in Nagasaki, and the strengthening of their faith were all due to the intercession of our Blessed Mother. We cannot explain the establishment of churches in Nagasaki without referring to our Blessed Mother.

Father Kolbe loved the Immaculata with all his heart, and the Knights who greatly venerated the Immaculata easily became popular among the Catholics of Nagasaki. Of course we should give credit to the efforts of the Knights, but we also should not overlook the fact that Marian devotions like these were deeply rooted among the Nagasaki Catholics.

The terminal port of the *Nagasaki-maru* was Kobe. It is doubtful that the Knights of the Immaculata would have been liked so much, had they gotten off the ship anywhere other than this port in Nagasaki.

After saying their prayers, Father Kolbe and the two friars entered the Bishop's residence.

Following Threads from the Newspaper of that Time

Unfortunately, Bishop Kyunosuke Hayasaka was away on a

Bishop Hayasaka accepted the Knights of the Immaculata in Nagasaki.

trip to Shikoku in search of a philosophy professor for Oura Seminary. As reported in the newspaper of that day, the other priests were also absent, attending the funeral of the late Father Shimauchi at Nakamachi Church. The only priest available was the seventy-two year old Father Paulo Ryo Matsukawa. The old Father Matsukawa heartily welcomed the visitors who had come from so great a distance. Father Kolbe is said to have read into that scene an image of the tender father whole-heartedly embracing his prodigal son who had returned home covered with dirt.

That first encounter with a Japanese priest had a deep impact on Father Kolbe. During the six years he lived in Nagasaki, Father Kolbe admired the old Father Matsukawa as a spiritual director and adviser, and showered him with love and respect.

For his part, Father Matsukawa took a special interest in Father Kolbe's work, and as the Knights of the Immaculata often found themselves in one sort of difficulty or another, he consoled, encouraged, and helped them. Eventually the other priests returned from the funeral. The arrival of the Franciscan friars was the immediate topic of conversation among the five priests. Father Wasaburo Urakawa (later bishop) made the decision as Vicar General to let the friars stay at the Bishop's residence until Bishop Hayasaka returned.

Father Kolbe wrote in a letter: "The Bishop has been absent for a few days. Initially, the Vicar General was difficult, but when he learned that I can teach philosophy in the local seminary, he changed his attitude. He wanted to write to the Bishop to inform him of it, but finally he advised me to write the letter. I wrote the letter and delivered it to the Vicar General. May the Immaculata direct all things! Other priests also want to ask the Bishop for his permission. I hope that he lets us stay here."

Right next to Oura Cathedral is the Bishop's residence, an old red brick building. I wondered which rooms were set up for guests? Brother Zeno and I went there in the summer of 1964. There were private compartments in a second floor room closest to the sea. Brother Zeno told me, "We waited here for the Bishop to return and every day the three of us, first in my room and later in Hilary's room, would gather and pray earnestly that Our Mother Mary's work in Japan would be successful."

This is how the first Knights of the Immaculata spent their first night in Nagasaki. According to the Nagasaki Meteorological Observatory, it suddenly rained around 8:00 p.m. The Nagasaki sky must have been dark.

Let's go back to the old Nagasaki Shimbun newspaper I read in the Prefectural Library. It must have also been kept in the residence of the Bishop, but there was no way Father Kolbe could read a Japanese newspaper. However, only one month later, Father Kolbe and his friars published 10,000 copies of the first *Knights of the Immaculata* with Japanese printing types. The amazing life of the Knights of the Immaculata in Nagasaki had begun. As we read in the newspaper, "the Hongouchi Reservoir filled up after a night of heavy rain." Later Father Kolbe bought land within a stone's throw from the reservoir and built a single-story wooden friary there. I could not help thinking that there was some kind of implicit thread on the pages of this old newspaper that connected us to Father Kolbe and his Knights.

Fifty years have passed since they set foot in Nagasaki. Father Kolbe has been canonized a saint, and Brother Zeno was called to heaven on April 24, 1982, the same date on which they arrived in

Nagasaki. He was ninety years old. Brother Hilary, who had played the role of Mary as the group's cook, went back to Poland, lived out his life as a friar, and died at the age of seventy-one.

April 24, 1980 — that year, the date also fell on a Thursday. The fiftieth anniversary of the arrival of the Knights of the Immaculata in Japan was celebrated with great jubilation in their friary in Hongouchi-machi. There were hundreds of flowers before the statue of (then blessed) Father Kolbe in the garden of the friary, and it looked all the more glowing for the decorations! The spring sunlight softly enveloped the grounds. The deep green water of the reservoir, the source of life for the citizens of Nagasaki City, spread out before the statue of Father Kolbe.

The eighty-three year old Koya Tagita came from Nagoya to participate in the anniversary celebration. He said, "The reservoir is none other than the spring of Father Kolbe given to the citizens of Nagasaki. And we may also add, a grace bestowed by Our Lady." Mr. Tagita, a university professor, lived with the Knights under the same roof when they first settled in Oura, and this opportunity led him to convert from the Ittoen new religion to Christianity. He read a haiku with great feeling:

> In all green trees
> Shining brightly
> The source of the Blessed

April 24, 1930, was a long day, a historical day that marked the start of the Knights of the Immaculata in Japan.

CHAPTER 2

In and About Oura

Foreigners fit in well with Oura: the cathedral, the former Dutch residence; stone-paved slopes; foreign friars, their habits blowing in the spring breezes, blended into the neighborhood.

Publishing the First *Knights* in the Month of Mary

Staying at the residence of the Bishop, the three Knights of the Immaculata waited and waited for Bishop Hayasaka to return. Ten days had already passed, which they felt was too long. Bishop Hayasaka eventually returned one night in May. No sooner had he returned than Father Kolbe went to see the Bishop in his room and told him of all his plans for the future. "We have come from Poland, where our Franciscan friary called Niepokalanów has a printing office and publishes the magazine called *The Knights of the Immaculata*. We want to set up a branch and publish the magazine here."

Bishop Hayasaka had another plan which he suggested to Father Kolbe.

"The post of a philosophy professor at Oura Seminary is vacant at present. I went all the way to Shikoku to find one, but there was no one suitable to fill the position. I heard that you have degrees in philosophy and theology. Would you be willing to give lectures in philosophy for us?"

Having shared their own needs, they found an agreement that satisfied them both. Perhaps it was Divine Providence who led to this agreement. Bishop Hayasaka granted permission to set up a branch of the Knights of the Immaculata and to publish the magazine, and Father Kolbe became a philosophy professor. It was May 5, 1930.

Once permission was granted, Father Kolbe promptly went into action. As May is the month of our beautiful Mother Mary, he wished to publish the first issue of *The Knights* within the month. At the time, the magazine was to be published as a supplement to the *Catholic Diocesan Newspaper* for the faithful of Nagasaki Diocese. Father Kolbe wrote manuscripts for the first issue in Latin and Italian. These manuscripts included "What is a Knight of the Immaculata?" "Where is the Statue of Santa Maria?" "Saint Therese of the Child Jesus" and others. He wrote freely about these subjects. Fortunately, the fellow priests and the students of the seminary translated them into Japanese. He visited the Society of Mary, which ran Kaisei Junior High School, to ask them to contribute an article to the first issue. The Society of Mary had a long history in Nagasaki, and it also ran Meisei Commercial School in Osaka. "If you want to buy a printing machine, I will introduce you to our brothers in Osaka," said the principal.

Father Kolbe acted swiftly. He took a train on Friday to Osaka to look for a printing machine over the weekend. He stayed at Meisei Commercial School and went with a German Marianist to look for a manual printer, which he bought for 650 yen, along with 145,000 printing types for 300 yen, and then he promptly returned to Nagasaki.

Father Kolbe had to give lectures at the seminary. He and two other friars moved from the Bishop's residence to the seminary on the cathedral grounds. But they had to find their own house, and it was left to Brother Zeno to look for one.

"It is very important to teach philosophy in Nagasaki. The population in Japan is eighty million, and there are eighty to a hundred thousand Catholics living among them, sixty thousand of whom live in Nagasaki. There are students here from other dioceses, too. What a valuable job it is to teach the young people who hold the future of Japan in their hands!" Father Kolbe confidently wrote this to a priest in Poland.

The friars' efforts were fruitful. On May 24th, just one month after their arrival, as many as 10,000 copies of the first long-awaited *Knights* were printed. It was a marvelous event! The next day, Sunday the 25th, following morning Mass, people witnessed the foreign friars distributing *The Knights* to the public in the streets of Oura. The friars handed out copies and, in return, they received contact cards from people in order to send subsequent issues of the magazine to them. Their habits blew gently in the spring wind, a scene that captures very well what Oura represented. Brother Zeno said, "I distributed 267 copies by eleven o'clock in the morning, according to my notebook."

Walking around Oura with Brother Zeno

In August 1955, Brother Zeno returned to Nagasaki for the first time in a long while after having visited many places throughout Japan to help poor people and those in devastated areas. Then he showed me a small notebook, his diary of 1930, in which simple Japanese words were written. Using the notebook as our guide, we walked around Oura, a memorable town for him. While walking, Brother Zeno told me the reason why the friars

Brother Zeno looked back on the day of arrival after he visited Oura Cathedral.

came to Japan: "During the First World War many children became orphans in Poland. The Japanese Red Cross Society worked most diligently to help them; in fact, they aided 3,000 orphans. This was the first time Poles heard of Japan. A bishop in Poland recommended we pray for Japan; Father Kolbe came up with an idea to inform the Japanese of the Immaculate Mary. In the Polish edition of *The Knights*, he published an article about Bishop Hayasaka, the first Japanese bishop, so Japan remained in the heart of the Polish Knights, and hence, we came to Japan."

I think this simple explanation is typical of Brother Zeno. We strolled along the seaside in Oura.

Brother Zeno further said, "We could not stay in the seminary forever, so we looked for a house. Back in those days, there were Russian soldiers in Oura. There were Jews among them, and there was a synagogue for them. We call it *bożnica* (God's house) in Polish. It was near the coast of Oura. An old priest found it for us, so we decided to rent the old synagogue. Let's go there now."

The synagogue was located in the center of town. Having once served as a place of worship, the two-story red brick structure had a solid foundation.

"At first, we planned to make the second floor a chapel and bedrooms, and the first floor a printing room. However, the house had many bedbugs — all over the place. We called an exterminator to get rid of them, which cost 10 yen. As the old priest had bad eyesight and poor hearing, he did not notice the problem. One Catholic told us we could not live in such a house, so in the end we decided not to rent it and began the search for another location. Let's go see it."

We crossed Benten Bridge, and came to the slope leading to Oura Cathedral. In the middle of the slope there was a large European-style wooden house.

"This is the house. We lived here for one year," Brother Zeno said.

It was a two-story, square building. Looking at the house from

The friars lived in a big house on the right side of Oura Cathedral for one year.

the gate, there was a woodworking shop in the front, and a residence for three families in the back.

The tall columns, the high ceiling and the lattice windows were the original as when Brother Zeno lived there. He seemed to feel nostalgic while moving around the house. There is a photograph of Brother Zeno cooking while fanning a *shichirin* (charcoal stove). "I cooked here," he said, pointing to the patio.

There is a letter from Father Kolbe at that time: "We have rented a house, which may be too large for us, for nine months at the total cost of 405 yen. During this time we have to build our friary. We moved here on June 2nd; we just drank water and ate bread and bananas for lunch and supper on that day. Things have become relatively normal, but there are still many difficulties including translation from Latin to Japanese and the lack of a Japanese editor. Printing types have already arrived, but they are still lying bundled on the ground. As it takes more than three months to obtain the authorization of subscription-rate postal delivery, we must pay as much as 2 sen (one-hundredth of 1 yen) per copy. Although a manual printing machine was set up, we have neither a trimmer nor binder. Paper is terribly expensive, and there is no more money."

However, *The Knights* they printed seemed to have been well received. A request arrived from Tokyo with the payment in advance for 150 copies of the first issue, and they also got new subscribers. The skies over Nagasaki were clearing up for the Knights of the Immaculata!

Start of Their Life in the Cradle

To digress a little from the subject, one day in April 1978, Mr. Masayoshi Hashizume of Nagasaki City visited me at the friary of the Knights of the Immaculata.

His story was as follows: When he was giving swimming lessons on the beach, he got to know two grandsons of Mr. Robert Walker, captain of an English ship, who had visited Nagasaki in the early years of the Meiji era. His elder brother, Mr. Wilson Walker, had also been a sea captain, but later left this employment, started a business in Nagasaki and built a hotel for foreigners in Oura. Although his business prospered, he died in 1914 and the hotel was changed into Amenomori Hospital, which, in spite of its fame, was also closed around the late 1920s and was later abandoned.

"Brother Zeno rented this vacant hospital," said Mr. Hashizume. He emphasized the importance of preserving the former hotel and other European style buildings in Oura district. Just as we were talking about it, a fire reportedly broke out in Oura, and the former hotel, of all things, was burned to the ground and one child was killed. I rushed to the scene of the fire. Such a tragedy! The house I had visited with Brother Zeno was completely destroyed! I was saddened to see that the house, in which Father Kolbe and other friars had endured many hardships over the course of a year, was no longer standing and the life of a child had been lost.

The encounter with Mr. Hashizume enabled me to meet Mr. Shikamatsu Fujikawa (born in 1897 and eighty-one years old then) who had worked as a rickshaw driver at Amenomori Hospital. I met him deep in the mountains in Ureshino, Saga Prefecture. He had been in charge of the maintenance of the former hospital from its closure until the explosion of the atomic bomb.

Mr. Fujikawa said, "I remember Father Kolbe and Brother Zeno very well. In those days there were four large vacant buildings in a space of 5,000 square meters in Oura, and nobody lived there. Foreigners in strange attire came there to rent one of the buildings. That is why I remember them well. They printed blue magazines with a manual device."

His son Tsuneo, a second year elementary school student then, had often visited the friars, because he was interested in the printing machine. Tsuneo, who had been brought up in the former hospital, made a valuable sketch of the grounds at that time. There was a pond 10 meters in diameter, an artificial miniature hill, a tall camphor tree and a king sago palm. Father Kolbe and the two friars converted the first floor into a printery, an editorial room and an office, and the second floor into bedrooms. It is regrettable that the house burnt down, but we can say it was the cradle of the Knights of the Immaculata. Of the four buildings, one burnt down, two others had been demolished before the fire, and the last one remains as a designated Cultural Property.

On June 12th, a month and a half after his arrival in Nagasaki, Father Kolbe left Nagasaki for Poland on the *Shanghai-maru* ship, in order to participate in the Provincial Chapter. Several seminarians went to see him off. He visited the two friars who were stationed in Shanghai, went from there to Dalian by ship, and travelled via Harbin and Siberia by train, arriving at Niepokalanów in Poland on July 3rd.

The two friars who remained in Nagasaki lived in the spacious Western-style building. As there were no beds, they slept directly on the floor. There was no furniture and there were no good kitchen utensils. The local Catholics could not ignore the situation, so they brought food items such as lard or meat.

At the end of June, the second issue of *The Knights* was published again as a supplement to the *Catholic Diocesan Newspaper*. The two friars strived somehow to publish the third issue by themselves in their printing office. Brother Zeno went to Osaka in the middle of July and bought a trimmer. He only knew three Japanese phrases then: "It's old." "It's bad." "Please give me a discount." The same German brother took care of Brother Zeno, who fortunately, could understand a bit of German. Brother Zeno returned to Nagasaki Station after ten in the evening. He was overloaded with too much baggage to handle on his own. Just then a man walked right up to him.

"May I help you? Where are you going?"

"To Oura..."

When Brother Zeno arrived home with the man, the door was locked! Brother Zeno decided to enter through the window and said, "Give me a shove."

The man gave Brother Zeno's rump a hefty push.

Brother Zeno thanked him, and said, "Give me your business card," intending to send him an issue of *The Knights* at a later time. The man gave it to Brother Zeno, but of course he could not read the Japanese letters written on it. Later on, a Japanese Catholic translated the content and found out the stranger was a police detective.

The third issue of *The Knights* was not published even as July drew to a close.

In August the two friars from Shanghai, Brother Seweryn and Brother Zygmunt, came to Nagasaki, because, despite their best efforts, their work in China was not a success. However, Brother Seweryn had fortunately learned Chinese characters, so he could contribute a little to selecting printing types. He later became an expert in type-selection, and worked hard at the friary of the Knights of the Immaculata in Nagasaki. But eleven years later, just before the Pacific War, he went to the USA.

The friars manually turned a printing machine.

The four friars left in charge of the printing did their best, and eventually published the third issue at the end of August. In spite of the delay, this third issue was the first *Knights* they published by themselves while selecting types, turning the printing machine by hand and finishing the copies with the trimmer. (There is a photograph of them turning the printing machine.) On the colophon of the third issue, the publisher was designated as "The Knights of the Immaculata" in Chinese characters, whereas it was written as "The Knights of the Immaculata Maria" in the two previous issues.

Who dared to delete Maria? Was it a wicked plan? It seems some Japanese person did it without permission, thinking the name of the publisher was too long. Weren't their lives and their faith all based on the Virgin Mary? Why was her name deleted then? Nevertheless, the Polish Knights (who did not understand what was going on) were cheerful and filled with joy and gratitude.

CHAPTER 3

The Friars and a Visitor from Kyoto

One summer day, after the friars had started their missionary work, a strange man in a cheap, Japanese kimono, claiming to be a person of "Ittoen," visited the Knights of the Immaculata in Oura.

Ittoen with Blue Eyes

When Father Kolbe came to Nagasaki for his missionary work, he was suffering from lung disease. He had been sick for ten years, so right away he looked for a doctor in Nagasaki.

The clinic of Doctor Ken Takahara, expert in respiratory diseases, was located in Ginyamachi. As he himself had experienced lung disease, he could understand how the patients felt. He was a devout person who looked after the poor. Brother Zeno used to go to the clinic to get medications for Father Kolbe, but it took quite a long time to go from Oura to Ginyamachi on foot. Mr. Kunijiro Kozone, who ran a pharmacy for foreigners in Oura, kindly suggested to Brother Zeno, "As I am a good friend of Doctor Takahara, I will get a prescription from him and give you the medicine for free." Mr. Kozone, who was a friendly person, delivered the medicine to the residence of the Knights of the Immaculata. Mr. Kozone was a follower of "Ittoen" (Garden of Light), the new religion based in Kyoto.

When he was young, he had been faced with a serious problem

in his life, and it was Tenko Nishida of Ittoen who had helped him solve the problem.

Tenko Nishida (Tenko-san) was widely known as a religious man among the intellectuals of those days, and he was also a man who practiced his faith in his daily life. He went around shops, packing up goods or pushing carts voluntarily. He used to visit families where he would chop firewood or clean toilets. He lived together with other fellow members of Ittoen, while sharing their food and money as a single community. With the motto of no possessions, he devoted himself to the life renewed by the Light. If we express his life in the Western context, it was exactly the Franciscan way of life. The faith of Ittoen, which sought a life of penance, no possessions, and service without pay, had spread throughout Kyushu, and there were seventy to eighty followers in Nagasaki, which was the second largest number after Fukuoka.

Tenko Nishida of Ittoen visited the friars in Nagasaki. (On the right side.)

In July 1930, the followers of Ittoen invited Tenko-san to a summer workshop. They lodged together at Korin Temple and experienced the religious life. As the elder brother of Mr. Kozone was the leader of the local branch, Mr. Kozone and his family took care of Tenko-san.

The ancestor of Mr. Kozone had been a wealthy merchant who had founded Dejima-island during the period of national isolation; his grandfather, Kendo Kozone, was also a famous merchant who supported the imperial activists, like Ryoma Sakamoto or Kaishu Katsu during the Meiji Restoration. In Nagasaki City there is a town called Kozone-machi which Kendo established by reclaiming land in the sea. As the bronze statue of Kendo Kozone was just completed, Mr. Kozone took Tenko-san to see his grandfather's statue during the workshop, because Tenko-san had written the inscription for it. On the way to the statue, Mr. Kozone took Tenko-san to the Knights of the Immaculata, telling him, "There is an Ittoen with blue eyes in Oura."

However, the friars were absent, so Tenko-san was not able to meet them.

After the workshop finished, he visited Oura again. He must have been very much interested in the friars. Tenko-san wrote about the events of that day in his diary, which is a valuable document.

"On July 20th, I visited Bishop Hayasaka in Oura, and talked with him for two hours. Then I visited the Franciscans, who came from Poland and lived in a room in the former hospital down the hill from the cathedral. They have spread a straw mat on the floor with blankets being laid on top. Their faces were very gentle as they welcomed me. On one side of the room, there is a printing machine and a Japanese helps the friars with printing. One Franciscan is named 'Hilary' and the other 'Zeno.'"

On that occasion, Mr. Kozone did not accompany Tenko-san.

No Possessions Makes Peaceful Faces

The next time, when kimono-clad Tenko-san visited the Western-style building of the former hospital, they were there — those two friars with the blue eyes. In their Franciscan habits, they looked like something he might have seen in a picture book. They wore black in spite of the summer heat. Their garb was ankle length. A white cord, tightened around the waist, hung with knots on the right side. On the left hung a rosary and a cross. They also had a cape with capuche. They looked the way a Franciscan should!

"They are barefoot," blurted out Tenko-san to his two companions in spite of himself.

The friars eagerly beckoned them to come into the room. They lived a humble life; there was only a straw mat on the wooden floor with blankets being spread on it. 'Is this a bedroom?' he thought to himself. There was no furniture. They used a wooden box for oranges as a desk.

Although Tenko-san was surprised at their life of extreme poverty, he was fascinated with their beautiful eyes. Their faces were full of peace. He thought that it must be the outcome of selflessness and having no possessions. Although Tenko-san and the friars could not understand each other's language, he intuitively felt that they were like old friends. He said, "In spite of the difference of nationality, the way to the true life is one."

The friars invited Tenko-san to come into the next room, the printery, where a printing machine was set up, and Japanese printing types were laid out. "They are trying to print by themselves in order to spread their religion," Tenko-san thought, as he himself had also a printing office in Kyoto and was publishing the magazine *Light*.

In that moment, Brother Zeno handed a copy of *The Knights* and a medal of Mary to Tenko-san, saying, "We are friends." Tenko-san was deeply impressed by these simple friars.

He wrote very frankly:

"Like pilgrims, they have come from a distant land to Japan, without knowing Japanese. They devote themselves to the Virgin Mary and their gentle faces show no anxiety. Neither of the friars is covered with any of the dirt of the world. Precisely because they have dedicated themselves to lives of no possessions, they are able to maintain such a peaceful demeanor.

Although there are many who have kind faces in the world, I have scarcely seen men whose faces show such kindness as these two. We were simply happy and thought that we would like to do everything we could for these friars."

The next day, Tenko-san came back to see the friars with a camera. He probably visited them again to reaffirm his initial impression. The friars, especially Brother Zeno, were glad to take a picture with Tenko-san. There is a precious photo of them with Tenko-san in the middle. He wore a humble kimono with a black belt, Brother Hilary being taller than Tenko-san, and Brother Zeno shorter. When he said that he would send the photos as soon as they were printed, the friars repeatedly replied: "To Poland, to Poland!"

Friars live a life of chastity. They do not touch women nor do they live with them. Though Tenko-san was accompanied by a female member, she was not allowed to enter the room.

Tenko-san felt many things, comparing his life to that of the friars. He wrote about the diversity of his life: "They are pure and distant from the secular society. I have a wife and children and lead an ordinary life. I have a lot to worry about and have to deal with problems more complicated than those of the Franciscans." However, the encounter with the Knights of the Immaculata left deep and memorable impressions on Tenko-san.

Although he was not able to personally meet Father Kolbe on this occasion, he must have been very pleased to meet real Franciscans whom he had previously only known through books. This encounter exceeded all his expectations! He left Nagasaki with a firm conviction that Ittoen also existed in Europe.

He wrote a detailed thirteen page article about his encounter with the Franciscans in the September 1930 issue of *Light*.

Father Kolbe Visits Ittoen

Three months passed. The summer became a memory, the fall had now arrived and Father Kolbe had returned from the Provincial Chapter in Poland. On October 4th, he himself visited Ittoen in Yamashina, Kyoto. He spoke in German, and a fellow member of Ittoen interpreted for him. There is a document verifying Father Kolbe's visit to Ittoen. When Father Kolbe arrived at Ittoen, Tenko-san was absent. To begin with, Father Kolbe spoke about religion with the members of Ittoen.

"The purpose of the life of Ittoen is to eliminate every conflict in the world, and to bring about true peace. Therefore, the members lead a life of penitence, mendicancy, and service, and when we abandon our ego, we can hear God's voice."

"How do you practice your religion, then?" asked Father Kolbe.

"We adore the essence of various religions. Each of us worships the religion he believes in," the Ittoen members replied.

Father Kolbe is said to have repeatedly insisted that "We can never accept the essence of other religions. If there is only one truth, then there is only one true religion." A while later, Tenko-san returned and this was his first meeting with Father Kolbe. They greeted each other gently, and that eased the tense atmosphere.

Tenko-san said, "As we have things in common in how we live our lives, I feel an unconditional closeness with you. Please feel at home with us whenever you come here." Father Kolbe replied, "Thank you for your previous visit. Unfortunately, I was away in Poland, and regrettably, we were unable to meet at that time. We came to Japan to further the publication of our magazine in order to spread the Gospel. I hope we will exchange our *Knights* for your *Light* every month." They exchanged lively conversation and then Father Kolbe was treated to a special dinner which he enjoyed, saying, "This is my first time eating Japanese food."

The document states, "During the dinner, Father Kolbe recalled that that very day was the feast day of Saint Francis of Assisi. Everyone was very pleased with this coincidence."

There was a stage set up in the garden. A member said, "Soon, over there, all the members will take part in the drama which Tenko-san produced." "That's fine. But you had better put the statue of Our Lady in front of the stage," said Father Kolbe. Tenko-san replied smiling, "We always hold the image of Mary in our mind." "I would like you not only to keep it in mind, but to express it little by little," said Father Kolbe, smiling back as they both bid farewell to each other.

What has since become of Ittoen? After the Second World War, Brother Zeno often visited Ittoen and renewed old friendships. The Ittoen followers had numbered tens of thousands throughout the entire country before the War. Tenko-san became a member of the House of Councilors after the War, and Ittoen carried out active movements in the political and social arena.

In 1967 Tenko-san laid his old and weak body down in a thatched hut of Ittoen. A Polish priest of the Knights of the Immaculata visited him then. The priest said, "I went there wearing the habit so that he could recognize that I had come from the friary of Father Kolbe." He gazed at the habit with obvious nostalgia, perhaps recalling the friars' habits he had seen in the Oura sunlight. He reached out his hands, and grasped tightly the cross that hung from the priest's cord. His hands were so beautiful! The hands of the old man who devoted himself to service and introspection all his life, were shining white and nobly.

Tenko-san could no longer speak. He just continued gazing at the cross as if he were contemplating its mystery. The priest who visited Tenko-san had an account to share: when he was a seminarian in Poland, he received a letter from Father Kolbe that said, "Please pray for the following Japanese with whom I have made very good friends." Four or five names were written on it, and each was allocated to one seminarian. The person assigned to the priest was unexpectedly Tenko Nishida. The priest had prayed for Tenko-san for thirty-five years ever since then.

As the priest could not stay long, he said farewell and began to stand up, but Tenko-san would not release his hold. The priest tried to release the cross from the hands of Tenko-san, but in vain. He had no choice but to leave it in the hands of the old man and then, he went on his way. After some time, Tenko-san finished his long life at the age of ninety-six and went to heaven.

When the Knights of the Immaculata started spreading the Gospel through publications, many people observed with great interest these Polish Knights living in holy poverty. Some were priests; some were Father Kolbe's seminarians; others were lay Catholics — pharmacists, butchers, paper dealers, and so on. It was especially significant for the Knights of the Immaculata that Mr. Tenko Nishida, who had a different standpoint, looked after them. No moment in a life that is directed by God is wasted.

Recently, Mr. Kunijiro Kozone, eighty-eight years old, visited me and told me he greatly admired Brother Zeno. "Father Kolbe wasn't very physically strong, so he didn't walk around Nagasaki for propagation. It was Brother Zeno who spread the mission of the Knights of the Immaculata. He didn't understand Japanese well, which actually contributed to the propagation. He practiced the religion not by his words but by his demeanor, which is very important. As the Knights of the Immaculata are involved in education, I want them to emphasize 'action' in their education, as Ittoen does. 'Action' is real, human education. Just preaching in a church is not enough. Father Kolbe published the magazine, but it was Brother Zeno who disseminated the word of God through action. The Japanese empathized with the pure deeds of Brother Zeno, as they did with Ittoen. Brother Zeno said to me that he would never forget my family name, Kozone. Do you know why? His mother's name was Anna Kozon."

It was the old Mr. Kozone who showed me the valuable diary entry of Tenko-san for July 20, 1930.

CHAPTER 4

The Seminarians Depart

*Poland, an eastern European country full of cherries.
From there to the country of cherry blossoms. National borders
do not exist for the Knights of the Immaculata.*

Cultivate the Seedlings You Planted

The seedlings of the Knights of the Immaculata were planted in Nagasaki. Whether one should dig them out or give them sunlight (funds) and water (human resources) was the greatest point of contention at the Provincial Chapter held in Poland in July, 1930. With a report on the mission in Japan, Father Kolbe participated in the Chapter in Lwów, which is now in the Republic of the Ukraine, but was a city in eastern Poland before the Second World War. The seminary and the provincial office of the Order of the Conventual Franciscans was situated in this city and the meetings were held there.

When a seminarian studying in this seminary heard that Father Kolbe had returned, he suddenly proposed to Father Kolbe, "I want to work in the mission in Japan. I want to live with you."

Father Kolbe wrote down his name, "Mieczysław Mirochna" and advised him, "I will tell of your desire to the Provincial, but you must pray that God's will be done."

And so, the conference began. In Nagasaki there were two friars left behind doing the best they could. Father Kolbe argued that establishing a branch of their Order in Nagasaki was appropriate for the following reasons:

1. Nagasaki was where Franciscans had been martyred.
2. Seventy percent of Japan's Catholics were to be found in this city.
3. The Bishop of Nagasaki was favorably disposed toward the Knights of the Immaculata and permited them to establish a branch and to publish *The Knights*.
4. The number of copies already printed had reached 11,000 and even the pagans had gladly welcomed the magazine.
5. Nagasaki could be a foothold for China, India, etc.

Seminarian Mirochna offered to work with Father Kolbe in Japan.

Of course there were opposing views as well. "Father Kolbe is adopting an unusual approach for the Order." "We don't have enough funds or human resources to send to foreign countries for missionary work."

At the center of the uproar, Father Kolbe felt himself severely tested. But he absolutely believed in the Immaculata. While opposing views were being stated, Father Kolbe lowered his head and prayed the Rosary quietly. But the trial did not last long. The former Provincial calmed the opposition down, and the present Provincial Father Kornel Czupryk advocated the necessity of spreading the word of God and expected that they would get enough funds and human resources if it was God's will. Finally, approval was given to cultivate the seedlings in Nagasaki. The guidance of the Immaculata was also at work here.

After the conference, Father Kolbe headed for Niepokalanów with seminarian Mirochna, who was on summer vacation. (Niepokalanów was the friary of the Knights of the Immaculata in Poland and was located in a suburb of Warsaw.) At the station of Lwów, a large number of priests who had attended the conference were waiting for the train home. So that Father Kolbe might not aggravate those priests who were against the propagation in Japan, he covertly took Mirochna, got into a different train car from the other priests and warned Mirochna not to put his head out the window.

In the car Father Kolbe took his favorite autobiography of Saint Therese and suggested to Mirochna that he read whichever chapter he liked. Father Kolbe said, "The philosophy lecture in Japan is held in Latin. I'm teaching philosophy there. What is your level of Latin? I'll give you a test." He then had Mirochna translate the constitution of the Order of the Conventual Franciscans from Latin into Polish.

After twelve hours the train arrived at Szymanów. It was a long trip which crossed Poland. Most of the priests had already gotten off the train. Father Alfons, the younger brother of Father Kolbe, came to the station to meet his elder brother. He was the guardian of the friary of Niepokalanów, which was located near the station. The construction of the friary had started on a vast expanse of land three years earlier (in 1927), and the printing office was already built where about eighty friars published 300,000 copies of *The Knights of the Immaculata* every month. Here, the seedlings of the Knights had started to grow at last.

The Big Dream of Spreading the Knights of the Immaculata Around the World

Here, I will explain the difference between the Order of the Conventual Franciscans and the Knights of the Immaculata.

Father Kolbe was a priest of the Order of the Conventual Franciscans. He pursued one ideal all his life: to increase the number of the faithful who consecrate themselves entirely to Immaculate Mary. For this purpose he established a sodality whose members wear the Miraculous Medal, consecrate themselves entirely to Our Lady, and read *The Knights of the Immaculata*. This sodality, also named the Knights of the Immaculata (Latin: *Militia Immaculatae*), was established for lay people.

There were Conventual Franciscan friars who sympathized with Father Kolbe's ideal and joined him in order to participate in the movement of the Knights of the Immaculata. They did not form a new religious order, but rather a friary called Niepokalanów, according to the ideal of the Knights of the Immaculata within the Order of the Conventual Franciscans which had seven hundred years of tradition. The friars of Niepokalanów consecrated everything to Our Lady, spread the movement of the Knights of the Immaculata, printed and published *The Knights of the Immaculata* by themselves, and lived the strict religious life of the Order of the Conventual Franciscans. The base of the Knights of the Immaculata in the West was Niepokalanów, and its base in the East was in the Japanese city of Nagasaki.

When Father Kolbe arrived at Niepokalanów, he confided his big dream to seminarian Mirochna. "Based in Nagasaki, I will establish branches in China, India, and Arabia, and publish *The Knights* in each language. Then more than one billion people, more than half of the inhabitants of the world, will be led by the Immaculata! This is not a mere dream but something we must realize as soon as possible." Father Kolbe's eyes shone serenely.

While awaiting permission from the Provincial, Mirochna stayed at Niepokalanów. He was very much taken by the friars of Niepokalanów because, after having read *The Knights*, he entered the minor seminary there. Father Kolbe showed him the church and said, "The most important place in Niepokalanów is the church. But there is another vitally important place here. Do you know what it is?" Mirochna thought that it might be the printing office, the administration office or the electrical room. Then Father Kolbe took him to the sickroom and said, "The crosses that the brothers are bearing here will bring about the grace of God. Sick people are the treasure of the friary. We cherish them very much. They are the best workers here."

Seminarian Damian, who was spending his vacation in Niepokalanów, also applied for missionary work in Japan. Both seminarians eagerly waited for permission from the Provincial. But in spite of having endured a long wait, they could not get permission. On the contrary, strange rumors started to spread around: "Father Kolbe is trying to take the seminarians to Japan against their will."

At a loss, Father Kolbe called the seminarians and said, "Go to the monastery in Łagiewniki, where the Provincial stays. Meet him in person and apply for the missionary work by yourselves. It depends entirely on you whether you go there or not. I will stay here and pray for you." Just to make sure of how to proceed, Mirochna asked, "If the Provincial is not there, what shall we do?" Father Kolbe answered, "Then you have to come back here immediately! I say immediately!" This word "immediately" strangely remained in Mirochna's heart. He started out with joy in his heart, as the monastery in Łagiewniki was a place where he had previously received religious training, and where his teachers and, above all, his brother Father Juliano, lived.

Both seminarians traveled in silence and prayer. They got off at Zgierz station, hired a horse cart from there, and headed for the monastery in Łagiewniki. When they came close to the gate of the monastery, they saw a horse cart coming toward them. Was it the Provincial? No. In looking at it closely, they could see it was Mirochna's brother, Father Juliano! Both horse carts stopped as if frozen with amazement.

"Where are you going?" asked Mirochna's brother.

"I was just going to see the Provincial," answered Mirochna.

"The Provincial is not here," said his brother.

"Oh, is he away? And where are you going, my brother?" said Mirochna.

"Good timing! I'm just going to see you," said Father Juliano.

Having said that, he immediately began to severely criticize Father Kolbe! "I heard that you would like to go to Japan. Is it true? I won't allow it!"

As Father Juliano spoke with vehemence, tears welled up in Mirochna's eyes. "Let's go to the monastery and talk it over at length," said his brother. It was then that Mirochna remembered what Father Kolbe said: "Come back immediately!" Mirochna obeyed that command and said, "I must go back immediately."

Father Juliano urged his younger brother to go to the monastery and talk the matter over with him, saying he himself would take responsibility for everything. But Mirochna would not hear of it. His brother said, "Then, nothing can be done! I'll take you to the station at least. Ride in my cart." During the ride, Father Juliano repeatedly slandered Father Kolbe and demanded Mirochna leave Father Kolbe and come back to the seminary. The brothers parted ways with the matter unresolved, and the two seminarians returned to Niepokalanów. Mirochna broke down in tears at the feet of Father Kolbe. Mirochna was bitterly disappointed.

Father Juliano arrived soon thereafter to visit Mirochna. It appeared as if he had been following close behind. This time Mirochna said once and for all with determination, "My dearest brother, I thought you would always help me as my blood brother. But I was entirely disappointed with your words. I have also heard critical opinions about Father Kolbe. But what's wrong with him? He loves the Immaculata, lives in poverty, and tries to develop the works of Mary in the world. What's wrong with that? Whatever you might think about Father Kolbe, I will follow him and go to Japan, even if you are against it."

His words were inspiring, full of zeal and conviction. After many hours of discussion, his brother finally yielded to him.

Father Juliano said, "I get it. I will no longer object. Go your own way. The reason you haven't received permission from the Provincial yet is because I have prevented it. I will ask him to grant you permission."

The brothers, at last, took leave of each other with bright faces. This would be the last meeting between Mirochna and Father Juliano, who was killed by Nazi soldiers during the Second World War. After the meeting, Father Juliano flew to Kraków where the Provincial stayed. Soon after that the two seminarians got permission to go to Japan.

On the Trans-Siberian Railroad

Mirochna went to say goodbye to his parents in Voynich where they lived. They were deeply religious and gave him their blessing to go to Japan with genuine pleasure. The five siblings all gathered for the occasion. He got only half the day off from Father Kolbe so he could only stay home from the morning he arrived there until the evening when he had to leave. The reason was that back then the trans-Siberian railroad train ran only about once a week.

Mirochna's father begged him repeatedly, "Stay just one night, as it might be our last meeting in this world." His father even sent a telegram to Father Kolbe whose reply, which would have allowed Mirochna to stay overnight, arrived too late; by then, Mirochna had already left! And that was the last time he saw his parents.

When Father Kolbe and the two seminarians left Niepokalanów, he took them to the room of his brother, Father Alfons, to say goodbye. Father Kolbe knocked on the door but there was no reply. He opened the door quietly and noticed that his brother was sleeping at his desk presumably from fatigue. "Let's leave him alone, as he is sleeping. We will sacrifice saying goodbye to him for the sake of Japan," said Father Kolbe as he left the room. This also was the last meeting of the two brothers. Four months later Father Alfons died suddenly from overworking and late treatment of a disease of the abdomen.

The twenty-two-year-old Mirochna and the twenty-one-year-old Damian, along with Father Kolbe, said farewell to Poland. They departed from their homeland where there were plenty of cherry trees bearing fruit to the country in the East where cherry blossoms bloom. The three travelers changed out of their habits and put on laymen's clothes to board the trans-Siberian rail. When Polish women saw them in lay clothes, they cried. People in Poland, a Catholic country, could not imagine the friars not wearing their habits. But there was no other choice when one travelled through Communist Russia. In those days, Polish people were extremely afraid of Russia. Whenever the young seminarians saw soldiers with guns at stations in Russia, they felt frightened!

At times, they were interrogated or tested in Russian; and the trans-Siberian train journey took about one long, anxious week before it entered Manchuria. There, they finally felt it was safe enough to change back into their habits.

As it was summer, they were often thirsty. Father Kolbe asked a vendor on the train for something to drink. "What do you want?" asked the vendor. "Well, I'll take this white water," said Father Kolbe and pointed to a 1.8 liter bottle. People around were staring at him with great curiosity. He had no way of knowing that it was cheap Japanese distilled spirits! In Poland, alcoholic drinks (which were colored) and clear water were sold on trains. No sooner had he tasted the seemingly clear water, than he spat it out! With a disappointed look, he threw the bottle from the train window into a big river below. The train ran from Manchuria through Korea to Busan where they took a ferry boat to Shimonoseki, Japan. Then they took another boat to Moji where they boarded a train for Nagasaki.

As soon as they stood on Japanese ground, Father Kolbe said,

"Now, we are in Japan. Start your mission."

But the seminarians were far from feeling like spreading the word of God in Japan's oppressive summer heat. They wore thick habits made in Poland and even had overcoats over their arms — they could barely walk! But Father Kolbe, although in poor health, walked with a steady gait.

It was Monday morning, August 25th. Four friars came to the station to meet Father Kolbe and the two seminarians. Two of the four friars lived in Nagasaki and the other two had come to Nagasaki from Shanghai ten days earlier. The seven Knights rejoiced together. They went back to the friary in Oura and, after they had put down their baggage there, they celebrated a Mass of thanksgiving in Oura Cathedral. For Mirochna, these last two months had been filled with one difficult trial after another. But finally he arrived in Japan, which he had longed to see.

The two seminarians entered the Oura seminary in September. Although they had been looking forward to coming to Japan for a long time, crosses they would have to carry were awaiting them. Summer in Nagasaki was more hot and humid than one could imagine in Poland. They sweat a lot and were annoyed with mosquitoes — and there was no shower facility. The meals were very humble. Damian suffered a nervous breakdown, returned to Poland within the year and later left the Order. Three months after his arrival in Nagasaki, Mirochna was continually ill for many days, vomiting and suffering from stomach disorders. He was hospitalized and underwent surgery. Initially, he was confused by these setbacks. But once he endured these challenges patiently, and once he had been restored to health, he worked vigorously. He was guided personally by Father Kolbe who taught the seminarian the spirit and virtues and academic knowledge necessary for a priest. Mirochna was ordained a priest while Father Kolbe was still in Nagasaki.

After Father Kolbe returned to Poland, Father Mirochna worked as principal of the minor seminary established by Father Kolbe in Nagasaki and was appointed guardian of the friary and director of the novitiate there. Father Mirochna trained many Japanese friars, admirably protected Father Kolbe's legacy during and after the Second World War, and made the seedlings of the Knights of the Immaculata flourish in a wonderful way.

Only after looking back on one's long life can one see the guidance of Our Lady. In 1980, when Father Mirochna was seventy-two, he gently recalled: "I came to Japan because I just wanted to live with such a noble man as Blessed Father Kolbe." Father Mirochna himself must have also been guided to Japan by the Immaculata, as part of God's mysterious Providence.

CHAPTER 5

An Encounter with Holy Poverty

*A strict Protestant preacher changed his life
after encountering the Franciscan friars.*

The Seven Samurai

Two seminarians arrived at Nagasaki from Poland. As a result, the number of the Knights of the Immaculata in Oura was now seven. They were, so to say, seven samurai who gathered under the banner of Our Lady. This was in late summer of 1930.

The seven were Brother Seweryn, who set type for the printings with a dictionary of classical Japanese in hand; Brother Zygmunt,

"Seven samurai" gathered under the banner of Our Lady.

who was completely absorbed in writing shipping addresses; Brother Zeno, who was the busiest friar of all with shopping, distributing *The Knights*, and everything from carpentry to repairing shoes; Brother Hilary, the cook; Father Kolbe, editor of *The Knights* and professor at the Oura seminary; Mirochna and Damian, who were his students at the seminary. Totally by coincidence, the day when all seven gathered for the first time was the Feast of the Seven Joys of Mary! Father Kolbe was very pleased with this providential start and said, "Let's do our best to be the seven joys of Our Lady."

At the Provincial Chapter in Poland, it was decided to carry on with the missionary work of publishing in Nagasaki, so they did everything possible to get the delayed publication back on schedule. The biggest hurdle was translating the manuscripts into Japanese and the next biggest difficulty was picking out the types. Brother Seweryn, who had learned some Chinese characters in Shanghai, rolled up his sleeves and did his best, but sometimes he could only pick out two and a half lines of type a day.

Besides publishing *The Knights*, it was urgent to find a piece of land in Nagasaki City. Oura was just a provisional residence. They looked for more spacious and cheaper land in the less central area of the city. They needed land where they could build a printing room and a novitiate, but they also wanted to build a minor seminary and grounds in the future. It was also urgent for them to cut their living expenses to the bare minimum and allot the money saved to publication and propagation.

All the expenses were covered by money from the friary of Niepokalanów in Poland. Every year, they needed more than 400 yen at the currency value of that time. They had little income from *The Knights*. The magazine cost 2 sen, including postage. As the postage cost the friars 2 sen, it meant that the magazine itself was free. Since it did not qualify as third-class mail, they increased the pages of the magazine to twenty-four from the eighth issue (in 1931), and raised the price to 3 sen. In most cases, they handed out the magazines for free. But having observed the friars' poor but honest lives, many offered donations or other forms of support, and their number gradually increased.

We know how frugal their lives were at that time from the letters of Father Kolbe or the witnesses of those who experienced it. They could have beef, potatoes, or milk only rarely — foods which Westerners had regularly. They mainly ate bread and soup with a small amount of carrots and wheat; and they drank tea in enamel cups. The diet was low in nutrients, and soon even a stray cat living with them died of malnutrition. A Catholic butcher, finally unable to ignore the situation, sometimes brought them lard and inexpensive meat.

Father Kolbe lived in Nagasaki for six years but he left few things behind. He did not leave his habit, shoes, spectacles, or his prayer book. Only a simple desk with a chair made by Brother Zeno and a notebook entitled "Nagasaki Diary" written in Polish, are preserved in the friary. Father Kolbe started using the desk from the Oura period. When we read his diary, we often come across the name "Yamaki" in it. Yamaki refers to Mr. Toshio Yamaki.

It was Mr. Masami Iwanaga, a Catholic in Urakami, who brought Mr. Yamaki to Oura for the first time. Father Kolbe wrote in his diary: "Mr. Yamaki is a pastor and a secondary school teacher. He was brought up in an ardent Protestant family. He respects Saint Francis of Assisi." According to the reminiscence

Mr. Yamaki met seven Franciscans living in holy poverty and his life was profoundly altered.

of Mr. Yamaki, Father Kolbe had great difficulty translating his manuscripts. He wrote them in Latin and a seminarian in Oura translated them into Japanese. But the seminarian was also busy; so if the translation took longer than expected, there would be a delay in publication.

Mr. Yamaki recollected, "Then I proposed that I would help Father Kolbe, as I could understand Italian. He was very pleased with my proposal, saying that it was providential."

As Father Kolbe had studied in Rome, he was fluent in Italian. I can just imagine how Father Kolbe must have smiled with joy upon hearing this. The encounter of one person with another is indeed something providential. Sometimes the course of a person's life may be completely changed, as was the case with Mr. Yamaki. He met seven Franciscans living in holy poverty and his life was profoundly altered.

He Saw Saint Francis There

Mr. Yamaki was thirty-six years old at that time. He was born in Nagasaki City and taught at the Chinzei Secondary School, founded by the Methodist Church. His father was a scholar of the Chinese Classics and taught Japanese and Chinese Classics at the Kwassui Girls' School, also founded by the Methodist Church. His mother was an experienced Methodist evangelist. As his parents were Protestants through and through, he was raised in a strict family. He did not drink alcohol, smoke cigarettes, or go to the theater; he led a life centered on the church.

When Mr. Yamaki was a boy, he dreamed of being a professor of Methodist theology. When he studied at Kwansei Gakuin College in Kobe, he listened to a lecture on Dante by Mr. Oga, a famous scholar of Dante, and was fascinated by this great poet. Wishing to read *The Divine Comedy* in the original language, he mastered Italian, which later provided him with the opportunity to get to know Father Kolbe in a more personal way.

Mr. Yamaki's interests extended from Dante to the history of the Middle Ages. After a while he discovered Saint Francis of Assisi, a saint of the Middle Ages. Finally, he became more fascinated with Saint Francis than Dante. He transferred from Kwansei Gakuin College to the faculty of theology of Aoyama Gakuin College.

Mr. Yamaki explained that he was captivated by Saint Francis for the following reasons:

1. As he was brought up in a very strict faith, he longed unconsciously for something calm, quiet, and comfortable in Christianity. He found it in the gentleness of Saint Francis and the love with which he called the things in nature "brother and sister." Through his familiarity with Saint Francis, he was able to come into contact with the life of Christ.

2. The life of Saint Francis, who lived in perfect holy poverty, was nothing other than the life of the Holy Gospel. Through Saint Francis, the Holy Gospel was no longer something of a time two thousand years ago, but now was merely seven hundred years old.

3. There was great interest in Saint Francis at that time. Many biographies of Saint Francis, including *The Little Flowers*, *The Life of Saint Francis*, and *The Mirror of Perfection*, among others, were published one after the other.

Having received a strict Methodist education, Mr. Yamaki was brought up with the Holy Gospel at the center of his life; and through his discovery of Saint Francis he was able to find the spirit of the Gospel of seven hundred years ago. However, he had not yet encountered its spirit in the reality of his own time. But his passion for academic research relating to Saint Francis was quite unusual. He wrote papers about Saint Francis in his notebooks — numbering more than a dozen — and collected all the original texts and materials he could find.

After graduating from Aoyama Gakuin College, he was licensed as a pastor and taught at a secondary school in Kyoto, as well as at Kwansei Gakuin College. In the fall of 1930, he came back to Nagasaki. Upon his return, he heard that some Franciscan friars had come to Oura. He visited Father Kolbe for a utilitarian purpose: he wanted to make use of him for his academic research. However, what he found there was not an object of research but the real life itself.

Brother Seweryn rolled up his sleeves and picked out types.

He witnessed a poor diet and simple life there. It was presumed that no one saw or would ever see such miserable food in any other religious order in Japan. As Father Kolbe tried to maintain the life of Saint Francis so rigorously, even some fellow friars thought that he might found a new religious order.

The friars had no money at their disposal and were completely obedient to their superiors. They were not allowed to go out without permission; they lived together and were dedicated to their work. Their publications were done as missionary work and without any intention of making a profit. Besides, they were joyful and lived in fraternity and placed their faith in the Immaculata. Where did these practices come from? Mr. Yamaki found the love of Saint Francis in the Polish knights.

One day, an employee from a paper store came to ask for payment. With a look of innocence, Brother Zeno, who received him, said while shrugging his shoulders, "Our Lady hasn't given us money yet. Please wait for a while." The employee murmured, inclining his neck doubtfully, "Where is your lady? Is she a rich woman? I have come here three times, only getting the same answer."

There was no stove even for the New Year. There was no fire at all, and it was snowing. After the New Year's party, Mr. Yamaki visited Father Kolbe, who seemed to have been waiting for him to ask him to translate his manuscript. "I cannot write anything, as my fingers are numb with cold," said Mr. Yamaki. Then Father Kolbe brought him hot tea in an enamel cup and said, "Please drink this. It will be like a stove inside you."

After completing his translation, Mr. Yamaki took his supper with the friars and Father Kolbe invited him to sit on his own chair. They ate in silence and after the meal, they read the Holy Gospel. After a while, the silence ended at the sound of a bell and then they started talking quite merrily. Though living in poverty, the habits of the seven friars fitted the atmosphere well and their life reminded Mr. Yamaki of "the little flowers" of Saint Francis. As all spoke in Polish, Mr. Yamaki could not understand what they said. When everyone laughed, he did not. After hearing Father Kolbe's interpretation into Italian, Mr. Yamaki had a good laugh all by himself.

Father Kolbe seemed to be especially friendly to Mr. Yamaki, who was often mentioned in his diary: "He is a good Protestant." "He helped me with my translation then." "After that he went to church to preach." "He has not become a Catholic yet but he said that his heart was in the Franciscan family." "He thinks it's time for him to be a Catholic." Mr. Yamaki is often referred to in this way in Father Kolbe's diary. Mr. Yamaki was a mighty helper for the Knights of the Immaculata.

When Father Kolbe bought the land of Hongouchi, which measured about 25,000 square meters, he promised to pay 7,000 yen for it in five installments. If he could not finish the payment by the due date, he would forfeit the prepayment. This land was situated on the slope of a suburban area. It was not too attractive. What is more, there were as many as sixteen land owners. The next day, after Father Kolbe drew up a contract and paid 1,500 yen in advance, Mr. Uraoka, a faithful Catholic in Oura, anxiously visited Father Kolbe. Mr. Yamaki played the role of interpreter for him.

"Father, will you buy the land?" asked Mr. Uraoka.

"Yes, I will," replied Father Kolbe.

"Do you have the money for it?"

"Not at the moment."

"Will you surely get the money from Poland? Otherwise you will have to give up the 1,500 yen you have already paid."

Then Father Kolbe replied, "I don't know whether the money will be sent or not. If it is what Our Lady wishes, then we will surely get the money. If not — we will not get it. It's not what I should worry about, as everything depends on the desires of the Immaculata. I entrust it to her." "I am relieved to know your resolution." Mr. Uraoka did not say any more. There is an expression in Zen Buddhism: *A Zen priest gives thirty blows of the stick*. While acting as interpreter, Mr. Yamaki felt indeed as if he had received thirty blows of the stick of a Zen priest.

Mr. Yamaki was struck by Father Kolbe's trust. The spirit of Saint Francis was surely still alive there. He had thought it was absolutely impossible for people of the day to lead the strict life of Saint Francis in perfect poverty. Though the friars were human beings just as he, they were living the life of Saint Francis admirably, here and now. It was not, so to say, an unattainable flower on lofty heights.

He thought he should give more thought to the Catholic faith to which the Franciscan order belonged.

He had studied it as part of Church history, but from then on he would pursue it in relation to his own life. In this way, Mr. Yamaki came into contact with the Catholic faith. However, he did not convert to Catholicism in the Oura period. He had his own family reasons. Additionally, he had not been with the Knights of the Immaculata in Nagasaki for a long enough period.

Salary from Our Lady

Mr. Yamaki left Nagasaki and worked as pastor in Sendai for more than two years. Yet, ever since he had met Father Kolbe he had lost his enthusiasm to act as pastor. He courageously resigned his post and went to Tokyo. He had no regular occupation and was at the bottom of his life. In the summer of 1933, his wife became ill. He did not even have money to send her to the hospital. Coincidentally, he received a letter from Father Kolbe who had temporarily returned to Poland at that time. Enclosed in the letter were 50 dollars, equivalent to 100 yen, and more than two months' salary for a teacher at that time.

The letter said, "I enclose the money, as I think you need it now. It's not from me. You worked very hard for the Immaculata. Therefore, it's a present from her to you. Please express your gratitude to her."

This unexpected present was sent to him although he had not informed Father Kolbe of his latest situation. Mr. Yamaki broke into tears, holding the letter reverently. He could now pay the hospital expenses with this money. At no other time had the phrase in the Holy Gospel, "So do not worry about tomorrow: tomorrow will take care of itself," penetrated more deeply into his heart.

In fact, when he resigned from the office of pastor in Sendai, he handed in his resignation to the Methodist authority saying, "Up to now, I have received my salary from you, but from now on I will get it from my God." He considered the gift as salary from Our Lady. All throughout his life he never forgot what he experienced on the day he received the letter from Father Kolbe. He understood clearly that the teaching of the Holy Gospel was true even for a man like him. This salary of Our Lady led him to the Catholic Church, and he was baptized soon after.

After the Second World War, he served as principal of Nigawa Gakuin, an elementary, junior, and senior high school, and served also as lecturer at Kobe Kaisei College and Sapientia University which was located in Amagasaki. In 1979, he was stricken with heart disease and bedridden.

One day, I visited Mr. Yamaki who was recuperating at home in Himeji. While lying in bed, he was reading French and German books, and learning Spanish. There was a picture of his wife near him. The wife of his eldest son said, "I have lived with my father-in-law for twenty-three years, ever since I got married. He has always been united with Father Kolbe. Rather, I should say he rests in Father Kolbe. He gives off a brilliance like today, when he talks of Father Kolbe." In fact, his face was radiant and he talked a lot.

He said happily, "Father Kolbe always said '*veritas una*' (truth is one). If I hadn't met Father Kolbe, Saint Francis would have been only an object of my research."

This short statement by Mr. Yamaki remained in my mind for a long time. These were the last words of a man who lived his long life with great care, always seeking the Way. I saw the image of old Saint Francis in this aged teacher. Three months later, he was called to Heaven at the age of eighty-five. Father Kolbe, who often said *veritas una* to Mr. Yamaki, would have been the first person in Heaven to meet him.

CHAPTER 6

Every Day Is Mary's Day

*Oura is filled with memories of Father Kolbe:
the statue of Santa Maria in the cathedral;
stone steps leading up to the seminary and its classroom
where Father Kolbe taught philosophy to the young students.*

The Philosophy that Father Kolbe Taught

Morning comes early in Oura, a cosmopolitan district in Nagasaki City. Day broke with the sound of the bell at Oura Cathedral. Polish knights, whose friary was near Oura Cathedral, also

Seminarians in kimono were photographed with their philosophy professor, Father Kolbe.

started their activity early in the morning. They woke up at five, after which they joined Father Kolbe in going to the cathedral as Bishop Hayasaka had not granted permission to celebrate Mass in the friary yet.

Having a breakfast of only bread and tea after Mass, the friars started printing at once. Their entire life consisted of publishing *The Knights*. Father Kolbe and the two seminarians went to Oura seminary, where Father Kolbe was a professor of philosophy.

On September 22nd, Father Kolbe made the following entry in his diary: "I lecture eight hours a week, at nine every morning, and again at three-thirty on Tuesdays and Thursdays." He lectured on philosophy in general, including ethics, psychology, metaphysics, and natural theology. He taught diligently for two years from April 1930 to March 1932 with few lecture cancellations.

The wooden building of the "Latin Seminario" built by Father Petitjean in 1875, more than one hundred years ago, is still in existence. It is designated as an Important Cultural Property by Japan. More than thirty minor seminarians boarded there at that time; however, Father Kolbe did not teach in this building. Seminarians of the philosophy course boarded at the missionary school above the cathedral and heard Father Kolbe's lectures there.

The stone steps, which lead up to the former missionary school, still remain as they were. The external appearance of the building was totally changed and it is now a convent. However, inside the building we can still see the traces of the former school. There are three semicircular windows, like in a church; and ten columns, originally set on the terrace, are displaced beautifully inside the room now. I am delighted with the consideration of the sisters who preserved the building carefully. In this small room Father Kolbe lectured philosophy with a passionate gaze through his spectacles, and taught how one should live.

Fourteen seminarians belonged to the philosophy course, eleven of whom were from the diocese. They wore kimonos in the first year and soutanes in the second year. The other three seminarians — Mirochna, Damian, and Aleksy — who joined from the second year, belonged to the friary of the Knights of the Immaculata.

Six of the fourteen seminarians are still alive (in 1980): Father Banri Nakashima, Father Shiro Iwanaga, Father Shizuo Iwanaga, Father Totaro Nakata, Father Mirochna, and Mr. Gen'ichi Eguchi. As ten of the fourteen seminarians became priests, we may say that the percentage of the seminarians who were called to the priesthood was amazingly high.

Always Praising the Students with "Bene!"

Father Kolbe gave all his lectures in Latin, as he had not been in Japan for long and could not speak Japanese, except for a few phrases. Latin was the common language in the Catholic church in those days, and all the ceremonies of the church, the liturgy, and prayers were carried out in Latin. Therefore, after completing the secondary education, seminarians studied Latin hard. However, Latin is very difficult to learn as it is not a modern language. It took quite a while and required much effort to master this difficult language. The Latin proficiency of the philosophy students was insufficient. As they had to study the difficult philosophy with their inadequate knowledge of the language, we can understand how arduous was the task of carrying out the lectures. "Nevertheless, Father Kolbe tried very hard to make the students understand the lectures one way or another," said Father Nakata. When seminarian Nakata was puzzling over a difficult question, Father Kolbe motivated him to answer it, encouraging him gently: "Dicas! (Tell me!) Dicas!" And when seminarian Nakata could somehow answer the question, he repeated "Bene! (Good!) Bene!" In addition, the textbook, which Bishop Hayasaka directly obtained from Rome, was a laborious and high level one written by a famous professor of the Pontifical Gregorian University. Father Kolbe had studied in this university for three years and earned a doctoral degree in philosophy at the age of twenty-one.

A keen professor, Father Kolbe gave lectures in his own way using simple examples. To the great relief of the students, he let them cross out some parts of the textbook before the exam, excluding them from the scope of the exam, saying, "Omittamus. (We omit them.)"

He often said, "Bene! Bene!" How tenderly his "Bene!" touched the hearts of the young Japanese students!

Exam was a big challenge for the students. According to Father Shiro Iwanaga, they always had to have oral exams, which Bishop Hayasaka and Principal Urakawa attended. Although Father Kolbe advised his students, "If it is difficult to answer in Latin, you can answer in Japanese," the students did whatever they could to reply in Latin in the presence of the Bishop and the Principal. Then Principal Urakawa often smiled wryly and Bishop Hayasaka grinned. But Father Kolbe would repeat "Bene!" as usual and evaluated the students generously with "optime (best)."

Father Kolbe told interesting stories, explained their undertakings, and sometimes made requests of the students at the beginning or the end of his lecture. In the first lecture, Father Kolbe asked students to translate a Latin phrase into Japanese. Seminarian Hatada, who became a priest later and passed away in 1960, wrote down "mugenzai no seibo no kishi" and it became the Japanese title of *The Knights*. Mr. Gen'ichi Eguchi, whose study had been interrupted by illness — much to his chagrin — had the following memory to share:

> In one class Father Kolbe said, "I want a new printing machine. The Immaculate Mary will take care of it." Several days later he said, "A man in Tokyo gave us a donation. The Immaculate Mary will see that everything is all right." And the next time he said with delight, "I finally ordered a new printing machine from Poland. The Immaculate Mary will fulfill our hope." After quite a while he gave thanks: "We

received the new printing machine at last. The Immaculate Mary fulfilled our hope."

While repeating "The Immaculate Mary" as if he were praying the Rosary, Father Kolbe just asked that Our Lady's will be done and thanked her for it. There is a saying that "every day is a good day," but in the case of Father Kolbe, it is better to say that "every day is Mary's day."

The spot Father Kolbe loved most was the Maria statue in Oura Cathedral that was involved in the discovery of hidden Catholics. Father Kolbe took pleasure in praying before this statue of Santa Maria on the way to and from the seminary. His prayer was by no means lengthy. He prayed for a short time, but enthusiastically, at the place where the hidden Catholics had courageously confessed their faith after hiding it for two hundred and fifty years. What triggered their confession was the statue of Santa Maria. There may be no other mystical place like this in the world! Father Kolbe, who prayed to Our Lady, left a deep impression on the seminarians. When I asked Father Kolbe's former students what impressed them most about him, they unanimously mentioned his praying before the statue of Santa Maria.

One student said, "I can't forget Father Kolbe's beautiful, shining eyes!" In the depth of his pure eyes there must have been a hidden textbook of philosophy.

The seminarians who learned philosophy from Father Kolbe for the full duration of two years were promoted to the theology course. Two of them went to Rome, and two went to Paris. The other seminarians went to the Major Seminary in Tokyo. Subsequently, Father Kolbe left the seminary.

After Professor, Editor

The distance between Oura Cathedral and the friary of the Knights of the Immaculata was only a little less than a hundred meters. When Father Kolbe completed his duties with seminarians

Father Kolbe wrote letters and manuscripts until late at night.

and came back to the friary, his busy life as editor and guardian started. Through his diary and letters we can get a glimpse of what Father Kolbe's life was like then.

From September 2nd to the 5th, there was a retreat for the confraternity of the Knights of the Immaculata, which quietly began its activity as an organized group. At the end of October, Brother Seweryn was able to pick and set type. Father Kolbe rejoiced: "Glory to the Immaculata Mary! At last our colleagues are capable of handling Japanese types — something we have long awaited!"

November 1st. All Saints' Day. A group of seminarians came to help Father Kolbe. In fact, they must have felt especially close to him. They often came to help him with writing addresses or printing the magazine. But they often got into mischief, according to Brother Zeno.

Brother Zeno was multi-talented and had various skills. Although he could do anything, he especially liked working with machinery; he assembled the German printing machine and repaired it when necessary. But somehow the machine he bought in Osaka did not feed paper smoothly and often tore it. Then the seminarians made fun of Brother Zeno, singing a song they made up themselves with a humorous melody.

Father Kolbe wrote: "November 15th. A fourteen-year-old boy came to help us. He is not baptized. I told him that he would be a good friar, if he worked hard. I hear now some Japanese shouting outside, 'delicious *obiad*.'" *Obiad* means lunch in Polish. The name of this fourteen-year-old boy was Tatsuo Tanizaki. He was a junior high school student. He received a copy of *The Knights*, which Brother Zeno had distributed in front of the school, just a few days before. That is why Tanizaki came to visit Father Kolbe and the other friars, of course without his father's knowledge.

The boy grew familiar with the friars and ate obiad with delight. He sometimes sat surrounded by the big friars, who learned the basics of Japanese from him. We can just imagine this heart-warming scene!

On December 4th, after more than six months since the arrival of the Knights, the first Japanese wishing to be a friar visited them at last. This seventeen year old man from Urakami was an apprentice tailor. He was short, wore glasses, and was likely to be exempted from the military service because of a slight disability in his leg. Father Kolbe rejoiced at the first Japanese Knight, and cherished him. By the participation of this Japanese, their lives became considerably more convenient.

Brother Zeno distributed *The Knights* as usual, everywhere in the city. One day he walked about handing out copies to the factory workers, saying, "If you want to continue to read the magazine, I will send it to you. Please write down your name and address here." He had them write their names and addresses in his notebook. There were some wise guys who wrote fictitious names like Mataemon Araki, who was a great swordsman during the time of the persecution of Catholics.

Brother Zeno brought the list of the addresses carefully home, and had his Catholic helpers write them on the envelopes. When a helper said, "As this is a false name, I cannot ship it," Brother Zeno insisted to send it anyway, as he had obtained it with effort. The Catholics who helped him were puzzled with his insistence, because the story titled "Mataemon Araki" had been published as a series in the Nagasaki Shimbun Newspaper and was very popular just then.

At that time Father Kolbe wrote in his letter, "We are leading a poor life. We don't drink milk. We haven't seen a cow. We haven't thought about meat. We don't eat Western food. We eat rice, wheat and noodles of wheat flour. Potatoes are a luxury."

One day Mr. Uraoka, a Catholic butcher, gave a large amount of beef to the friars, so that they could get more nourishment. Brother Hilary, who was in charge of cooking, was astonished to see so much beef for the first time since their arrival in Nagasaki. He exclaimed, "it will be our first feast in a long time!" as he put all the meat into a pot and began to boil it. Since the meat was too much, the lid popped up and one could see inside the pot.

At that very moment, Bishop Hayasaka appeared in the friary and said with a grin, "I thought you lived in poverty, but you have a potful of meat. I've never seen such a feast even in the Bishop's residence." Brother Hilary went into a panic, and tried to explain in Japanese that it was a present but he was at a loss for words. Father Kolbe intervened and explained the matter in Latin. Bishop Hayasaka certainly had known of the generous gift and consoled Brother Hilary by saying, "I am well aware of your hardship."

At that time, there was no kitchen in their building, so the friars cooked either outside or on the terrace, so Bishop Hayasaka could easily look into the pot. On a rainy day, another visitor saw a friar cooking rice with an umbrella and said, "He opens an umbrella so that the soup in the pot will not get diluted."

The year was drawing to a close and soon it was December 24th, Christmas Eve. It was the first Christmas in Japan for the Knights, and they prepared a feast. The boy, Tanizaki, also joined the dinner party in the evening.

Before the party, everyone had a big *oplatki* (Christmas wafer) in their hands and broke a piece of it, exchanging one part with each other, saying "Merry Christmas!" and they ate together. This is a Polish custom on Christmas Eve. Tanizaki, quite bashful, was warmly accepted into the friendly atmosphere of the Franciscans. Father Kolbe wrote in his diary on that day, "A Japanese boy confided to me that he wants to be a Catholic." Tanizaki's father was an educated person and at first opposed the idea that his son would become Catholic. However, after three years Tanizaki was baptized, and soon thereafter, his father was also baptized under the guidance of Father Kolbe.

The Christmas Midnight Mass was celebrated in the beautifully decorated Oura Cathedral. The Oura seminarians served at the Solemn Christmas Mass and sang hymns, which was the tradition since the foundation of the cathedral in the Meiji era. The Latin hymns sung by Father Kolbe's students were wonderful! Father Kolbe served with humility as a deacon in the Mass celebrated by Bishop Hayasaka and prayed with gratitude at the altar.

So the year 1930 was coming to an end. It was a memorable year for Father Kolbe who came over to Japan from Poland under the banner of the Immaculate Mary. At the same time, it was the first of the next six years abounding in hardship and suffering.

CHAPTER 7

An Incident in the First Winter

*A statue of Jizo, a Buddhist guardian deity of children,
was placed in a bush on a mountain slope.
The Knights bought the land, and when they removed
the statue of Jizo, they found a cross there.*

Sacrifice on the Feast of the Immaculate Conception

The Knights were getting ready for their first winter in Oura. Seven months had passed since their arrival in Nagasaki. December 8th, the Feast of the Immaculate Conception of the Virgin Mary was approaching. It is one of the most important feasts of Our Lady, whom Father Kolbe venerated at the risk of his life; and also, the title of the magazine, *The Knights of the Immaculata*, was derived from the feast. Therefore, they had a special practice of praying and sacrificing for nine days before the feast out of love for the Immaculata. What would they sacrifice to Our Lady this year?

The publication of *The Knights* had gotten on the right track, and the December issue reached 20,000 copies. The manual printing machine was replaced by an electric one. If they had enough funds, they could print more copies. The future looked bright! Of course there were some small difficulties, but the Knights' ship was running through calm seas at full sail.

Sometimes though, Our Lady requires immeasurable sacrifices. On the day before the Feast of the Immaculate Conception, a telegram arrived at breakfast. Father Kolbe read it and said, "Let's kneel down." The seven Knights knelt and Father Kolbe recited the prayer for the dead. After praying, he read the telegram from Poland. "Father Alfons died a praise-worthy death. Everything is in order." Then the friars wept with surprise and sorrow for the first time. Father Alfons was the guardian of the friary of Niepokalanów and Father Kolbe's younger brother.

"It's incredible that Father Alfons died suddenly," said one of the friars.

Would there ever be a bigger sacrifice than this? It was thanks to Father Alfons, who protected the headquarters firmly in both financial and human resources, that Father Kolbe was able to spread the word of God in the East. Father Kolbe might have to go home in this situation.

However, Father Kolbe behaved nobly then. He was not upset at all. He just said, "I envy him," and accepted his brother's death with serenity. "It is just before the Feast of the Immaculate Conception. He was called by the Immaculata and he went back to the Niepokalanów in Heaven. I'm certain that he is one with the Immaculata now. So I'm really envious of him," Father Kolbe said from the bottom of his heart. Seminarian Mirochna remembered Father Alfons, asleep from fatigue at his desk in his room four months before, on the day Mirochna left Poland. In this way the funeral Mass of Father Alfons was celebrated on the Feast of the Immaculate Conception. The friars sang a requiem in mournful tone.

This had been an historical feast for the Franciscan order for several hundred years, which paved the way for the Immaculate Conception of the Virgin Mary to become a dogma of the Catholic Church. It was a tradition of the Order to celebrate it for eight days after the feast.

At this time, there occurred another worrisome event for the Knights of the Immaculata: Seminarian Mirochna was hospitalized because of peritonitis. He had arrived in Nagasaki with Father Kolbe at the end of August and had started to attend the Oura seminary in September. But from that time on, he had been feeling ill; in the autumn, he began to vomit and suffered from abdominal pain. Yasuro Fukahori, a Catholic doctor, advised him to go to the hospital and have an operation. Mirochna appeared to have acute appendicitis.

According to the letter which came from Poland later, Father Alfons died of acute suppurative peritonitis. Having heard that he needed to have an operation, Mirochna went to the hospital in a gloomy mood.

Father Kolbe Faints

The year 1931 began and seminarian Mirochna underwent the operation just after the New Year. Father Kolbe came to the hospital on that very day. The abdominal operation took more than two hours and the patient suffered from severe pain during the entire time, as the anesthesia was not very effective. When Mirochna was brought to the recovery room after the operation, his face was pale. With one look at him, Father Kolbe fainted. Nurses quickly took care of him and let him rest in the next room.

They spoke of Father Kolbe: "He is surely the elder brother of the patient." They must have felt that he had warmer affection for Mirochna than the real family members. After a while, Father Kolbe regained consciousness and went back to Oura. Father Kolbe himself was suffering from lung disease and always ran a slight fever. Nevertheless, he brought Communion to Mirochna every day.

The operation was not completely successful. In a letter, Father Kolbe expressed his suspicions about Japanese medicine. The wound was still open and pus came out of it. Seminarian Mirochna thought he might need another surgery, as he watched the grey clouds in the winter sky from day to day. Then he received a telegram from the Provincial who advised him to return to Poland. He wondered whether he could ever become a priest. The hospitalization cost 3 yen a day; in addition, the operation and the treatment were fairly expensive. Mirochna understood well that the Knights of the Immaculata had no money at all to spare.

Father Kolbe referred to the hospitalization in his letters several times: "If a seminarian comes to the mission field and is afraid of hardships and adversity, he had better stay quietly at home." "I paid 200 yen in hospital costs. 200 yen is half as much as our monthly expenses for living and missionary work. I paid the cost willingly, because I know that the Immaculata will bless us even more." He also wrote, "Mirochna's recuperative power is weak. The Immaculata may have her own idea." Father Kolbe suffered things he could not share with others but he was never disappointed in the Immaculata.

Father Kolbe said to Mirochna, "Our Lady will look after your illness." "Sick people are the treasure of Niepokalanów, whose sacrifices will bring the grace of conversion to the readers of *The Knights*." "Even if you are called to Heaven now, there will be a great glory for you as you stand before the Immaculata, because you were willing to devote your life to Japan. There is no more honorable thing than to die in the mission field." This was exactly the resolution of the Knights of the Immaculata. And seminarian Mirochna persevered through his trial.

At the beginning of February, Father Kolbe visited Mirochna in the hospital and said, "Brother Zeno has been engaged in finding land." The Knights were renting one of the four buildings on a property down the hill from Oura Cathedral. The owner of this land proposed to sell it to them, including the buildings and the garden, for 45,000 yen, or 30 yen per 3.3 m². They didn't have that much money. They were looking for a cheaper, quieter, and more spacious property.

Finding Land in the Hilly Section

At any rate, Brother Zeno's method of trying to purchase land was amazing, if a bit too bold. He was not very proficient in Japanese.

"I want to buy land." "It's too expensive!" "Please give me a discount." Handling these simple phrases skillfully, he tried to buy land. Mostly, he relied on the good will he engendered with his beard and gestures.

This is what I heard from Brother Zeno: One day a water supply worker, wearing a cap, told him that there was land for sale. The worker brought him to Inasa Shinto Shrine and called aloud, "Priest!" The Shinto priest came out and the worker ran away. Brother Zeno just stood there.

The priest asked, "What's the matter with you?" "I want to buy land," answered Brother Zeno. "Which land?" asked the priest. "This land, here! I want to buy it cheap!" The priest got angry: "Don't be ridiculous! I won't sell it! I must ask you to leave!" It turned out the worker had played a prank on Brother Zeno.

In the middle of February, when Mirochna was still in the hospital, Father Kolbe said, "We finally were able to find a piece of land." Brother Zeno added, "This time it's not the water supply worker, but a city employee." He had told Brother Zeno that there was an estate for sale in Hongouchi, and asked him whether he would be interested in buying it. Brother Zeno went out there to the outskirts of town. The estate was on a thickly forested hillside. Most of the land was not flat, but covered with bushes. Sixteen owners possessed this land in common. The land covered an area of 25,000 m^2 and cost about one yen per 3.3 m^2. The landowners required a payment of 7,000 yen within three months.

The funds which would be sent from Poland amounted to 10,000 yen. After paying for the land, there would be a remainder of 3,000 yen. With this money, the construction of the friary was in sight. Although there was a person who wished to donate an estate in Urakami, Father Kolbe preferred the land on the hillside. He thought it was the will of Our Lady to buy it, because they could build a Lourdes grotto there. Brother Zeno, however, was against it, and he was still attracted to the estate in Urakami.

One day Father Kolbe visited Yoshitaro Komori, who lived along the national highway, to negotiate the land purchase. When Father Kolbe arrived, Mr. Komori was by the well which enshrined the "Water God (Suijin)." Father Kolbe asked in Japanese, "Where is the master (Shujin) of this house?" "Shujin" sounded like "Suijin." Then Mr. Komori said to himself, "This 'Dutch' person is religious, because he says Suijin." All the foreigners were called Dutch in Nagasaki. Afterwards, he realized that Father Kolbe said Shujin instead of Suijin, and laughed out loud with his family.

The landowners proposed the following conditions:

1. When signing a contract, a reliable Japanese priest or a lay person should be present.
2. At the beginning, 1,500 yen should be paid as a deposit.
3. If the rest of the price is not paid by the end of May, the deposit would not be refunded nor the land transferred, and the house built on this land will be confiscated.

There was an untold reason why the landowners imposed such severe conditions. The friars came to realize later that no one had cultivated the land since the Edo Period.

There were bushes and bamboo trees that grew thick around there. Legend had it that the graves of persecuted Catholics were located here and a rumor spread that people saw will-o'-the-wisp there.

Previously there were three people who had tried to buy the land to build a villa. But they all gave up when they heard the rumors. One of them tried to plant seven hundred Japanese apricot trees but he gave it up for fear of being cursed, because so many human bones were dug up in the process. That's why the landowners did not touch the land themselves.

"I don't care about those things." Brother Zeno was cool as if nothing of this mattered. Sure enough, many human bones and old coins were found when they reclaimed the land in order to build a friary. Stones engraved with a cross were also found. Father Kolbe reported to Bishop Hayasaka that the land seemed to be the place where persecuted Catholics were buried. Bishop Hayasaka was delighted and said, "It's a very good place, as the blood of Catholics was shed there."

After the purchase of the land where the friary of the Knights of the Immaculata presently stands was decided in this way, seminarian Mirochna was finally released from the hospital where he had been for two and a half months. The cold winter was passing and spring was just around the corner. The winter in Nagasaki is not as severe as in Poland. As it got warmer, his health improved. Although the incision from his surgery had not healed yet, he went to the hospital in between taking classes in philosophy at the seminary.

Discovery of the Crucifix of the Ancient Catholics

Bright spring days also reached Mirochna, who was fully recovered after being discharged from the hospital. One Sunday, the Knights went for a walk from Oura to the land in Hongouchi. As one could see the city of Nagasaki at a distance from the hilltop, Father Kolbe was pleased with the location. But the slope was covered with bushes. Father Kolbe said, "Japan is a mountainous country. So it is appropriate to build Niepokalanów here. We will possibly be able to build a Lourdes grotto. This land is very good. People don't like to buy this land, because there is a graveyard down here. There may also be graves of the persecuted Catholics in it."

There were no houses around there but a narrow road from the mountain to the graves. Beside the road there was a huge stone, on which a Jizo statue about one meter in height was enshrined. It was probably built for the repose of souls. Twelve Poles in habit took a picture near the statue.

"Let's build a seminary around there and its school ground near here." Father Kolbe was already nurturing his dream and imagined Japanese boys playing around there.

A crucifix of ancient Catholics was found under a Jizo statue.

Seminarian Mirochna was rather pessimistic: "Where can we build a house on such a place? It's in the mountains! Is it possible to build a seminary here?" Father Kolbe said, "See how the Japanese people do. They are building wonderful houses in the mountainous areas. Let's follow their examples."

As Father Kolbe had imagined, a seminary was built after only five years and the school grounds also came to be, where nineteen students from Nagasaki City, the Goto Islands and Hirado enjoyed playing sports.

With apologies to Jizo, the statue was retired and carefully relocated by the townspeople to the head of a trail up Mt. Hikosan. In the autumn of the year when the seminary was founded, a crucifix was unexpectedly found exactly where the statue had been. It was a strange coincidence. The size of the crucifix was 11.5 cm long and 5.8 cm wide. The Christ on the crucifix was worn away and roundish.

According to a local historian, it was made three hundred years ago and another crucifix in the same mold has been kept in the Tokyo National Museum. Presumably, hidden Catholics carefully preserved it at the risk of their lives, prayed before it secretly and passed it down to their descendants. And it was Father Mirochna, who had just become a priest after recovering from his illness, who took charge of the crucifix which a seminarian had found and brought to him.

Father Mirochna served as principal of the minor seminary after Father Kolbe, who had returned to Poland after seeing the first class of students enter the seminary. Holding the valuable Christian relic in his hands, Father Mirochna hoped to show it to Father Kolbe, who was in Poland then, and definitely would be delighted by it.

Father Mirochna thought that this was exactly the land the Immaculata wanted for them. When the atomic bomb was dropped, the land was protected by the mountain and suffered little damage from the bombing.

The crucifix of the hidden Catholics became one of the most important treasures of the Knights of the Immaculata. Silently, it speaks to us of the "secret faith" of those who had to pass many years under harsh persecution. Even if not as severe, we all have to undergo harsh winter seasons in our own lives. "It's an unforgettable memory of how we found this land in Hongouchi." Father Mirochna seemed to be recalling that winter when, as a seminarian, he suffered from illness.

CHAPTER 8

Establishing *Mugenzai no Sono* (the Garden of the Immaculata)

One year had passed since the Knights came to Nagasaki and started living in Oura. On a sunny day after much rainfall, they moved to Hongouchi where they lived in severe, holy poverty.

No Potatoes in Japan?

In January, 1931, while Father Kolbe was still in the provisional friary in Oura, he wrote a letter to Poland in his own room: "First of all, about money. The funds which Niepokalanów granted us must be used for the glory of the Immaculata. We must not use it for other purposes, however wonderful they might be. We merely are managers of the donations received from the members of the Knights of the Immaculata and the readers of *The Knights*; we are never permitted to use it arbitrarily. The money should be used only to make the whole world belong to the Immaculata.

Next, personnel. We would like to have a brother who can work simultaneously as a zincographer, a photographer and an editorial staffer, and has a holy soul, completely consecrated to the Immaculata. He should be able to use Latin and other languages. English is especially necessary."

Father Kolbe wrote no further than that when the bell rang for lunch. He went to the dining room. When the silence was broken after lunch, he asked the brothers who would be the best to join them in Japan. They suggested Brother Romuald Mroziński and Brother Celestyn Moszyński. He wrote their names in the letter he had begun before lunch.

In the friary of Niepokalanów Father Florian served as guardian after the late Father Alfons. Father Florian called the two brothers mentioned in the letter. They were both twenty-one years old and full of vigor. Brother Celestyn was born in Kiev in Russia and a little thin. Brother Romuald, the son of a gardener, had a good physique. Both of them hoped to go to Japan; Brother Romuald especially had prayed secretly for this.

Finally, both of them were to leave Poland for Japan. As Brother Celestyn was born in Russia, it was dangerous for him to take the Siberian Railway. Travelers through there sometimes went missing. Therefore, he took a steamship. Brother Romuald had to travel independently. As the cars of the Siberian Railway were for four passengers, Father Metody and two seminarians, Aleksy and Ludwik, accompanied him. Father Metody was the first priest of the Order of the Conventual Franciscans to go to Japan, except for Father Kolbe. So Father Kolbe looked forward to his joining them very much: he would be able to write manuscripts in Italian, as he had studied in the seminary in Assisi and could speak the language.

Father Kolbe wrote "travel information to the missionaries departing via Siberia for Japan" in a long letter. It showed precisely how to buy tickets; things to bring like teapots and some canned food, how to buy bread; how to give tips, necessity of blankets, convenience of air pillows; absolute necessity to lock one's luggage, currency exchange; to be vigilant at night on the train; and Japanese words necessary for traveling like fune (ship), eki (station) or kisha (train). We can see here evidence of how considerate Father Kolbe, the veteran traveler, was for others.

On an early spring day in the middle of March, Brother Celestyn arrived in Kobe alone. Half a month later, the other four arrived in Nagasaki. Brother Romuald was impressed by the vast ocean he had seen for the first time in his life at the Korean Straits. He also ate bananas in Nagasaki for the first time.

The number of the members in Oura was now twelve: two priests, four seminarians and six brothers. Ludwik and Damian went to Tokyo to study at the major seminary there.

As Father Metody came to Nagasaki, Bishop Hayasaka said to Father Kolbe, "You don't have to come to Oura Cathedral for Holy Mass. You may celebrate Mass at the friary. But the Eucharist should not be reserved there yet." They went to Oura Cathedral for Benediction of the Blessed Sacrament and Sunday Mass.

Without time to recover from the fatigue of the long journey, Brother Celestyn started working hard as a clerk and Brother Romuald as a printer. He said, "We didn't have a paper folding machine at that time, so we folded paper by hand. When it comes to folding paper, I'm second to none. I flatter myself that I folded 3,000 sheets in a day. My fingers were blood stained."

Brother Romuald worked hard as a printer.

But Brother Romuald was annoyed with the poor meals. He was not willing to complain about it, but he could not fight the good fight on an empty stomach. He rarely saw a Western meal but ate mostly rice or udon noodles. Above all there were no potatoes, which he had eaten so often in Poland! Brother Zeno, who was in charge of shopping, told Brother Romuald that there were no potatoes in Japan, and gave him none. Brother Romuald, not knowing about Japan, thought it was true that there were no potatoes in the country. Day after day he could not eat any potatoes! But one day he saw a female farmer going up the road to the cathedral, carrying a basket full of potatoes. By chance, Brother Romuald saw her from the window on the second floor.

"There are potatoes!" he cried out in Polish. He ran to Father Kolbe, saying "I found potatoes! There are potatoes here in Japan. I saw them."

"Okay! Okay! Let's buy them," Father Kolbe gently answered. Then Brother Zeno came in a hurry and said in a loud voice, "I don't buy potatoes, because they are expensive!" But Father Kolbe bought the potatoes. The farmer was very happy that foreigners bought them, and said waving her hand, "Please buy potatoes again!" Brother Romuald, who could not understand a single Japanese word, waved his hand modestly. The following Sunday, the potatoes were cooked in a Polish way, and enjoyed by all. Brother Zeno also ate them, muttering "Expensive! Expensive!"

Surprised by a Fight among the Carpenters

By the time Brother Romuald arrived in Nagasaki, it had already been decided to buy the new plot of land. It was a forlorn, hilly place covered with weeds and bamboo grass at the foot of Mt. Hikosan. Father Kolbe asked Brother Romuald, "What do you think about this land?" In truth, Brother Romuald was disappointed to see the place. "I can see only bushes and bamboo grass. Wherever can we build a house?"

Father Kolbe consoled him: "It's all right; since the Immaculata wishes it to be, we can definitely accomplish it. Let's do our best to make her wish come true."

Brother Zeno and Brother Romuald cut the bamboo grass, opened the land, and most importantly, installed the statue of the Immaculata. They followed the example of the foundation of Niepokalanów. Brother Romuald tied a towel around his head in the Japanese fashion for the first time and worked hard. Some local residents helped them. There exists one photo taken at this time. There are friars and local residents in front of the statue of the Immaculata. Father Kolbe is also among them and a young woman can be seen at the right. Several dozens of pictures of Father Kolbe were taken in Nagasaki but this is a rare picture, the only one in which a woman is included.

In April, Brother Zeno, Brother Romuald, and Brother Celestyn poured concrete for the foundation of the first building which would be a temporary one-story, wooden house, 8 meters wide and 24 meters long.

Brother Zeno suggested building the house by themselves in order to save money. Besides printing the magazine, they bought lumber and started the preparations at Oura. However, as they were not professional carpenters, the pieces of lumber did not fit well. Brother Zeno had built a house with bricks in Poland, but he had never built a Japanese house with timber and roof tiles. Sometimes, he took the wrong measurements and Brother Romuald chiseled holes in the wrong places, so their undertaking made no progress at all. It was surely too much for them! Finally, the Polish friars got confused and they left the construction to Japanese carpenters from the town.

So, the professional carpenters started to build the house at Hongouchi. Just when things were starting to go well, a serious incident happened on May 7th. It was the day of the frame raising ceremony, according to the diary of Father Kolbe. Some local carpenters came to the ceremony uninvited and began to complain that they were upset because the town carpenters had invaded their territory. The quarrel developed into a fight. The town carpenters, being in the minority, were severely injured and abandoned the house construction.

Father Kolbe wrote in his diary: "The carpenters fought. Five of them were arrested by the police." The fight must have been fairly fierce. The friars who usually lived a quiet life were shocked by it all. Besides, the weather changed suddenly that night, with heavy rain and violent winds. The friars were afraid that the framework might be damaged by the rain and wind. They were so worried about the house under construction that Brother Zeno and three other friars ran the four kilometers from Oura to Hongouchi in the rain.

When they finally arrived at the building site, the local carpenters were propping up the house so that it would not fall down in the heavy rain. How considerate of them! It was hard to believe that they had fought with the town carpenters so terribly. The friars expressed their gratitude to the local carpenters.

Father Kolbe was worried about how the affair might turn out. He temporarily stopped the construction to allow the matter to settle down; then he invited both groups of carpenters and made the following suggestion: The town carpenters would make the roof and the inside walls. The local carpenters of the neighborhood would do everything else.

The local carpenters agreed to this proposal, as they could also get work for themselves. But the town carpenters were not satisfied with this proposal. They insisted they would do the whole job themselves. And several days later, thirteen town carpenters assembled at the building site and they all together completed the house nicely in just one day, including the roof and walls. The house could be built so quickly because it was just like a barracks, which was quite fitting for Franciscan friars.

The friars, including Father Kolbe, were delighted. Father Kolbe wrote in his diary of May 13th, Wednesday: "The Immaculata sent us thirteen carpenters. They finished everything very quickly. Mr. Yamazaki, the carpenter who undertook to build the house, gave us a donation of 5 yen 50 sen before he went home."

A Friar Playing Hide and Seek

The long-awaited house was completed and the time came for the friars to move in. Their year in Oura was about to end. Father Kolbe decided they would move on May 15th, since they would have to pay the rent for the following month, if they postponed the move for one day. But since it rained heavily on that day, it was impossible for them to move under those circumstances.

On that very day, Father Kolbe was to depart for a Eucharistic Procession in Miyazaki. Mr. Lo-Pa-Hong, a Chinese millionaire, visited Nagasaki to donate the baldachin for the Procession. He came to Oura to meet Father Kolbe, whom he had met when Father Kolbe had gotten off the ship at Shanghai on his way to propagating the Faith in Asia. He had taken care of Father Kolbe there. Mr. Lo was the president of the Shanghai Electric Railway and ran a children's home and a nursing home at his own expense for the sake of social welfare. He had promised to support Father Kolbe's missionary work. So, out of gratitude to Mr. Lo, Father Kolbe decided to take him with him on the trip to Miyazaki.

Before starting off on the trip, Father Kolbe emphatically said to the friars, "Tomorrow is Saturday, the day of Our Lady. Be sure to move to the new location no matter what!" The next day it was still raining a little. About noon the weather cleared up and one could see the blue sky. With this good weather, the friars began to move enthusiastically. They carried the printing machine in a carriage. The May blue sky seemed to celebrate the bright future of the Polish friars. "This is definitely the blessing of Our Lady. As Father Kolbe always says, everything goes well if we do it with the Immaculata. We will be blessed if we are obedient to our superior." They were grateful and hurried to Hongouchi.

Saturday, May 16, 1931, was the beginning of the friary of the Knights of the Immaculata at Hongouchi. It was the second spring since they had landed on Nagasaki. However, there was still no window glass, nor even window frames in the new residence. "I immediately ordered them from a local carpenter," said Brother Romuald.

The one-story house of 192 m² consisted of a chapel, a guardian's room for Father Kolbe, a room for seminarian Mirochna, an office, a room for typesetting, a printing room, and a room for both dining and shipping. As no other room was included in the house, a kitchen was made in the open air, and for a toilet there was only an outhouse. The friars slept, believe it or not, in the attic! One could see the roof tiles from within and also the sky between the gaps.

At night they pulled down the ladder beside the printing machine and went up to the attic. As the Polish friars were somewhat tall, they often hit their heads on the beam. On the first night, Brother Romuald could hardly sleep because there were so many mosquitoes. The house was surrounded by bushes, so of course there were a lot of mosquitoes.

The next day was Sunday. Mr. Uraoka, a Catholic butcher in Oura, came to see how the friars were doing. Brother Romuald complained, waving his arms about: "Oh! It's terrible!" Mr. Uraoka said, "It's no wonder you couldn't sleep. We, Japanese, use a mosquito net. It's necessary here." Then he went off to buy a mosquito net for them.

Father Kolbe came back from Miyazaki to Hongouchi, by way of Kagoshima. His residence was no longer in Oura; those unforgettable days in Oura were over.

Father Kolbe called the land in Oura "Grodno in Japan" and the new land in Hongouchi "Niepokalanów in Japan." It was translated "Mugenzai no Sono" in Japanese. Grodno is the name of a city that then was located in the eastern part of Poland. It was the cradle of the Knights of the Immaculata. It was at the friary in Grodno where Brother Zeno entered the Order.

"May 29th, Friday. We paid off the entire price of the land," wrote Father Kolbe. With this payment, the land and the house finally belonged to the Knights of the Immaculata. Glory to the Immaculata!

On May 31st, the last day of the month of Mary, Bishop Hayasaka came to see the friary. Brother Romuald recollected the day: "Bishop Hayasaka was very pleased. When he came up, the stairs were covered with mud. He asked, "Where is the chapel? And the Eucharist? Not yet? You may now reserve it in the chapel." It was a great joy for us that we could reserve the Eucharist. Father Kolbe told Brother Hilary, who was responsible for cooking, to prepare something for the Bishop. But there was nothing, not even suitable dishes or chairs! There were only cans used as cups. Therefore, Brother Hilary fled and hid in the bamboo grove. It was as if he were playing hide and seek. He didn't appear, no matter how long we waited. Father Kolbe was very sad. We searched for him and finally brought him back. I don't know whether Father Kolbe gave him some words of admonition."

I can imagine that the young friar squatted down sadly in the bamboo grove, as there was nothing to entertain the Bishop with. The image of this despondent foreign friar may even evoke pity. But in fact, they all lived in the midst of holy poverty. We may say that the poorest life like this is truly Franciscan.

CHAPTER 9

Caramels from Our Lady

In spite of all of the hardships, there were also plenty of graces from the Immaculata. Father Kolbe named these graces 'caramels,' a delicious sweet.

A Shiny Black Desk

From the temporary friary in Oura the friars brought to Hongouchi a printing machine, printing types and a paper cutter, but no beds. They brought one more thing: a desk Father Kolbe used every day. This simple desk was made by Brother Zeno from rough and cheap boards.

They carried the items from Oura into the new barrack-styled friary. Today the wooden one-story building does not exist. It stood on the site of the present inner court in front of the printing office of the Knights of the Immaculata Publisher. The courtyard is overgrown with weeds.

The printing machine and the printing types have been disposed of. Only the desk of Father Kolbe is still carefully preserved in the Father Kolbe Memorial Museum. Everyone who visits the Knights of the Immaculata can touch this well-thumbed, shiny black and broad desk. If one pulls the drawer, one can easily see how crudely it is made. The boards were not smoothly planed and overall, the desk is poorly constructed. On the wall behind the desk there is a big photograph of Father Kolbe writing a manuscript. As we see in

Father Kolbe's room is preserved in the Saint Kolbe Museum.

this picture, Father Kolbe sat at this desk and continued writing manuscripts and letters, working very hard for six years in Nagasaki.

Father Kolbe wrote letters almost constantly. The addressees include the Superior General of his Order in Rome, the Father Provincial in Poland, the Guardian of Niepokalanów, and other friars. He often wrote to his mother too. The letters reached a huge number if we include those to individual persons. Fortunately, all of them were preserved in Poland. All the letters which Father Kolbe wrote during his stay in Japan were translated into Japanese and published in December 1980. It was indeed a laborious undertaking, but because of it we are able to know exactly the life of *Mugenzai no Sono* (Niepokalanów in Japan) in its early stage and the ideas of Father Kolbe.

The Knights moved from Oura to Hongouchi in May, 1931, and experienced there the rainy season in June and the hot summer in July and August. I shall quote from Father Kolbe's letters what happened during this period.

Firstly, his frequent requests for money stand out. As Father Kolbe often writes things like "we have no money," "please send money," "we need money," in his letters, his image as a "saint" might almost be tarnished. For example: "As we don't have 68 yen, we can't install electricity. We turned the machine by hand. And today, Brother Seweryn vomited blood. He presumably bled from his lungs."

"There is a tall embankment just behind the building. We need to remove it, as it blocks out the sun. In the rainy season, the dirty water came from the embankment into the rooms. There are too few of us to cope with the work. If we employ workers, it costs 200 yen." "Because of the lack of money, we have to go down to the public well to collect water. In the summer women and girls go around half naked there, which is intolerable to see. To build a link to the water supply network would cost 130 yen." "I imagine how embarrassing it must be for you to keep getting nothing but constant requests for 'money, money.' But we really need it. The walls of the house have gaps everywhere. The land should be fenced in, as the friary is on it. But the Immaculata knows everything and she will provide."

It was the friary of Niepokalanów in Poland that paid all their expenses.

Salt around Feet

Father Kolbe still went to Oura Seminary with two seminarians every day to teach philosophy. He continued doing so a year after their move. "I go to the Oura Seminary to teach Japanese students who will become priests in the future. In the absence of a bicycle, it takes almost an hour to get there and one more hour to get back. It saves no time to go by street car." "Will some Polish reader of *The Knights* help us? We need one bicycle — well, really three bicycles, as there are three of us going to the seminary. Will someone help us to cover the exterior walls with clay; remove the embankment to let the sunlight in; build a fence; purchase a printing machine and pay off the debt in this mission country? I well know times are bad now, but…"

The last resort was to cut back on the friars' living expenses.

Secondly, the toughness of the friars, like oak trees, stands out in the letters. Father Kolbe evaluated: "Brother Zeno, Brother Seweryn, Brother Celestyn, and Brother Romuald serve the Immaculata sincerely, with all their souls. They are strong like oak trees."

It was the first Japanese summer for Brother Romuald who is now (in 1981) seventy-two years old and resides in the Nigawa friary in Nishinomiya City. It is pretty hot in the summer in Nagasaki. Sweat streams down even if one does nothing! As Brother Romuald used his large body as the motor of the printing machine, his situation was most serious. Sweat literally poured down from him like a waterfall! The floor he was standing on got drenched with his sweat, and white salt remained afterwards.

Brother Romuald recollected: "As it was very hot, I sweated heavily. Gazing at it [the sweat], Father Kolbe said that it was for the sake of Our Lady. Once the sweat dried, there was salt left behind. As Brother Celestyn didn't want others to notice it, he kicked it around with his foot until it disappeared."

Brother Celestyn went to Manchuria during the Second World

War, fell ill and died there after the war. About two months had passed since the Knights moved, and they were now allowed to use the motor, which made the printing work easier. When Brother Seweryn worked until 1 a.m., Brother Romuald followed and worked until morning. Brother Romuald reflected: "As Brother Seweryn felt sorry for me, he worked until about 2 a.m."

At five o'clock in the morning the printing work stopped; then the friars prayed to God, meditated, and celebrated Mass. After that the regular work started. The workers were few. There were two priests and two seminarians. Two other seminarians were studying in Tokyo. Among the brothers, Brother Hilary had bad eyesight and Brother Zygmunt was engaged in office work. Brother Marian Sato was the first Japanese brother. Those who actually did heavy work were the three brothers: tough Brother Romuald, Brother Celestyn, and Brother Seweryn.

Brother Zeno was busy distributing *The Knights*, making contacts, shopping, and cooking. He always said, "I'm busy. I have no time," and went shopping late in the morning. He returned after noon and then the brothers got busy. He ordered: "You make a fire!" "You peel potatoes!" As Brother Zeno was an elder, they followed him reluctantly, while grumbling. Lunch time was never certain. After lunch, they visited the Blessed Sacrament, followed by a brief rest.

Brother Romuald looked back: "When I was tired and going to rest, Father Kolbe said, 'Please start working at once. You should reflect on whom you are working for.' This single word of advice was enough for us. Brother Celestyn and I worked hard without a break."

No doubt Father Kolbe had a firm trust in the Immaculata that she would surely be pleased if they did the work for her. This conviction certainly was transmitted to the brothers as well. Being encouraged by Father Kolbe, they dedicated themselves to their missionary work.

Day for the exhausted brothers ended in the attic. They went up to the attic in order to sleep. Then the roof tiles in front of their eyes, which had been cooked by the daytime sun, annoyed them, emitting heat. In winter snow fell in through the gaps. Presumably, they spent sleepless nights in this foreign country. They must have had a lot of hardship, poverty, and complaints. Yet, nonetheless, the new life and undertaking of *Mugenzai no Sono* started up.

Father Kolbe used a colorful expression that there were a lot of devils in Japan. "For every devil you may have at Niepokalanów in Poland, there are 10 devils here, since they know well the reason why we came to Japan." "The devils are not happy we have put down roots here. We are weak. With the help of Our Lady we shall laugh them off while whistling away." There seemed to be a reason why Father Kolbe felt the resistance of devils. At that time four colleagues were unable to fulfill their dream and returned to Poland. Since this was the first setback for Father Kolbe, we can infer his inner suffering from his letters. The first one among them was Father Metody, who stayed only half a year in Japan. Father Kolbe had high expectations of this young priest. But unfortunately, Father Metody, who had not come from Niepokalanów, could not understand Father Kolbe's devotion to the Immaculata and his spirit of holy poverty. Father Metody was opposed to Father Kolbe and only wanted an ordinary religious life and ordinary Marian devotions. Father Kolbe wrote: "He has not accepted the spirit of the Knights of the Immaculata yet. He uses a beautiful wicker chair and places a small pillow or blanket on it. According to him, those who want to live with greater rigor should join more rigorous religious orders; otherwise we should observe the way of the Conventual Franciscan life. I'm afraid that this spirit of lacking preference for holy poverty has begun to infect the other friars. However, he is a good person and does nothing to upset me."

Although he did not share the spirit of the Knights of the Immaculata, Father Metody was never a troublesome person. He heard the friars' confessions and carried out ordinary religious life. He simply could not follow the spirit of total devotion of Father Kolbe for anything. But his discomfort significantly disturbed the atmosphere of the friary. This really pained Father Kolbe all the more. He asked the Father Provincial earnestly: "If you select someone to replace him, please send one who would be willing to dedicate himself entirely to the Immaculata, to live in the poverty of Saint Francis and to die for the Immaculata in the midst of plenty of suffering and labor." "I regret having to use the money of Our Lady for their travel expenses to return home."

Seminarian Damian had a nervous breakdown, Brother Hilary suffered from an eye disease, and Brother Zygmunt completely lost enthusiasm for missionary work. They all went back to Poland with Father Metody.

At present (1981), Father Metody is said to be serving as a priest in a town in the south of Poland. Meanwhile, Father Kolbe was beatified and is widely respected in the Catholic Church. How does Father Metody feel about it? Father Mirochna visited him several years ago but the old priest turned away from Father Mirochna and refused to meet him. I cannot but feel pity when I think of this priest turning his back on his fellow Knight.

Whatever May Happen in This World

In 1931, the Manchurian Incident broke out and war clouds started to gather in the skies over Japan. Father Kolbe wrote prophetically, "Something is going to happen in the world. But nobody can rob us of anything but our lives as we dedicate ourselves entirely to Our Lady. Even if we lose our lives, it will be wonderful for us. At that very moment we will be able to do the best work with both hands to lead the whole world to the Immaculata." I would like to say that this passage truly predicted Father Kolbe's own future. For Father Kolbe, Japan was the training hall for his future death. One might see Father Kolbe's resolution in his eyes. There was a lot of internal and external hardship in his life then, but there was also a lot of support and consolation from the Immaculata. Father Kolbe named these encouragements "caramels Our Lady gives us."

I would just add a note here: In some biographies of Father Kolbe, caramels are regarded in the opposite sense as sufferings, which is inaccurate. Brother Romuald said, "Caramels are sweets. They mean consolation, support, and graces. Our Lady gives us caramels so that we are not discouraged by hardships. These are necessary for weak souls. But those who love are not satisfied with consolation or pleasure. They wish for nothing other than hard bread." He told me the following episode:

> When I was helping with cooking, the sugar ran out. We usually bought a 60-kilogram straw bag of brown sugar. Living without sugar is a great sacrifice for us from the Western world. But we didn't have money to buy it. However, the crisis didn't even last one day. In the afternoon, an old man from Urakami came to see us and made a contribution to Father Kolbe. The amount was just equal to what we needed to buy brown sugar. Father Kolbe said, "Our Lady has given us this money. She wishes that we buy brown sugar." So Brother Zeno went to buy it. In fact, we had simple faith at that time and received direct support from Our Lady.

This is truly a heart-warming Franciscan episode. But after pleasure comes pain. Father Kolbe referred to his suffering: "We received caramels from Our Lady almost every day in May. But in June, I suffered a distress I had never experienced before."

This distress that Brother Romuald could never forget was that Father Kolbe was questioned by the new apostolic delegate.

"The new apostolic delegate came to Nagasaki for inspection. Someone passed him inaccurate information that convinced him that we were here without permission from Rome and he gave me a stern reproach. Yet, when I brought a document from the Congregation for Religious and showed it to him, he recognized our legal status."

It was a great shock for Father Kolbe, who valued obedience above all, to have been reproached by a high-ranking priest. It is said that Father Kolbe returned from Oura Cathedral and wept before the friars.

CHAPTER 10

Garden Covered with Snow on the Fiftieth Year

Pope John Paul II dedicated both a red and a white garland to the statue of Blessed Kolbe, where the first printing office had been built.

Two Helpers

Three months had passed since the Knights had moved to Hongouchi. The summer heat had peaked and it was now the middle of September, 1931. By this time, the friars were missing four members who had returned to Poland. However, two dependable helpers came to Nagasaki from Niepokalanów on September 13th: Brother Grzegorz Siry, twenty-nine years old, and Brother Sergiusz Pęsiek, twenty-four years old.

As the path of the four members who left Nagasaki and that of the two new members who started out from Poland might meet in Moscow, Father Kolbe made special efforts to ensure that they would not encounter one another.

Brother Grzegorz liked the English language. He had been studying English before he became a friar. After he had entered Niepokalanów, he left his precious dictionary behind in the office, thinking that he would not use it any more. When Father Kolbe returned to Poland to join the Provincial Chapter, he found it there. He asked, "Whose dictionary is this?" The name Stanisław was signed on the back page. "Who is Stanisław?" It was the secular name of Brother Grzegorz. "Do you speak English?" "Yes, a little…" "We need those who understand English. Let's go to Japan, then."

The way Brother Sergiusz was called to his religious vocation was a little peculiar. His home was located near Niepokalanów. His father was a carpenter and he helped his father. One day when Father Kolbe visited them, he ordered a chest of drawers. Brother Sergiusz and his father completed a wonderful chest and brought it to Niepokalanów. Then Father Kolbe said to him, "The chest has entered the friary. Now it's your turn to come here." Brother Sergiusz said that he decided on his vocation when he heard Father Kolbe's words.

At that time, he was twenty years old and had to take a physical examination for conscription. He would rather be a friar than go into the army so he entered Niepokalanów. The friary ran quite short of goods and the friars lived in extreme poverty then. There was no extra furniture for a new volunteer. Hardly had he entered the friary than Father Kolbe said, "As you are a carpenter, make the bed you'll sleep on yourself."

At first, Brother Sergiusz made a simple bed and slept on it in a hut he fixed up. Then he started to work under his senior, Brother Zeno, who had been a difficult person to deal with for many years. His work was rough and imprecise. He was shrewd and sometimes just took off without a word to anyone. Brother Sergiusz said that it had always been a great sacrifice for him, the young friar, to work with Brother Zeno, who often miscalculated and wouldn't give him a break. Conflict often happened between them and each time he was reproved gently by Father Kolbe.

Walking in the garden, Father Kolbe advised him: "In the friary we all have our seniors. You and I must be obedient to them, because they show us the will of Our Lady. In your case, Brother

Zeno shows it to you. Therefore, strive to obey him as readily as possible. It is necessary to control yourself at first. You must be a good friar, a good person. Keep this in mind and obey what Brother Zeno tells you to do, and you'll be able to keep profound peace in your mind.

If you have some troubles, please confide them to me anytime. But the most important thing is to pray. If you pray, you can overcome any trouble and any suffering. Do you understand? Then go to work, Maria!"

Prophecy of a Gypsy Woman

Brother Zeno left for Japan with Father Kolbe for the missionary work. Brother Sergiusz succeeded Brother Zeno and became the master carpenter of ten fellow friars. He finally felt relieved but it did not last long. One day Guardian Florian said to him, "Won't you go to Japan?"

Brother Serigusz thought, Brother Zeno is in Japan, but Father Kolbe is also there; I want to see the merciful Father Kolbe! After deliberation, he made the decision to go to Japan. When he arrived at *Mugenzai no Sono* in Nagasaki and looked at the humble barrack friary, he shouted in Polish in spite of himself: "This barrack was built just in the same way as the early buildings in Niepokalanów!"

Father Kolbe frowned to hear it and took Brother Sergiusz to the attic. The floor boards, on which the friars directly slept, had not been planed smooth. Brother Sergiusz, as a carpenter, was startled to see them and wondered why they had not been planed. That night as Brother Sergiusz slept on the floor, looking at the roof tiles above him, he thought "I've finally come to this land in the distant Orient." The following episode tells the reason why he felt that way.

When he was twelve years old, a group of gypsies arrived at the village in caravans. The villagers were afraid of them: cows and oxen, hens and cocks often disappeared, when they came. They stayed in the village ten to fifteen days. During this period, the villagers took turns keeping an eye on them.

One day, a middle-aged gypsy woman came to Brother Sergiusz's house. She said, "Would you give me something?" His mother told him to give her some flour. The boy climbed to the attic and came back with a wash basin full of flour. His mother was in a bad mood, because he brought too much and generously gave it to the gypsy woman, who then looked at the boy and said, "You will not eat the bread of your country in the future. You will live to be eighty-two years old." And she turned to Brother Sergiusz's mother and said, "A big problem will happen in your home soon." Then she disappeared.

It was true! The gypsy woman's prediction came true. Soon after that, a bovine infectious disease spread and his family barely escaped a great loss. Fortunately, his family survived. She had also predicted that he would not eat the bread of his country; and he started to eat the bread of Japan from this day. If her prediction came true, he thought, I will live to be eighty-two. But to him, that was in the very distant future.

This is how the young friars, Brother Grzegorz and Brother Sergiusz, started their work in Japan. Father Kolbe ordered Grzegorz to serve as receptionist and accountant. "The next day after I came to Japan, I became receptionist. I remembered just one Japanese phrase then. 'Wait a minute, please.' And then I would run and get Father Kolbe." Brother Sergiusz took charge of construction with the carpenters, and also of cooking, instead of Brother Zeno. Then all were relieved because they would be able to eat lunch at a regular time from then on.

By 1981, fifty years had passed since the two men had come to Japan. During these years, full of hardship, many things happened: the death of Father Kolbe, who sacrificed his life out of love; the hard days during the Second World War; the Atomic Bombing and the reconstruction after the war — the world was entirely changed.

Fortunately, Brother Sergiusz had been blessed with good health and turned seventy-four in 1981. He is my reliable senior. This year, he had a great joy which had not been predicted by the gypsy woman: Pope John Paul II, his fellow countryman, visited the friary of *Mugenzai no Sono* (the Knights of the Immaculata) which our revered Father Kolbe had established.

Prior to the visit of Pope John Paul II, Brother Sergiusz received a letter written in Polish from Father Domański, the leader of the confraternity of the Knights of the Immaculata in Rome. In the letter the relationship between the Pope and Father Kolbe was written as follows:

> John Paul II shows special love and respect for Father Kolbe. He is from Poland as is Father Kolbe, and served as an archbishop of Kraków before becoming Pope. Father Kolbe lectured philosophy at the Major Seminary of the Order of the Conventual Franciscans in Kraków, after he came back home from studying in Rome. As Auschwitz, where Father Kolbe was killed, belongs to the parish of Kraków, John Paul II often visited the starvation bunker and prayed there when he was a cardinal. When he became bishop, he placed the letter of M on his crest after the Marian devotion of Father Kolbe.
>
> When Father Kolbe was beatified ten years ago, John Paul II served as spokesman before a number of reporters who crowded together. When he was cardinal, he built a modern beautiful church consecrated to Father Kolbe at Nova Huta, a suburb of Kraków. The World Synod of Bishops declared that Father Kolbe was a good example for catechists. There had been a movement to build a church consecrated to Father Kolbe in Auschwitz, and, recently, permission for its construction was finally granted by the government.
>
> When John Paul II was in Kraków, he often visited the friary of Niepokalanów with his fifty to seventy fellow priests,

celebrated the Mass, preached a sermon or went into retreat. Through his visits, he inhaled Father Kolbe's spirit of love. John Paul II often preached a sermon about Father Kolbe and I (Father Domański) heard it at least twenty times after his papal inauguration.

Pope John Paul II didn't meet Father Kolbe in person because of their generation gap, but the spiritual ties are very strong. He was elected pope on October 16th, which was the day Father Kolbe started the Knights of the Immaculata in Rome. This may show the existence of a providential relationship between the two men.

Father Domański ended his letter in this way.

A Red Garland and a White One

Pope John Paul II arrived at Haneda airport in a foggy rain. It was just when the TV show, "You at Three O'clock," was being

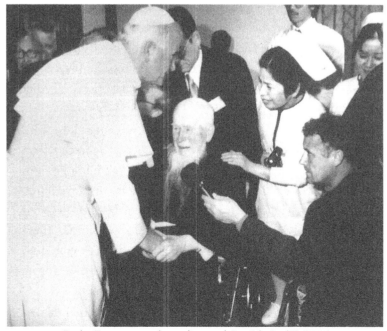

Brother Zeno was granted an audience with Pope John Paul II. (1981)

broadcast. He went to Saint Mary's Cathedral. After the Mass, a touching scene was aired on TV throughout Japan: Brother Zeno was granted an audience with the Holy Father.

I videotaped this scene and have watched it repeatedly. My impression can be summed up in the statement that Pope John Paul II is truly our Holy Father. He bent himself forward as if he embraced Brother Zeno, and talked to the old friar who was under medical treatment: "I am Pope. I came from Poland. I talk to you in Polish. Fifty years ago you came to Japan with Father Kolbe. Thank you for your work." He showed his love to Brother Zeno, while stroking the old friar's head and rubbing cheeks with him. Brother Zeno said in a feeble voice, "Ojciec Święty (Holy Father)!" and burst into tears in spite of himself.

Before coming to Japan, Pope John Paul II had received a special training in Japanese for two months from Father Nishiyama who lived in Rome at that time and accompanied the Pope to Japan as his official interpreter. Father Nishiyama also had a close relationship with Brother Zeno. Just after the Second World War, Brother Zeno built an orphanage in the friary of the Knights of the Immaculata for children who had lost their parents during the war. Father Nishiyama was brought up in that very orphanage. This connection between Brother Zeno and Father Nishiyama is an amazing one.

Pope John Paul II is said to have brought rain to Tokyo, but snow to Nagasaki. After the snowstorm — which was rare in Nagasaki, located in the southern part of Japan — had finally stopped, the Holy Father arrived at the friary of the Knights of the Immaculata in the evening. Those who felt the greatest joy were the Polish friars, who had come to Japan in the era of Father Kolbe and were still continuing their missionary work at that time. They were seated on the pew nearest to the chair of John Paul II.

Father Mirochna was there; and so were old friars such as Brother Romuald, Brother Grzegorz, and Brother Sergiusz. Brother

FATHER KOLBE IN NAGASAKI

Polish friars amassed around Pope John Paul II with joy. (1981)

Grzegorz had come to meet the Holy Father from the friary of Konagaimachi, 50 kilometers outside Nagasaki City. When Pope John Paul II came into the church, they broke out into cheers, "*Ojciec Święty! Witamy!*" (Holy Father! Welcome!) The Pope gradually proceeded to the altar with a smile, giving everyone his blessing. Then he knelt on the prie-dieu and prayed.

He did not move at all. The cheering voices suddenly quieted down. There was only silence — not a sound was heard. It was a long prayer. The Holy Father was probably filled with the thought that he finally came to the place where Father Kolbe had once breathed. After a while, he stood up and explained "why I came to this friary" quite long in English. Then he chanted his own "prayer for the Immaculata" in Polish and finally, everyone prayed the Lord's Prayer in Latin.

When he left the church, the Polish friars, whose joy had reached a peak, broke rank and amassed around him. He might possibly have sensed a comfortable atmosphere of home and the nearness of Father Kolbe. He seemed to be relaxed in spite of being tired.

GARDEN COVERED WITH SNOW ON THE FIFTIETH YEAR

I had asked Brother Sergiusz, "What will you talk about, when you meet the Holy Father?" He answered, "In August next year, 1982, the 600th anniversary will be held in Częstochowa, which is a famous pilgrimage town of Our Lady in Poland. Six hundred years will have passed since the icon of 'the miraculous Black Madonna' was housed in the monastery. As the Holy Father is to participate in the anniversary, I would like to ask him to canonize Father Kolbe there in Poland. It's my one and only desire." However, he had no opportunity to speak with the Holy Father in the crowd.

According to the schedule, the Holy Father was to stay in the friary of the Knights of the Immaculata for twenty-five minutes, but in fact, he stayed there for sixty-five minutes. After a while, he went out into the garden, which was nothing but a yard, where Father Kolbe had constructed, with great worry and difficulty, the first building with a printing office. There is no trace of the building and no one can remember what life was like there in those days, except a few Polish friars.

There was snow on the head and sleeves of the statue of Blessed Father Kolbe in the garden. And then a memorable event for the Knights of the Immaculata happened. The Holy Father presented both a red and a white garland to the statue of Blessed Father Kolbe. The white and the red garlands symbolize the life of Father Kolbe.

According to his biography, Father Kolbe was a very naughty boy. "What will become of him?" His mother was anxious about his future. One day, when he was praying at the altar, Our Lady appeared to him and showed him a red and a white crown and asked, "Which one do you want?"

He answered, "I want both." "If you want both, you must be better." After this event, there was a big change in him. This episode was made public after Father Kolbe's death. The white crown represents the chastity of those who are called to the priesthood; and the red crown represents the love of those who dedicate their lives for others.

Having welcomed the Holy Father, Brother Sergiusz reflected: "Looking back on the day I arrived at *Mugenzai no Sono* fifty years ago, it's like a miracle that the Polish Pope visited our friary. It's amazing that we have such a great person among us Poles."

Whenever Brother Sergiusz, a poor friar, talks about the Holy Father, his eyes become gentle and filled with tears.

NOTE: Brother Sergiusz passed away at the age of one hundred and three in 2010. Father Kolbe was canonized by Pope John Paul II in the Vatican on October 10, 1982.

CHAPTER 11

Some Petty Daily Incidents

After having read "The Knights of the Immaculata," those seeking the truth or seeking to enter the Order frequently knocked at the door. Among them were some who were merely after the poor Western friars' bread.

After Brother Grzegorz and Brother Sergiusz arrived from Poland, the friars' homeland, *Mugenzai no Sono* was full of life. In his delight, Father Kolbe entertained them with fried eggs, which were precious, as if he were trying to overcome the fatigue of their long trip. They brought many presents which reminded the friars of their homeland. Before their departure from Poland, they had received a letter from Brother Zeno which said, "There are no potatoes in Japan. Bring some. Bring also rye seed." They brought plenty of potatoes and rye seed, as requested. In addition, they brought sausages, which were genuine, stuffed, intestine casings shaped like bamboo tubes and were very delicious! It all added up to eight large suitcases.

In the evening on the day they arrived, Father Kolbe said, "Let's thank Our Lady for being able to welcome the two new brothers. The project in Japan is not ours but belongs to Our Lady. We are nothing but her little instruments. She is trying to accomplish this great project with these humble instruments. An instrument must move at the will of the one who uses it.

"Let's try to be perfect instruments of Our Lady, regardless of time, place or circumstance. If we make such an effort, we cannot fail. We can surely expect to make great progress. A man is not measured by external greatness but according to how he loves Our Lady and by a heart that sacrifices and prays. Brothers, in order to be perfect instruments of the Immaculata, we always have to pray for her help. To pray to her is not at all a difficult thing. It is enough just to invoke her name in your heart all the time."

The next day Father Kolbe assigned their share of duties to Brother Sergiusz and Brother Grzegorz. "Brother Zeno, you are in charge of shopping from today. If there is something you need, please write it on a slip of paper and put it in the box in front of my room. Brother Sergiusz will check the box twice a day and Brother Zeno will buy the items that I signed onto. Brother Sergiusz will be in charge of cooking, which has been assigned to Brother Zeno up to now."

In addition, Brother Sergiusz was in charge of carpentry and maintenance. Brother Grzegorz was assigned to reception and vestry. He kept a small amount of money as a receptionist for those who were going into town. As he did not know a single word of Japanese, he just bowed his head repeatedly when he received guests.

Replacing Brother Hilary, who had returned home during the summer, Brother Zeno had been responsible for cooking. He boiled rolled barley instead of rice; as he did not use enough water, it often scorched. "Brother Zeno often added tea to it, in order to save the rolled barley," said Brother Grzegorz. Anyway, most of the food Brother Zeno served was instant. The Poles have a staple diet of potatoes. It is unimaginable for them to live without potatoes. Therefore, it is quite natural that everyone in the friary wanted to eat potatoes. But Brother Zeno hardly served them, giving as his reason that there either were no potatoes, or they were too expensive. But all you had to do was go to town and you would see potatoes in the grocery stores and they were not so expensive. It was troublesome to peel them, though, so Brother Zeno served udon-noodles instead, which were easy to cook.

He admirably tried to cut down on expenses, so for firewood he would gather the bamboo grass that grew everywhere around them or tree roots. Therefore, he was delighted when the two friars brought sausages! Brother Sergiusz said, "We hung them up in the attic, cooked them sometimes with potatoes and ate them. It was a banquet for us."

Brother Sergiusz was in charge of cooking, carpentry and maintenance.

However, one day the precious sausages were stolen! When Brother Sergiusz climbed up to the attic, in order to put on their usual feast, the sausages were gone. Who would have stolen them? The costly food which we brought all the way from our homeland disappeared! The truth behind this small incident never came to light. However, another similar incident happened three days later.

Brother Sato came into the room, crying out in a strange voice: "Thief! Thief!" The foreign friars got ready for an emergency and gathered under the ladder. Father Kolbe tried to climb up to the attic but seminarian Nishiya stopped him, saying, "It's dangerous!" If someone was hiding, he might assault Father Kolbe out of desperation. So Father Kolbe put his hat on a stick, and pushed it up into the attic quietly. In such an emergency, Father Kolbe would wear his hat and bring a stick from his room. But no one was there at the time. The thief must have slipped away, while Brother Sato went to call for the other friars. The sausages were targeted by someone from outside the friary. Father Kolbe said smiling, "There is someone who is poorer than we are."

"However," I said to Brother Sergiusz, "it's surprising that Father Kolbe took a stick in his hand." He answered, "Father Kolbe often got swellings on the neck, stomach, or feet. So he used a stick to support himself when he walked. Besides, he told us to wear a black hat whenever we felt danger. One night some suspicious man was walking around. Father Kolbe put his hat on and went out with a stick. It was a police detective walking his rounds."

The Japanese Who Tried to Enter the Friary

Kunihiko Amaki had been searching for the Truth since the Oura period. He was about twenty years old. In July 1931, he became the first person who was baptized at *Mugenzai no Sono*. Father Kolbe wrote in his letter: "He came from Oura to work without any compensation, studied the catechism, understood the Faith, and received Holy Baptism, after having overcome a lot of

Various Japanese seeking the Truth knocked at the door of the friary.

difficulties. His Christian name is Marian. He said that he read *The Knights*, and that's why he wanted to become Catholic." It seems to have delighted Father Kolbe that the first Japanese Catholic was born as a fruit of *The Knights*.

Young Amaki brought his friend Susumu Hara who was about the same age with him to the friary. Hara lived in Oura and his family worshiped the Shinto deities and Buddha. Those who were suffering from illness or difficulties in life came to ask his parents for advice. They prayed to the deities and Buddha, and gave those sufferers solutions. In sharp contrast to his family's circumstances, Hara came to visit Father Kolbe to work without recompense. He started working from morning, took lunch and supper, and went back home. He continued this routine for more than a year.

About twenty years ago, I met Mr. Hara in person. He said, "I picked out types, wrote addresses, packed *The Knights*, helped with cooking, plowed the field, and did other chores. When I look back on those days, I'm thankful that they allowed a cub like me to work there. I was not baptized but could lead a pure life like friars.

"After that I received Holy Baptism from Bishop Furuya in Osaka. With a certificate stating that I worked at the friary of the Knights of the Immaculata, I was exempted from the test of the catechism and became Catholic. If I hadn't met Father Kolbe, I would not have become Catholic. Of course, my parents were against it, and I had many troubles. However, in spite of having been brought up in a family of a Shinto and Buddhist shaman, I have well maintained my faith so far and, besides, I'm serving as president of the Society of Vincent de Paul in Oura church. It's because I had a good memory of Father Kolbe that I have kept my faith."

Seminarian Nishiya, whom I mentioned previously, was the son of a photographer who lived near Suwa Shrine in Nagasaki City. He had graduated from a junior high school under the old educational system. Tsutomu Nishiya, called Paul, was a big man with a strong frame. He was enthusiastic but had a violent temper. He went around passing out *The Knights* and if someone threw it away, he slapped the person across the cheek! On Christmas Eve in 1931, he received Holy Baptism with Antoni Yoshida. There remains a photo that they took with Polish friars including Brother Sergiusz.

Father Kolbe wrote about Antoni Yoshida in his letter as follows: "The young man, being taught the catechism now, came across one of our brothers in the street who was handing out *The Knights*, and he visited us. He said that he wants to work with us. Every day he comes to work without any form of reward. His family and his relatives are all opposed to it. In fact, his father disowned Antoni on his deathbed, even though he was the eldest son. Since then, he has been living with us and he wishes to be a brother after he is baptized."

Paul Nishiya also longed to be a seminarian right after Baptism. Father Kolbe often made entries about the activities of Nishiya in his Nagasaki diary at that time: "Nishiya went to get firewood." "Nishiya brought in as many as four people: two wrote addresses and the other two went to town, which was crowded with visitors for the Nagasaki Kunchi Festival, to distribute *The Knights*." "Nishiya went to Nakamachi and stayed there to take care of several dozen people who fled from the Shanghai Incident," and so on.

According to the Rule of the Order of the Conventual Franciscans, one could become a novice in the Order after at least three years since Baptism. Moved by the enthusiasm of Nishiya, Father Kolbe took the trouble to obtain a special exemption from the Holy See. However, "easy come, easy go" as they say, Nishiya left *Mugenzai no Sono* within a year.

A letter written by Father Kolbe at that time says: "In May we celebrated the second anniversary of our arrival in Nagasaki. During lunch, the young Amaki who sat next to me, stood up and said, 'If you had not come here, I would be still a pagan.' He said these words in gratitude to the Immaculata. So I felt deeply that the Immaculata used us as her instruments. Even if no one else had been converted except this man, all the efforts we had done so far would have been amply rewarded.

"However, the Immaculata made it possible for two more people to be baptized and soon, we will have three more. Another person received Holy Baptism in Osaka."

In this letter we can perceive the plentiful joy of a missionary who obtained one valuable soul.

A Dog Barks in the Middle of the Night

Through the distribution of *The Knights*, those seeking the Truth or wishing to be novices knocked at the door of the friary, but not all of them were the kind of men who could accept the Faith.

In the letter of March 14, 1932, to Poland, Father Kolbe reported in detail a case of petty theft that occurred in his daily life. Whenever I observe his behaviors in detail, I cannot but feel that he was not a mountain hermit but a warm-hearted man living close to us. So I quote the whole letter here:

> I was awakened by the insistent barking of our dog. The dog came right under the window of my room, and then went away from the house. I was tired, so I didn't get up and only strained my ears to hear if noise was coming from the chapel, but it was entirely quiet. The next morning I saw a man's footprints and scratch marks of our dog left on the ground around there. The dog didn't only awaken us with his barking but even bit the suspicious man. A few days before, I had told the brothers that the dog was not necessary and I was thinking of releasing it. However, it watches our house in the night. Because there are a limited number of brothers, a night watch would negatively impact their health and their work.
>
> After this incident, Brother Grzegorz, our treasurer, brought me the monthly account statement and informed

me that about 24 yen were missing from the total amount. At first I thought I should lock the door, but I changed my mind and worked out a plan. I told him not to tell anyone but to do a cash check every night. On the very first day, he reported to me that another 3 yen were missing. Then I urged Brother Grzegorz to place the lid on the box at a slant and check a few times a day, to see if the lid was moved. I informed the seminarians of the matter, and asked especially seminarian Mirochna not to go into the chapel after lunch, but to keep an eye on the outside. At that time we had a novice, a pagan who came to help us, and Antoni Yoshida, who had previously lived with us.

It's possible, someone else may have broken in, getting through the barbed wire, because there are no fences around our land. On the mountain side, the land is overgrown with bamboo grass near the building, so that one can easily get very close to it quite unnoticed.

Being vigilant, seminarian Mirochna sensed somebody and heard the door open. As he glanced through the window, he saw Antoni Yoshida opening the money box. The thief also looked at Mirochna and ran away quickly and disappeared. We didn't report it to the police, but just told those in *Mugenzai no Sono* to be careful. In fact, Antoni is a good soul. It saddens me that he must have given in to temptation. As he admitted himself, he has bad companions and I even heard that he has a relationship with a gang. If only the Immaculata could win them over!

The door of *Mugenzai no Sono* was open to one and all, but no one could predict the moral quality of the truth seekers or novices who came to us at that time. In fact, the first friar, Shigeo Sato, suddenly proposed to leave the friary in December, 1931, and walked down along the national highway to the town. About one hour after arriving at the station, he had second thoughts and came back crying. Father Kolbe wondered whether it was good or not, but he let him put on the habit again. In fact, there was a strict, penal regulation for those who went out of the gate of their own will if they were to be received again. According to Father Kolbe, in those early years the Japanese novices were not so reliable, so the Polish friars were the main driving force.

Kunihiko Amaki became a novice after Baptism, but he also left within a year. Brother Grzegorz whispered to me that Antoni Yoshida (who had been the subject of the theft incident) kept a close eye on Father Kolbe and the other friars who had come from a neighboring country of Communist Russia, and reported what he saw to the police.

I am not certain if he was, in fact, a pawn of the Special Higher Police.

CHAPTER 12

The Bearded "*Gyoja*"

*People in Nagasaki called monks "gyoja."
Father Kolbe's* gyoja *with their beards,
holding copies of* The Knights of the Immaculata,
soon attracted the attention of the townspeople.

Traveling around the Islands

On Sundays, Father Kolbe went with other friars to distribute *The Knights*. Brother Zeno distributed the magazines in the areas of Nagasaki City close to the friary when he went shopping. So on Sundays they went to fairly distant places like other cities or islands outside the harbor.

Father Kolbe made entries about the distribution in his Nagasaki diary: "Brother Zeno, Paul Nishiya, and other brothers went to Omura City with 3,000 copies of *The Knights* for distribution." "On holidays, brothers went out with the copies of *The Knights* in three groups. They came back with ninety-three new addresses."

Before departure, groups were organized with two members each: Brother Celestyn and Brother Romuald; Brother Sergiusz, who had just come to Japan, and seminarian Nishiya; Father Kolbe and Brother Marian Sato. Brother Zeno acted alone as usual. No one knew when, where, or how he parted from the other members, but he always came back with many new addresses in the evening. This was the first distribution for Brother Sergiusz who had been in

We can see Nagasaki City across the sea from Iojima island.

Japan only a month and spoke little Japanese. Even Brother Zeno was anxious about him and taught him some basic, key Japanese phrases: "Business card. Give me. Every month. I send you..."

They took a ferryboat from Ohato. It left the Port of Nagasaki and went around the beautiful islands. Father Kolbe gazed at Nagasaki's shining sea with his narrowed eyes. When the ferry arrived at Iojima, Takashima, or Nomo, the Western *"gyoja"* set off for various places with their copies of *The Knights*. Father Kolbe not only distributed the magazines but also tried to preach in the street. But Father Kolbe's Japanese was limited; when he could not find suitable words, Brother Sato spoke on his behalf. As Brother Sato had entered the friary one year before, he had picked up some Polish just by listening. Besides, he could almost read Father Kolbe's mind.

Brother Sergiusz recollected: "For the first time, I got the feeling that I was indeed in a foreign country. I was always in trouble; for instance, when I said, 'Give me a business card,' as I was taught, people talked to me in Japanese, because they assumed that I could speak the language. How could I possibly know what they said? At first, Nishiya explained that I was new to Japan and didn't understand anything. But he was perplexed as people came one after another."

Brother Sergiusz told me another episode: Paul Nishiya invited him to visit his friend's home nearby. However, out of reserve, Brother Sergiusz did not go with him but waited at the road side. Nishiya did not come back for a long time. Getting tired of waiting, Brother Sergiusz began walking. At last Nishiya seemed to have finished his business and appeared in the distance. He was waving his hands so that Brother Sergiusz might come to him. But his gesture was just the opposite of the European way. Brother Sergiusz thought his gesture was telling him to go away. Thinking it was rather strange, he went farther away from Nishiya, who got angry then and started to cry out in a loud voice. In short, Brother Sergiusz did not understand the Japanese way of beckoning at that time.

In the evening the friars had supper in high spirits. They were feeling joyful about the distribution. Sitting around the humble table together they talked about the failures, the number of new readers, and the lunch provided in a private home, etc. The conversation of "gyoja" reminds us of the propagation of the Faith in the era of Saint Francis, the founder of the Order. Father Kolbe chided Brother Sergiusz then: "What would you do if you got lost? You should learn Japanese at once." Brother Sergiusz said to me, "To tell the truth, I didn't want to learn Japanese, even after I had arrived in Nagasaki."

Father Kolbe's method of doing missionary work was publishing *The Knights*. He hoped to publish as many copies as possible until they reached every home. In order to achieve this goal, Father Kolbe thought seriously that he needed a boat for missionary work since Japan is an island country. Besides, he still had a dream to advance from Nagasaki as the base to China, India, and Arabia, and to publish *The Knights* in each language. Though the publication had not been successful in China so far, he had not given up yet: "The Chinese Catholic activist Mr. Lo-Pa-Hong promised to provide me with the funds for the publication. I want to publish *The Knights* in Chinese at any cost. The postage from Nagasaki to Shanghai is cheap. In addition, we have Chinese printing types." In this way, Father Kolbe still had hopes for China.

A solid foundation was laid in Nagasaki. In order to increase the number of issues, the machinery had to be improved. Brother Zeno went to Osaka in December, 1931, to buy a new printing machine which could print sixteen pages. The machine they had used so far was old and could print only eight pages.

Brother Zeno talked about the purchase: "I went alone. Father Kolbe didn't go. My Japanese was a little better then: 'Please give me a lower price.' The president of the company spoke Polish and Russian.

"When Japan fought against Russia, he was a soldier of the Red Cross. Among the Russian captives, there were Polish soldiers. The president was kind to me. He invited me to his house, offered me dinner and discounted the printing machine. He was kinder to me than my fellow brothers were. He came to Nagasaki and assembled the machine. The company burnt in an air raid. After the war, I looked around Osaka, but couldn't find him."

Father Kolbe wrote in his diary: "Brother Zeno brought back five hundred and fifty addresses of new readers from Osaka. The new printing machine cost 750 yen, a very low price. I earned 266 yen and 21 sen as my salary from the seminary. I used it to pay for the printing machine." Fortunately, a paper folding machine was sent from Poland, which reduced the time required for folding the pages compared to the manual paper folding which had been done until then. It was used for forty years and is now preserved in the museum of the friary.

With the introduction of this folding machine, the number of pages was increased from twenty-four to thirty-two, and the number of copies rose to 40,000. The first yearbook of *The Knights* was published. Even though the pages had increased, the price remained 3 sen. Father Kolbe had lofty aspirations.

The Best Consolation

People in Nagasaki called nuns "dotei-san," and monks "gyoja." At that time the Western "gyoja" of *Mugenzai no Sono* wore the black habits of the Franciscan order with cords around their waists and had beards as well. Their appearance became a topic of the conversations of the citizens. Their beards were quite full, as two years had already passed since they had come to Japan. I hear that they grew beards because they thought it common in Asia. Brother Zeno's whiskers were red at first.

The Western "gyoja" with beards worked with their own hands without uttering a word. It seemed to have touched the hearts of the people in Nagasaki. Even now, I often hear some old people proudly say that they had seen Father Kolbe. They were not able to distinguish Father Kolbe from Brother Zeno in the least. Every foreign "gyoja" in *Mugenzai no Sono* was Father Kolbe to them.

One day in August, Mr. Kushimoto, a medical doctor, came to the friary with a professor of Nagasaki Medical College. Father Kolbe spoke in German. The visitors were not baptized. Even though the topic Father Kolbe talked about was religion, they seemed to have liked it. From that time on, Mr. Kushimoto often visited Father Kolbe. Afterwards he left for Tokyo and wrote the following letter to Father Kolbe:

"I have had a lot of medals, but only as art objects. But I love the Miraculous Medal I got from you and I wear it with pleasure. I turn to Mary and I try to find peace in her." Father Kolbe introduced these passages in his own letter, and added very impressively: "This is the best consolation for our work, isn't it?" I think I can really understand the reasons for Father Kolbe's joy: he found here a Japanese who is going to love Our Lady!

Japanese Bonzes Don't Eat Meat

The first winter came since the friars had moved to Hongouchi. Although they had become accustomed to the bitter cold of Poland in Eastern Europe, life in the barrack-styled friary without heat chilled them to the bone! Father Kolbe expressed it very simply: "December 12th, it snowed a lot from midnight to morning. I couldn't sleep. The friars in the attic must have had an even more difficult time of it. The blankets became white and there was snow in the wash basin. But the brothers talked happily about Japanese snow at breakfast."

In addition to the cold, Father Kolbe had other suffering at that time. He had large swellings all over his body, from neck, back, stomach, down to his feet. "I'm suffering from boils all over the body. I had them cut out twice by a surgeon. The boils appear, burst, and then re-appear. During the Mass, one friar held me up. Also, I have a high fever. But there is nothing to worry about."

According to Brother Sergiusz, malnutrition caused these strange boils. In fact, after Father Kornel arrived at Nagasaki as Guardian of the friary two years later, the diet was improved and Father Kolbe recovered his health.

"We reduced food expenses to cover the costs of paper and postage. Now sardines are in season and very cheap. We often eat them."

After the uncooperative Father Metody had left for home, Father Kolbe still had a debt of 300 yen, because he had managed to get money for Father Metody's travel expenses. So payment to the paper dealer was delayed, and the dealer would not deliver paper to the friary.

"In most cases, the money from Poland arrives by the end of every month. This month we haven't received it yet. I wonder if it might have gone missing because of the Manchurian Incident. I have a lot to pay. The bakery and the milk dealer brought us their bills."

Consequently the friars had to cut their food costs. Even in such a frugal life, they nevertheless celebrated feast days with a banquet. The following is the episode of Brother Zeno and the meat.

It was Easter of 1932. Father Kolbe told Brother Zeno to buy beef for Easter which was the next day. Brother Zeno went shopping but he came back without buying it. So there was no meat for a banquet on the feast day.

"Brother Zeno, why didn't you buy beef?" asked Father Kolbe. "I didn't forget to buy it. The Buddhist bonzes don't eat meat. It's expensive. We also had better not eat meat," insisted Brother Zeno. There occurred a quarrel between them in Polish. Finally Father Kolbe said to Brother Zeno, "Go to town and buy beef at once!" Brother Zeno, flailing his hands with gestures typical of him, said: "Father, today is a feast day!" In Western countries all the shops were closed on feast days and it was customary not to do shopping at all. Brother Zeno couldn't imagine going shopping then. But Father Kolbe said with determination, "Brother Zeno, please go buy beef right now!"

Brother Zeno went out reluctantly and bought minced beef. "Brother Romuald, please cook it," said Father Kolbe. Brother Romuald made big hamburgers and the friars ate them with joy. He also baked a Polish pastry called a "*chrusty*." He said he has been making them ever since.

Even Father Kolbe seemed to have trouble with Brother Zeno's stubbornness. Father Kolbe wrote this memorandum: "Brother Zeno is very stubborn and is often quite unreasonable. But he becomes mild at night. He's been a friar all the way back to the period at Grodno. But most importantly, he came to enter the Order of the Conventual Franciscans, so he needs to change his way of thinking."

Even though Brother Zeno openly opposed Father Kolbe, the life of the bearded friars, including Brother Zeno, was pleasant. On Sundays they forgot all their troubles and went out to propagate the Faith through distribution of the magazine.

Father Kolbe wrote in his Nagasaki diary of Saturday, January 1, 1932, as follows: "Brother Zeno, Brother Severyn and others went by boat to Shikimi for propagation. Ninety eight fish cost 20 sen." Here fish means sardines. Brother Zeno may have bought them for their daily food on the way back from their missionary work.

There remains a camphor tree which survives from the time of Father Kolbe. Standing in the corner of the garden of the friary, it is more than ten meters tall now and its leaves are thick all the year round. In the spring fresh green leaves spread out and the hard leaves which have made it through the winter die and fall. Gazing at the camphor tree, I feel as if it passes on to us the spirit of the people of that time.

CHAPTER 13

The Goat Meat Was Tough

The friars formally invited Bishop Hayasaka of Nagasaki and entertained him with the meat of goats that had stopped giving milk, but the meat was very tough.

The winter came and seminarian Mirochna fell ill again. Father Kolbe wrote in a letter to Poland in January, 1932: "A doctor said that he would have to be operated on for a second time. I don't trust Japanese medicine. Some patients died after their operations. I have my reservations about this second operation." So Father Kolbe advised Mirochna to make the Novena to Saint Thérèse of the Child Jesus.

Saint Thérèse has been recognized as the Patroness of All Missions by the Catholic Church. Thérèse, a nun in France, lived a perfect ordinary life in the convent, died at the age of twenty-four, and was canonized.

Father Kolbe made a promise to her in Heaven: "If you send down a shower of roses (blessings) upon us, I will spread the word about you in *The Knights*." Some blessings may have been given in answer to this prayer as things changed for the better and "yesterday the doctors determined that surgery would not be necessary," wrote Father Kolbe in the following letter.

In February, Father Kolbe received a telegram from Poland permitting seminarian Mirochna to return home. "Mirochna had tears in his eyes. He doesn't attend the lessons in the seminary right now. He studies at home. I consulted with a trustworthy doctor and he advised us to wait and see. Mirochna has learned Japanese rather well."

The doctor advised Mirochna to eat more nutritious food. So Father Kolbe decided to buy a hen for eggs, and two goats for milk. He ordered Brother Zeno to make the purchase.

As Brother Zeno frequently walked around the town, he was able to make a quick purchase. He soon returned to the friary with a hen and two goats; however, the hen seemed to be too poor. "Will it really lay eggs?" Father Kolbe asked doubtfully. Then Brother Zeno answered, "Look! It has already laid one."

In fact, there was a snow-white egg! Actually, however, the dealer who had brought the hen had secretly placed the egg in with the hen. In the end the hen did not lay a single egg. The same thing happened with the two goats. Though they milked the goats, they did not give a single drop of milk. The friars complained about Brother Zeno in the dining room: "That's the way he does things. He was tricked into buying two useless goats."

Brother Zeno was at a loss and went to the dealer of the goats, saying angrily, "They didn't give any milk!" The dealer sneered at him: "If you really want milk, it's not enough to feed them grass. You have to let them drink water." He turned Brother Zeno away. Luckily there was plenty of grass at *Mugenzai no Sono* to feed the goats but they did not produce milk, just as the hen did not lay eggs. Brother Zeno lost the trust of other friars in short order. After that, Father Kolbe sometimes brought up this story of the goats in the presence of Brother Zeno, and amused the friars.

Four New Members Arrive

"A reporter of the Nagasaki Shimbun newspaper came to interview me. He took many pictures and asked questions." I got interested in this entry that Father Kolbe made in his Nagasaki diary at that time, and wondered what kind of article the reporter had written. I visited the Prefectural Library in Nagasaki City for the second time. Upon opening a file of old copies of the Nagasaki Shimbun of 1932 in the archive on the fourth floor, I found the story!

"A Story of a Monastery" was written in a three-part series on May 4th, 5th, and 6th. I was delighted to have found this article of fifty years ago. There was a picture on each of the three parts.

"Renouncing Five Desires, A Wonder on the Hill," "Enraptured in Silent Prayer Mornings and Nights," "Rules as Harsh as the Autumn Frost." These headlines written in old-style Japanese draw the reader's attention.

"Seen from a distance, it seems like a primary school in the countryside. If we approach it, it reminds us of a henhouse. Twelve friars including a priest live in this humble barrack. In the spring full of pleasure, they only lead a life of contemplation and work here. Don't they instinctively feel sexual urge? The friars say that they don't have time to think about earthly desires, nothing but God, prayer and thanksgiving..."

I can imagine the Franciscan friars living in the barrack house!

The twelve consisted of nine Polish friars and three Japanese: seminarian Paul Tsutomu Nishiya, Brother Marian Shigeo Sato, and novice Joseph Fusasaburo Yamashita, a student of Kaisei Junior High School. Yamashita became a Trappist priest later. The nine Poles were Father Kolbe, seminarians Mirochna and Aleksy, and six brothers in chronological order: Brother Zeno, Brother Seweryn, Brother Romuald, Brother Celestyn, Brother Grzegorz and Brother Sergiusz. Seminarian Ludwik left the Order several days before the interview.

On May 19th, four new members from Poland joined this religious family: twenty-seven-year-old Father Konstanty, Brother Kasjan, Brother Henryk and Brother Bartłomiej. Ever since Brother Kasjan Tetich came to Japan, he has devoted himself to cooking. He was born in 1902 and still lives in Nagasaki at present (in 1981). Brother Bartłomiej was nineteen years old then and lives in a friary in the United States now (in 1981). Father Konstanty had graduated from a university in Warsaw and came to Nagasaki as a philosophy teacher for the seminarians, including Mirochna. But unfortunately for Father Kolbe, he also became a rebellious priest (as Father Metody). Brother Henryk, a thin, twenty-two-year-old friar, lived fifteen years in Nagasaki but left for Niepokalanóv because of a stomach disorder after the Second World War. In 1980, he visited Japan for the first time in thirty-four years.

I asked Brother Henryk, "How was Japan at that time?" "Japan was a very quiet place. I thought Japan was not so rich. Poland was wealthier than Japan then. But now it's the other way around," he answered in fluent Japanese.

When the four members arrived at *Mugenzai no Sono*, the friars were busy with their work. Everyone was silent. They firmly repressed their great joy of welcoming fellow friars from their homeland. After a while Father Kolbe said, "Let's take a rest." Then it was time for tea and the friars hugged each other and rejoiced.

Brother Henryk continued, "The bedroom was in the attic, so I was not very happy. However, nothing could be done about that. Father Kolbe asked me to be patient. He said he would build a new friary soon. Living in the attic was hard."

What made the strongest impression on Brother Henryk was that the number of Catholics was small. "All the people in Poland are Catholic. I felt very lonely. When I saw many Catholics in the Eucharistic Procession in Urakami, I was very happy. Then I went to the site of the martyrdom of twenty-six saints in Tateyama. Our life was humble but I was consoled to know that the martyrs had suffered much more than we did." Brother Henryk was a tailor. Putting his profession aside, he occupied himself above all with sending out *The Knights*. He worked as a receptionist two weeks after his arrival in Nagasaki. He just learned one phrase: "Wait a minute, please."

I asked, "What do you remember about Father Kolbe?"

"We suggested to Father Kolbe that we could try another way of propagating the Faith. Polish missionaries worked in Africa then. We often read about their missionary work in Polish newspapers. Without printing, they taught the catechism and baptized many local inhabitants. Although we worked a lot from morning to night, we had no way of knowing what the results of our work might have been. That's what we thought, so we argued with Father Kolbe. Brother Seweryn worked hard and got angry once, saying that we had better change our method of work.

"Father Kolbe comforted him gently saying, "We don't know the result immediately but what is written doesn't disappear quickly. Someone will read it later. We will have results." Then Father Kolbe read the letter from a reader of *The Knights*, in order to encourage us and said that this reader had started to study the catechism after having read *The Knights*."

Brother Romuald said that the gentle Father Kolbe got angry once. When the young Brother Bartłomiej complained to him face-to-face, saying "It's meaningless to publish such a magazine," Father Kolbe retorted angrily: "That's what you always say! We are not in a business but doing missionary work." No matter what others might say, Father Kolbe stuck to his firm beliefs. He maintained that mass communication was the most appropriate way to propagate the Faith in the modern age and devoted himself to publication.

A Problem Tougher than the Meat

After Father Kolbe had surmounted one difficulty like crossing a mountain, there appeared a series of mountains. "Thanks to the three new brothers, our missionary work is going smoothly. Although they work tirelessly, Father Konstanty's nerves became weak and he didn't grasp the ideal of the Knights of the Immaculata."

No sooner had Father Kolbe felt relieved after Father Metody had returned home than Father Konstanty became a source of worry for him. Early on, he had hopes for him.

Father Kolbe wrote in his letter: "Father Konstanty still has quite a few different opinions. I comforted him by telling him that he would be able to understand more after finishing his training here."

In October came the Feast of Saint Francis of Assisi, the founder of the friars' Order. Two and a half years had passed since they had arrived in Nagasaki. Looking back on these years, Father Kolbe realized that he had not formally invited Bishop Hayasaka yet.

Father Kolbe invited Bishop Hayasaka and entertained him with goat meat.

So Father Kolbe decided to invite Bishop Hayasaka. Those goats which had not produced milk were cooked and served on that day! The hen had already disappeared. "As we had goats, we thought we had better not buy expensive beef. We decided to entertain the Bishop with the things we had on hand, in the spirit of Franciscan

THE GOAT MEAT WAS TOUGH

holy poverty. That's why we cooked and served the goats," said Brother Sergiusz.

The banquet hall was their dining room which also served as the workplace for the shipment of *The Knights*. It was really a poor table, quite appropriate for Franciscan friars.

The goats that had not given any milk were roasted whole but the meat was thin and tough! The friars themselves ate goat meat for the first time because, in Poland, the Jews owned the goats. Bishop Hayasaka knew what the friars were up against, so he put on a happy face the whole time and seemed as if he enjoyed the dinner.

The good-natured Bishop then, reflecting on those days when the Knights of the Immaculata first arrived in Nagasaki, opened up to them. "To tell the truth, I was not willing to take you in back then. If I hadn't, you probably would have had to take your big bags and go somewhere else. But our students would have been in a bind without a philosophy teacher. There were those opposed to you, and the problem was complicated. It was a problem tougher than this goat meat," he said with a laugh.

Brother Sergiusz added: "Once the Bishop had made sure that the project of the Knights of the Immaculata was basically on track, he confided in us, comparing the problem to the goat meat. After the Bishop left, Father Kolbe told us that Bishop Hayasaka told him frankly that he actually had accepted us willingly at the beginning, but he later wanted to expel us."

The reception of *The Knights* was not necessarily positive. There were articles that Japanese readers found difficult to comprehend like "The hands which witness that a man came back from Purgatory." The editing was pretty bad.

The Knights became an issue at a meeting of the Catholic Publishers in Tokyo. The complaint was that its rather poor content would be a hindrance to evangelization. The meeting was coming to the conclusion that the publication of *The Knights* should be stopped. But Archbishop Chambon of Tokyo said, "*The Knights* has been published under the imprimatur of the Bishop of Nagasaki. We'd better entrust it to him," and directed those at the meeting not to discuss this matter any further.

Father Matsukawa consistently supported Father Kolbe. (In the middle of the Polish friars.)

We could say that *The Knights* survived, thanks to Archbishop Chambon. But these critical opinions must have come as a great shock to Father Kolbe.

This affair gave rise to another problem: a Japanese priest responsible for the approval of publications entirely changed his attitude and came to dislike *The Knights*, since he had attended the abovementioned meeting. One day, Brother Celestyn brought the manuscript of *The Knights* for approval to this priest. Then he said in a sullen manner, "I don't want to cooperate with this magazine," and threw all of the manuscripts on the floor! Brother Celestyn's face turned red because of the terrible treatment by the priest. But he suppressed his anger and returned to Father Kolbe. The two friars knelt down and earnestly prayed to the Immaculata for a long time, which calmed their emotions.

Father Kolbe said, "Take the manuscripts to Father Matsukawa, then." Fortunately, the old Father Matsukawa was also one of the censors. Thereafter, they took the manuscripts to Father Matsukawa, who had shown his goodwill towards Father Kolbe. He received them politely and checked them with care. It was at that time that the merciful love of the old Father Matsukawa sank deeply into Father Kolbe's heart.

Since Father Kolbe put everything he had into the propagation of the Faith through the publication of *The Knights*, these serious criticisms and resistance must have caused him great distress. We may presume that this is why Bishop Hayasaka described the opposition as "tougher than the goat meat."

Father Kolbe made this entry in his diary: "October 4th, Tuesday. One seminarian received the tonsure on the Feast of Saint Francis, our father. Bishop Hayasaka came to our friary and ate lunch with us. After lunch we took a commemorative photograph." Tonsure refers to the ceremony through which seminarians are admitted to the clergy. The seminarian who received the tonsure on that day was seminarian Mirochna who had endured the illness. Father Kolbe hung the photograph taken that day on the wall. In front of the three-story friary that was still under construction, we can see Bishop Hayasaka, Father Aijiro Yamaguchi, pastor of Nakamachi Church, priests of the Franciscan order in Urakami along with the friars of *Mugenzai no Sono*. They had all been served the lunch of goat meat.

Poor thing! The life of a goat that does not give milk is short.

CHAPTER 14

The Map of India Buried in the Archives

India was the next target. Father Kolbe left for India, worrying about his hemoptysis. He wrote a letter in Japanese on the sea: "I will die soon. I don't have much time."

A Man of Many Hardships

When a man starts off on a journey, he usually consults a map and follows his dream.

In the Knights of the Immaculata in Nagasaki, there is an old, dusty atlas Father Kolbe once used. This large English volume published in 1924 comprises 290 pages. In the spring of 1932, Father Kolbe consulted the atlas in order to realize his long-cherished dream. His destination was India. He wanted to build the third Niepokalanów in India, which he had wished for a long

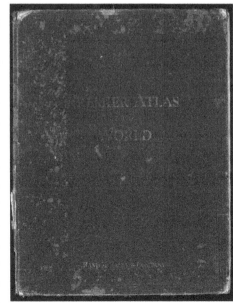

Father Kolbe consulted the world atlas in order to realize his dream.

time. He knew that he would not live long. Life is short. There was only one thing that he wanted to do in his brief lifetime: to make the whole world belong to the Immaculata as soon as possible.

He did not have much time. He had to realize his wish without delay. Once he had settled in Japan, his eyes were turned towards India, which lies in the middle of the Orient. India had a large population. It was an unexplored land for Christianity and he had a strong yearning for India.

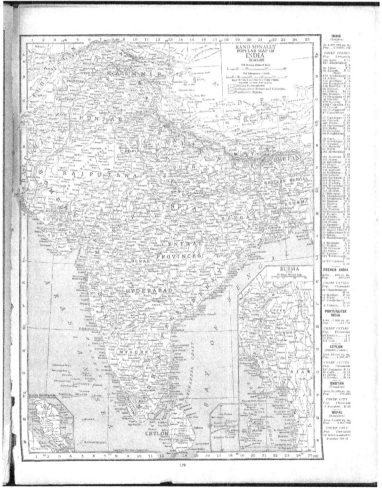

His eyes were turned towards India in the middle of the Orient.

Father Kolbe had a certain procedure when he set about a new plan. He looked for materials on his own and made a detailed plan, then submitted it to his superior, i.e., Father Kornel, the Provincial in Poland. After that, he left the whole decision to the Provincial. Sometimes he did not obtain permission. However, when permission was granted, he regarded everything as due to the will of the Immaculata, not to his own plan, and started his action promptly and perfectly. So Father Kolbe wrote to Father Kornel many times and informed him that he would like to go to India and build a new friary in southwest India. Father Kornel replied, "You may go to India, after Father Konstanty arrives in Nagasaki in the middle of May."

Looking back on those days, Father Mirochna, who was a seminarian back then, said, "The letter from the Provincial said that he would think about it and Father Kolbe might go there. As it could be interpreted both ways, I opposed his plan of going to India. Father Konstanty had just come here, besides the Provincial didn't say that Father Kolbe should go. The letter could be interpreted that the Provincial would consider the plan. Therefore, I said that it wasn't appropriate for him to go to India. But Father Kolbe said that he would go as the Provincial had permitted it, and he made preparations for the voyage. As soon as Father Konstanty arrived, he started out for India. Inwardly, I wondered whether it was a wise choice."

For Father Kolbe, who made obedience the most important foundation of his religious life, the subtle nuance of the Provincial's statement suggesting he might go must have sounded like a signal for departure.

What's important is to live not by one's own plan but by the will of the Immaculata. There must not be plans or acts coming from the individual. Everything comes from the will of the superior. Behind his will is the will of the Immaculata. This was the cardinal rule of Father Kolbe. It was this obedience that he stressed repeatedly to his fellow friars in his daily conversations and letters. At any rate, Father Kolbe was a man of many hardships.

Before his departure for India, he got those strange boils again on his arm. Brother Romuald remembered them very well: "They were terrible! Father Kolbe was in great pain. During Mass, he needed to be supported by the friars. In the morning, he was taking a rest just before Mass. When it was time for Mass after meditation, I went to get him from his room. As we tried to go out, carrying him in my arms, the door swung back and struck him. He fell down in great pain."

The friars thought it impossible for him to travel to India and advised him to put off the departure. Father Kolbe did not care much what they said and replied, "I still have several days. The boils will burst and I will be fine." And that is just what happened. The boils burst and he left on his own for India.

Japanese Language Not So Good

Father Kolbe was not necessarily free from all worries and anxieties. He wrote down his inner feelings before his departure: "The plan in China is not going well. The plan in Vietnam and Saigon was postponed. Other ideas have come and gone and the city which now appeared vividly before my eyes was Ernakulam in India. But I'm worried. I won't know until I get there and see the place. All for the Immaculata."

May 29th, Sunday. He left Nagasaki on an express train and arrived in Kobe the next day. He sailed from Kobe to India on a Japanese ship called the *Amerika-maru*. In his cramped cabin he still agonized over whether it was the will of the Immaculata.

"I have plenty of worries. I wonder whether the remark of the Provincial that he might think of the new Niepokalanów indicated I should make this journey for India." We are able to see some of his qualms in this memorandum.

The ship stopped at Miike Harbor in Kyushu and proceeded to

the East China Sea. He wrote two letters in Japanese on the sea, both short ones written in the Roman alphabet. Through them we may conjecture his level of the Japanese language.

This trip to India was made in 1932, more than two years after his arrival in Japan. Although he must have had plenty of opportunity to use Japanese as editor of *The Knights* and as professor at the Oura Seminary, he seems not to have been proficient in Japanese,- judging from these letters in the Roman alphabet. Sailing on the East China Sea with a distant view of mainland China, he thought back to the friars at *Mugenzai no Sono* and wrote to the Japanese brothers. We can find the names of seminarian Paul Nishiya and Marian Sato in the following letter:

"Thank you for the letter from Paul and the greetings from Marian.

As I go to Heaven soon, I can't lose a minute.

In which way?

By almost forgetting myself.

Doing penance by free will.

Loving truly only the will of the Immaculata and doing it perfectly.

I will die soon. I have little time.

You'd better remember it well in difficult times.

Good bye. I will send this letter from Hong Kong."

One can understand what he is saying but it was not written well in Japanese.

He wrote another letter which was much more difficult to understand as he sailed the South China Sea from Hong Kong to Singapore. The latter half of it reads as if all we have to do is to be a little flower like Saint Thérèse. However, I could not understand the first half at all, so I asked Brother Sergiusz what Father Kolbe meant. He was truly a friar from the same country who knew the spirit of Father Kolbe well. He interpreted the former half of the letter in this way: "If we have a great love for the Lord and the Immaculata in this small world, we will already enjoy the taste of Heaven on earth." "Oh I see!" I was really impressed.

In Father Kolbe's halting Japanese, I felt as though I were getting a glimpse of his heart. Although hundreds of Father Kolbe's letters are carefully archived, those written in Japanese are valuable, being very few. His Japanese was not very good, but he seems to have been satisfied with it then, as he wrote that he felt proud of his Japanese: "When I wrote letters in the Japanese language, a thought of pride suddenly occurred to me." This sentence was written on the same sea about one year later. He had left Nagasaki for Europe on the same course in April, 1933, in order to attend the Provincial Chapter.

"The instant I thought that I was able to express myself in Japanese, I felt my love for the Immaculata had cooled. The Immaculata does not like even a tiny bit of pride. When I gazed at the statue of the Immaculata, it seemed as though her eyes were scolding me."

While remembering writing letters in Japanese on the same sea, the humble Father Kolbe regretted his pride and sent this letter from Shanghai to the friars in *Mugenzai no Sono*.

Even Father Kolbe had a part of himself that was susceptible to pride. But to put a good interpretation on it, can we not say it might be ordinary human joy that he was able to achieve even that degree of success with such a difficult language as Japanese?

Roses of Blessing

Most days at sea were uneventful, but there were a few episodes during the voyage. One was on the first Friday after boarding the ship. At that time Catholics did not eat meat on Fridays, which were days of abstinence. Father Kolbe said to the waiter, "I don't need meat today," but he was served chicken at lunch. He then repeated to the waiter, "I told you that I didn't need meat." The waiter answered, "I thought meat meant only beef, as a chicken has two legs."

In Hong Kong, Father Kolbe got thirsty because of the torrid weather and drank plenty of soft drinks. His boils had gone down but his lungs ached constantly. He worried that he would cough up blood. Then in Singapore he wrote, "There were no tigers anywhere. Forty million people speak Malay. I keenly felt that we need another Niepokalanów here."

Once the ship entered the Indian Ocean, strong winds blew every day. During the Mass, the Sacred Blood almost spilt. At the end of June, he arrived at the coast of Malabar in southwest India via Ceylon. He went into the interior of India by train for two and half days. He met the Archbishop of the Syrian Rite and the Archbishop of the Latin Rite. There was no chance with the Syrian Archbishop because of the difference in the liturgy. The talk with the Latin Archbishop did not go smoothly either, as the Spanish Carmelites were already there and the Archbishop did not want another order coming in.

Just when Father Kolbe was about to lose hope, a flower petal that looked like a rose fell to his feet from the statue of Saint Thérèse of the Child Jesus, which stood in the corridor of the Archbishop's palace. Father Kolbe had established a special spiritual pact with her. He took this as a sign that there would definitely be a blessing coming. This small incident consoled the travel-weary Father Kolbe and gave him hope. Strangely enough, the situation took a turn for the better after that. The Archbishop took Father Kolbe to the site in his own car and promised to offer him spacious land and buildings. Although it was not conveniently located, Father Kolbe liked this quiet location.

A middle-aged Indian priest offered his cooperation. Father Kolbe asked him, "I will send articles and funds. So would you publish *The Knights*?" Father Kolbe sent a telegram to Poland, "Indian Niepokalanów was founded. Glory be to the Immaculata!"

Later he wrote, "Regarding Niepokalanów in India, it's hard not to see the hand of Saint Thérèse of the Child Jesus with whom I have a pact. In Kobe and during my travel I came across images and statues of Saint Thérèse everywhere."

Having finished the preliminary negotiations, he left for Japan on the ship, the *Angkor*. He sailed the same course he had taken, transferred to the Japan-China ferry in Shanghai, and returned to *Mugenzai no Sono* on July 25th. The trip took about two months. As he had plenty of time on his way back to Nagasaki, he wrote a detailed report to Father Kornel, the Provincial.

> We would like to ask for your consideration on the project in India. It is said, "Strike while the iron is hot." I envisaged the project to make the whole world belong to the Immaculata two years ago. Its first stage includes Japan, China and India. The inhabitants of these three countries add up to half of the global population.

He must have felt relieved when he got back to Nagasaki. He wrote a letter to his mother, Maria Dabrowska, after a long interval: "After sailing for eighteen days to the island of Ceylon, I travelled to the town of Ernakulam. As difficulties were piling up, I prayed many Rosaries. One of the roses that surrounded Saint Thérèse of the Child Jesus fell off. In the local language, 'Niepokalanów' will be called 'Amalam.' Rice ripens three times a year. There are poisonous snakes called 'cobra' in mountain areas. There are regions where contagious diseases are rampant. However, thanks to the Immaculata, I came through unharmed."

Father Kolbe was relieved, having finished his mission. All he had to do was to entrust it to his superior.

I asked Brother Sergiusz, "Why didn't the Indian branch come to fruition, after all of Father Kolbe's efforts?" The answer was very simple. "Because there were no friars who wanted to go to India."

Provincial Kornel suspended the India matter until the Provincial Chapter that was to be held the following year. It was reviewed anew again then but, in the Order of the Conventual Franciscans, there were no friars willing to go to India. "Why did Father Kolbe target Ernakulam, not a bigger city like Bombay?"

Brother Sergiusz replied, "When he travelled to Rome before coming to Japan, he met a major seminarian from India who recommended Ernakulam to him." "So Father Kolbe had a connection with an Indian seminarian." "That's right," Brother Sergiusz answered. After a while, he added, "Father Kolbe told me about an interesting vision when he came back from India."

Such was the vision: "Japan is preparing to wage war against Russia. Japan isn't afraid of anything, not even America. The Immaculata is leading Japan well. Japan may occupy the whole of Asia. Or they may occupy Europe. This is all good for the Knights of the Immaculata. Let's march out with the Japanese and propagate *The Knights*."

Strangely enough, he saw into the distant future and placed a good deal of his hope on the Japanese nation. Then he closed the map of India. The old dusty atlas has not been opened again since then. The old atlas which inspired Father Kolbe to follow his dream lies buried away in the archives of the Knights of the Immaculata in Nagasaki.

CHAPTER 15

The Dream of a Friar Sinking in a Swamp

All the Polish friars who came to Nagasaki were young and their monastic lives were still immature. One day, Father Kolbe told them about a dream of a friar who was sinking in a swamp.

Those with Psychological Difficulties

The young friars who came to Nagasaki from Poland had just made their temporary profession of vows. In order to become a friar one has to pass more than half a year as a candidate. Then he enters into the novitiate which lasts one year, puts on the religious habit of the Franciscan order, and receives a religious name. Brother Romuald and Brother Celestyn put on the religious habit for the first time at the friary of Niepokalanów.

In the friary there is an "order of calling" according to time of entry into the friary and the age. As Brother Celestyn was a half year older than Brother Romuald, Brother Celestyn was supposed to ascend the altar earlier than Brother Romuald. However, Brother Celestyn hesitated to stand up, so Brother Romuald ascended the altar first. "You'll be called Brother Romuald from now on." Actually, this was the religious name which Celestyn would have received. Through this accident both 'fraters' came to understand each other especially well. The novitiate is a period when the novices seriously try to discern whether they are suited to the religious life. Those who have passed through the novitiate can make their temporary profession of vows.

After both friars had made their temporary profession, they came to Japan for missionary work together. There are many troubles and hardships in the mission field. For the young friars, living in the mission field was like being tossed about on stormy seas. Brother Celestyn was gentle and good when he was in Poland. But after his arrival in Nagasaki, he lost the luster in his eyes and became a different person. Maybe it was due to the weather in Nagasaki or to loneliness. He got angry easily and was sometimes lost in thought. He did not move at all for a long time, but just gazed at the Holy Sacrament on the altar, seemingly not because of his devotion but rather due to his mental illness.

Brother Celestyn came to Japan for missionary work with Brother Romuald.

Brother Romuald worried much about him. When Brother Celestyn had been well, they had taken a long bicycle ride together to the Shimabara Peninsula in order to disseminate *The Knights*.

They pedaled bicycles, singing in Polish, "Between mountains and valleys echoes the voice of the praise of Mary."

Now, Brother Romuald felt very sorry for Brother Celestyn who frequently complained of headaches. He was lacking in concentration during work or meetings and he assumed an attitude of indifference. Nevertheless, he was narrow minded in a sense and could not excuse the small mistakes of others. When Brother Zeno

THE DREAM OF A FRIAR SINKING IN A SWAMP

was dozing in the chapel, Brother Celestyn pushed this senior friar aside, saying "Go to bed if you must sleep. Don't sleep here!" Father Kolbe, Guardian of the friary, could not ignore the situation. He himself had been suffering from tuberculosis, so he was especially kind to sick people. He called Brother Celestyn to the guardian room and let him lie on the bed, put a blanket over him and, kneeling down next to him, massaged his temples.

"I sometimes went into the guardian room and wondered what the matter was. Later I envied Brother Celestyn because he was loved so much by Father Kolbe. He also had a fever then... Father Kolbe was really like a genuine doctor," said Brother Romuald.

Brother Celestyn was assigned to the office work of *The Knights*. He could speak Japanese better than any other friar. Father Kolbe thought it better for Brother Celestyn to be in the open air. So, he let Brother Celestyn help Brother Zeno. Brother Zeno had no ill feelings against this young friar for having pushed him aside in the chapel, but his way of working was very severe with everyone.

For example, Brother Zeno once mixed water with a lot of cement in a hurry about ten minutes before the closing bell rang. Leaving his work unfinished in this way, Brother Zeno ran into Father Kolbe's room, saying with exaggerated gestures, "I can't waste cement." He extended his arms, and asked earnestly for permission to be excused from prayer. Brother Zeno always worked overtime, which was no problem for his rugged body, but it was hard on the younger friars.

At that time, they were constructing stone steps, and the load was heavy, according to Brother Romuald. "It was a severe burden in hot weather. Brother Zeno was very strict. We didn't have any breaks. When Brother Celestyn changed his clothes, I saw his skin was peeling off and stuck to his undershirt. How painful that must have been! His back was bleeding because of sunburn. We didn't have a bathroom at that time; it was built later on, around the time Father Kolbe went to India."

The fabric of the shirts they brought from Poland was thick. When they came back soaked in sweat after taking a walk on the hill behind the friary, they had no spare shirts to change into. "The fabric of shirts was poor. As the dyeing was of poor quality, my back was stained blue," said Brother Romuald.

Was Brother Celestyn ready to throw in the towel? Hardly! He did his best without becoming discouraged while Father Kolbe remained in Nagasaki. During the Pacific War, he went to Harbin in Manchuria. In the confusion of the postwar period, he took care of the Japanese internees, caught an infectious disease, and passed away early at the age of thirty-five.

An Incompetent Commander?

When I read a letter that Father Kolbe sent to Poland in August, 1931, I had to frown because of an unknown fact I found there.

What were the criteria of Father Kolbe for selecting the four friars, Brother Zeno, Brother Seweryn, Brother Hilary and Brother Zygmunt? I had not known why Father Kolbe took these four friars with him but through this letter I could understand everything.

Brother Zeno and Brother Seweryn were experienced friars from the time in Grodno. It was quite natural that they were chosen, but the reason Father Kolbe reluctantly chose the somewhat odd Brother Hilary was that there was no other possibility to choose a friar who had made his perpetual profession of vows. As for Brother Zygmunt, Father Kolbe wrote, "I was greatly mistaken because I let myself be deceived by appearances. It taught me a good lesson for the future." Reading his regret, I felt as if I had been dealt a blow on the head. It seemed to me too random a selection. I doubted whether Father Kolbe had good judgment as a commander, since it appeared that he had not accurately evaluated his subordinates.

If the commander was in such a state, the subordinates themselves must have had their own worries. It is obvious the friars who came to Japan were no saints. As Brother Hilary and Brother

Zygmunt were still young, twenty-five and twenty respectively, their religious life was immature. For that reason Father Kolbe had an even harder time.

As for Father Kolbe's aptitude as a commander, Brother Sergiusz gives an account as follows: "There were eighteen friars who transferred from Grodno to Niepokalanów. Brother Zeno and Brother Seweryn were among them. They worked very hard and were of sound mind. Father Kolbe believed that Brother Zygmunt was fine because he had experienced a Marian apparition in Niepokalanów; however, it turned out to be a fake! I still wonder how Father Kolbe could make such a mistake."

At that time Brother Zygmunt asserted that he had seen Our Lady.

After taking a breath Brother Sergiusz added, "Actually, Father Kolbe wanted to choose Brother Salezy, but he was an electrician and indispensable in Niepokalanów. Consequently, there was no suitable one to send to the Orient. We really didn't have enough members so Brother Hilary was chosen even though he didn't seem

Brother Zeno was always busy with cooking, shopping, laundry and other tasks.

to be suitable. He said he was indifferent as to whether he went or not. Although he lacked enthusiasm, Father Kolbe chose him because he thought it was better for Brother Hilary to go than not to go. There was no other choice than Brother Hilary."

Brother Zeno was forty at that time. He was the only middle aged friar among the others. He had no academic qualifications, but he was a man of all trades and second to none in his work. The following is an episode about his entry into the friary:

> Brother Zeno did not get married when he was in his youth. After he left the army at the end of the First World War, he took various jobs including peddler, tailor, shoemaker, and mine worker. Finally, he settled into ironworks. His varied career made him jack-of-all-trades. Then one day he made a resolution to become a friar for some reason.
>
> At first, Brother Zeno tried to enter the Order of Friars Minor Capuchin who had their hair close cropped and wore simple grey habits with sandals on their bare feet. All of them grew whiskers. Brother Zeno did not like whiskers, so he ran away thinking, "I'll look like an old Jewish man if I grow whiskers."
>
> Then he went to the Order of Friars Minor Conventual. The friars of this Order wore leather shoes in good quality, oiled back their hair and wore nice overcoats. Brother Zeno thought, "That's it!" Convinced this was the one for him, he applied for admission into the Order.
>
> The first friary he entered was in Grodno, an old town lying in the northeast of Poland which belongs to the Republic of Belarus now. He encountered Father Kolbe there by chance. Before Brother Zeno entered this friary, Father Kolbe had been there for three years. He continued the movement of the Knights of the Immaculata, printed and published the magazine of the Immaculata, *Rycerz Niepokalanej*, by himself. Through his encounter with Father Kolbe, Brother

Zeno's chic taste was swept away and he became the ninth Knight of the Immaculata.

"Brother Zeno can't kneel down in the prayer and always has to sit. The reason is that he lifted an excessively heavy beam during the rebuilding of the paper supplies warehouse. Neither the doctors in Grodno nor in Warsaw were able to fix his problem. Nevertheless, he is doing heavy work and eats much," wrote Father Kolbe. Friars came one after another from Poland. But it was absolutely necessary for all of them, including Brother Zeno, to reform themselves in order to devote themselves to the strict Franciscan spirt of Father Kolbe. Brother Zygmunt and Brother Hilary returned to Poland after only a year: the former left the Order and the latter remained a friar in Niepokalanów and died of illness at the age of seventy-one.

Father Kolbe had a lot of trouble with the friars. But the biggest trouble must have been the withdrawal of seminarian Ludwik and his later life. Ludwik came to Japan with Father Metody, Brother Romuald, and others. He was studying at the Tokyo Diocesan Major Seminary. But when he was expelled by Principal Father Candau in 1932, he left the Order and went to South America. Father Kolbe did not have much contact with Ludwik, who was almost always in Tokyo.

However, in October of the same year an astonishing incident was reported to Father Kolbe that the former seminarian Ludwik had pretended to be a priest and celebrated Mass! What a grave sin! Although Father Kolbe had no connection with him then, he felt severely responsible for the affair and was laid up in bed from the shock of it all.

Father Kolbe wrote in a sorrowful mood: "I had a fever and headache. I was laid up all day long. In order to put me at ease, the brothers tried hard to console me as if they were competing with each other. They said that there will be perfect consolation in heaven. I can't help loving these brothers." Father Kolbe was also weak. He often shed tears and suffered in Nagasaki. His life of six years in Nagasaki itself was kind of a novitiate for Father Kolbe, his period of trial.

One day, some time later on, Father Kolbe related the following dream to the friars: "I had a dream. One friar fell into a swamp and couldn't climb out of it. He was writhing in agony. He was gradually sinking in the swamp. I offered him a stick in order to help him. I hoped he would grasp it. But it was useless. I looked for someone who would help him. When I looked back, I saw two brothers laughing and playing, even though there was a brother sinking down. Then the brother sinking in the swamp cried out and I woke up."

This account was written down in a notebook by Brother Sergiusz. He said to me, recalling the day: "After Father Kolbe told us the story, one brother whispered to me: Giovanni Bosco (a 19th century Italian saint who founded the Society of Saint Francis de Sales) often had dreams, too. His were day dreams. Father Kolbe's may have also been a day dream."

A Friar Who Ate and Drank

When Brother Zeno came back from travelling around Japan after the Second World War, he told me the following story.

The first Japanese friar was Marian Shigeo Sato. He was short and had a slight walking disability. He was short-tempered and a little lazy. He was frequently sick.

He came down with a slight fever. Since Father Kolbe always took good care of sick people, he asked Brother Marian whether he would like to eat chicken, which was the best meal. Brother Marian answered "Yes, with pleasure" and ate the chicken. Then Father Kolbe asked, "How about wine?" Of course, he was not going to say no. Brother Marian answered "Yes."

However, when he drank the wine, his fever started to climb quickly. Father Kolbe was anxious about him and called Dr. Asada of the University Clinic and had him examine Brother Marian. Dr. Asada said, "We have good medication for this," wrote something on scratch paper and handed it to Father Kolbe. Father Kolbe forwarded it to Brother Zeno and said, "Make the purchase at the pharmacy at Nakagawa-machi."

When Brother Zeno showed it to the owner of the pharmacy, he burst into laughter in spite of himself! The written instruction was that the patient would recover, if he ate sweet potatoes, lotuses and carrots.

The owner said, "We don't carry these medications. You'd better go to the grocery."

At the end of the story, Brother Zeno said, "After eating plenty of vegetables, Brother Marian soon recovered," and exploded with laughter for the first time!

Brother Zeno's story corresponds to the report of Father Kolbe to the Provincial in October, 1932: "Brother Marian will finish his novitiate soon. He would like to make his temporary profession of vows. In fact, there have been several ups and downs. The Chinese and Japanese have a certain fickleness, which a foreign priest and a sister of another religious Order also recognize. Brother Marian sometimes loses his health, but the doctor considers his condition not so serious. He just needs to be careful about his diet. I am enclosing the opinions of the friars."

The story and the document corresponded to each other so well that I could see it as a "jigsaw puzzle."

CHAPTER 16

A Lighthouse Shining on the Mountain

*A woman from a brothel came to the reservoir
to commit suicide. She happened to look up and saw
the statue of Mary, the Immaculata.*

Building a Lourdes Grotto on the Back Hill

At that time, Suwa-shrine was at the end of the streetcar line. When Father Kolbe went to Oura Cathedral for confession, he saw a big fish in the streetcar. At first, he thought it was dead but, to his astonishment, he found it was still alive. But without water, it could not swim. Father Kolbe got off the streetcar at the terminal and continued thinking about the fish, as he headed for the friary on the hill: "When I go out into the world, I have difficulty breathing, just like the fish. The world is full of garbage. Once I have completed what I need to do, I want to go back to the friary as soon as possible." With this in mind, he took a rest at Hotaru-jaya (which means 'tearoom of fireflies'). He also considered reducing the number of times he would leave the friary. Crossing over an old stone bridge, he took a shortcut and climbed up some stone steps. When he came to the national highway, he could see a dozen or so Jizo-statues all in a row, the heads of which had fallen down along the road side. Since Father Kolbe was suffering from a lung disease, he had trouble breathing when climbing a hill. "But if we go out under obedience, we can have peace of mind, because the blessings of the Immaculata are with us." Thinking such things, he walked along the highway. Here and there, clear water that sprang up from Mt. Hiko pooled up in front of private homes.

A horse cart had stopped there and the horse was drinking the water. It was an idyllic scene of the 1930s. Going up along the national highway, one could see the dark green surface of the reservoir spread out before one's eyes. Turning aside from there, Father Kolbe went up a narrow path to the friary, gasping for breath.

Life in Hongouchi was going along quite smoothly and Father Kolbe built a Lourdes grotto, a cave dedicated to the Virgin Mary, on the hill behind the friary. Lourdes is the name of a small town in France. In 1858, Our Lady suddenly appeared to a girl eighteen times in Lourdes. And surprisingly enough, miraculous water gushed out of the earth that instantaneously cured many seriously ill people. Since then, the Lourdes Grotto has developed into the largest Marian pilgrimage site in the world.

Father Kolbe visited the Lourdes Grotto in France on his way to missionary work in the East and prayed in secret that he would build a Lourdes grotto for the glory of Mary as soon as he arrived there. This was one of his ardent desires. So when he looked for land in Nagasaki, with the grotto in mind, he chose the hilly land in Hongouchi in preference to the flatland in Urakami.

When we climb up the narrow stone steps that Brother Zeno built beside the printing office, we find a steep road leading up to a thick forest. To build a Lourdes grotto, you must have water, a cave and a Marian statue. Fortunately, there was spring water and a natural rocky formation. At first the friars put a statue of the Immaculata on the rock instead of Our Lady of Lourdes, probably because they did not have the right one. A statue of Our Lady of Lourdes has her hands in prayer with a rosary around her arms, whereas the Immaculata Statue stretches down her hands and opens her palms. The statue of the Immaculata was placed there on the first day of the Marian month, May, 1932.

Hongouchi was the starting point of the Nagasaki Road in the Edo Period. There was a lot of coming and going of travelers there. So there were many Buddhist statues and pagodas that attracted people's attention to the place. Halfway up the mountain was a place where the practitioners of Shugen-do (Japanese mountain asceticism) could stand under a waterfall. The local people were used to seeing Buddhist statues there but now they saw a Marian statue for the first time in their lives.

When Father Kolbe returned from the town, he often went to the Lourdes grotto to pray. One day, he was shocked to see, of all things, the Marian statue on the rock cruelly smashed to pieces. This happened not once, not twice, but three times! Father Kolbe wrote sadly: "On the day before the feast of the Seven Sorrows of Mary, someone again smashed to pieces the statue of Our Lady of Lourdes in front of which the faithful pray. As we found a stone among the broken pieces of the statue, someone presumably took aim at it and threw the stone against it. This is the third time. In addition, since it was broken heartlessly into very small pieces this time, it is certain that someone did it with an evil intent.

"What a terrible thing! That someone would treat so viciously the statue of Our Mother whom we love. We prayed for the repentance of the miserable person."

Sorrowfully, Father Kolbe put a new statue on the rock, with the hope that it would never again be destroyed.

The Second Building Becomes the Keep of the Castle

Since the Lourdes grotto was on a hill behind the friary, Father Kolbe always thought that he would like to situate the statue of the Immaculata where the people of Nagasaki could see it well.

When the second building of the friary, a three-story one, was completed in December, 1932, he placed a Marian statue on the roof. He lit it up with light bulbs at night, so that one could see it from a distance.

A Marian statue was placed on the top of the three-story friary.
(On the upper right of the photo.)

Brother Sergiusz, who was responsible for the construction said: "It was a square wooden building, 12x12 meters. The cost of building amounted to 2,200 yen. Just then the yen weakened against the dollar and fell from two yen to four yen to the dollar. Since we were using the dollar, this allowed us to complete the payment earlier than expected.

"With the construction of the new building, the friars could come down from the attic of the old building. We were exuberant all the more because we moved to the new building on the 7th of December, the eve of the Feast of the Immaculate Conception! How we expressed our gratitude to Our Mother Mary then!"

They did not have to sleep in the cramped attic of the printing office any more. In the dialect of Nagasaki we say *"yoka yoka"* when we approve of something, which corresponds to *"dobrze dobrze"* in Polish. Shouting *"dobrze dobrze"* repeatedly, they moved to the new building.

There was a kitchen on the first floor and a dining room on the second. The friars brought their meals to the second floor, climbing wooden stairs. A common bedroom was made on the third floor, where the friars, including Brother Zeno, slept. The second building was just like the keep of a castle for the friars.

The statue of Our Lady on the roof was splendid! Since it was placed so high, one could see it clearly from midtown Nagasaki. The roof was covered with zinc plates and there was a handrail around it. The friars could meditate, stroll or enjoy cool evening breezes up there. It was difficult to do such things on the grounds of the friary, since there were bushes, cuts of bamboo trees, snakes, centipedes, mosquitos, etc. Brother Zeno hated snakes and rats!

Those who went back and forth on the national highway stopped at the sight of the Western-style building which had suddenly appeared at the foot of Mt. Hiko, and looked up to the Marian statue. It was like a lighthouse shining on a mountain!

Soon after Father Kolbe had placed the long-sought statue there, he wrote: "The Immaculata draws a lot of souls to herself. We often witness unbaptized passers-by stopping and looking up to the Marian statue. According to the friars, they often asked what the statue is and one unbaptized woman asked about our lives and missionary work with interest. And the other day an unbaptized family visited us..."

This family had noticed a dark, square building on the hillside. The daughter said, "Something is on the roof of the house." The wife said, "I see something like a doll."

The father said, "Let's go closer to see what it is." The family stood in front of the door of the friary out of curiosity. Father Kolbe received them but there was a problem. In the friary there was a regulation of 'clausura' prescribed by the Vatican, i.e., women were not allowed into the friary.

"Unfortunately, I was only able to take the father to the foot of the Immaculata statue and to lead the mother and the daughter to the chapel. When they left, I gave each of them a Miraculous Medal."

Climbing up to the roof, one could see the mountains and the town of Nagasaki City, cars and carts going by on the national road and the reservoir full of water. I wonder what Father Kolbe was hoping to show the Japanese while guiding them around the precincts.

What he wanted to emphasize must have been the grace of Mary, which can be compared to the reservoir. Since Mary is as full of God's grace as the reservoir is full of water, we can participate in God's grace if we get close to Mary. The logic of Father Kolbe is simple. In the reservoir of Our Lady he wanted to find the mystery of the Mother of God. I believe the aim of Father Kolbe's missionary work was to manifest to the Japanese people the profound love and mystery of the Mother of God.

An Ill-fated Woman Visits the Friary

During the "Closed Country" period in Japan, Nagasaki was the only port town which had permission to trade with Holland and China. I don't know whether this is the reason, but the fact is that red-light districts and brothels flourished in Nagasaki.

There was a bridge with the interesting name of 'Shian-bashi (Consideration Bridge) in Nagasaki. One would get to the red-light district of Maruyama by crossing over the bridge. Philanderers used to stop at the bridge and consider whether they would continue on to Maruyama or not, which is said to be the origin of the name of the bridge. When one got to Maruyama, there was another bridge called 'Omoikiri-bashi (Resolution Bridge). Nearby there was yet another bridge called 'Amigasa-bashi (Braided Hat Bridge)." There was another red-light district around there and men crossed that bridge with a braided hat in order to conceal their identity out of a guilty conscience. The name of the bridge is said to have its origins in this legend.

In olden days, young girls who were sold to brothels were considered ill-fated. A woman from the brothel appears in Father Kolbe's memoirs. It happened just around the time when the three-story building was completed and the statue of the Immaculata was placed on the roof.

"Recently a woman about twenty years old came to *Mugenzai no Sono*. She was in an unfortunate situation. She didn't know her father and had been banished by her mother. After her foster mother had died, she was deceived and sold to a red-light district. After suffering more than she could bear, she escaped. She didn't know what to do and came to the reservoir to commit suicide. Then she saw the statue of Mary."

With disheveled hair, the woman went up the hill to the friary, as if she were drawn to it, and rang the doorbell.

"The Immaculata attracted this ill-fated woman to herself. We heartily received her. She was physically and mentally exhausted so we tried to give her a meal. But she wouldn't eat it for a while, as she was genuinely terrified. After I had spoken words of comfort to her, she finally looked better and took some tea with a bit of bread.

"She sadly said that she had resolved to commit suicide several times because of her misfortune. Once she tried to throw herself into water with stones packed in her kimono but fortunately her life was saved. It pained me to see her."

I tried imagining around what time she visited the friary, as there was no record of it. Perhaps it may have been in the evening or at night. Did she intend to commit suicide in the dark of night? I can imagine Father Kolbe's anguished look and the pale woman under the dim lights of the friary.

"I wanted to help her. After cheering her up, I prayed and put a medal of the Immaculata around her neck. Then I consulted a Japanese priest and took her to him, so that he could give her support from then on."

What became of her after that? Father Kolbe wrote a letter three weeks later and concluded it with a note on her future, looking bright: "She lives now with a devout Catholic family and is studying the Catechism."

He wrote, "The Immaculata leads the souls of the Japanese in this way. We don't know how she has spoken to the hearts of many Japanese since the statue of the Immaculata was erected two months ago. We will know everything only on Judgment Day."

Father Kolbe put his hope above all on the work of the Immaculata. To be more precise, the Knights of the Immaculata do not work by themselves according to him, but "it is the Immaculata who does the work." To let the Immaculata work freely — this best characterizes what Father Kolbe was about.

We are no more than simple instruments of the Immaculata. When we abandon ourselves and offer ourselves perfectly to the Immaculata, she can work freely. That is how Father Kolbe believed we best could find swift and perfect sanctification and the fruits of the propagation of the Faith. Father Kolbe wrote with emphasis: "The Immaculata is promoting her own Japanese *Mugenzai no Sono* with her mighty hands. The number of pagans who first knew Catholicism by reading *The Knights* is increasing now."

One Sunday, Father Urakawa walked to *Mugenzai no Sono* with six major seminarians. They visited the Lourdes grotto to pray. The Marian statue on the rock was safe. After the statue had been smashed to pieces cruelly for the third time, Brother Zeno went to negotiate with the chairman of the neighborhood association. He said, "It's inexcusable" and circulated a community notice to all the members of the association. After that, no one dared to destroy the statue of Our Lady.

Father Urakawa was the priest who had previously refused to cooperate with the Knights and had thrown the manuscripts of *The Knights* on the ground, when a friar had brought them to him. Now, he was visiting the Lourdes grotto! Father Kolbe made an entry in his diary on that day. "Auxiliary Bishop Urakawa took a walk with seminarians and came to see us. They went to the

Lourdes grotto. According to him, the Catholics read *The Catholic Newspaper* and *The Voice*, and the pagans read *The Knights*. He proposed to cooperate with us."

There must have been no better news for Father Kolbe. Father Urakawa, a good writer, wrote "Introduction to Catholicism" and "Our Holy Mother" as a series in every issue of *The Knights* since then.

The incident of Father Urakawa and the manuscripts was told to me by Father Mirochna, who was a seminarian at that time. There is, however, a sequel to this story: "After the Second World War Bishop Urakawa declared that he really had persecuted Father Kolbe. When, in his later years, he retired as Bishop of Sendai, he admired Father Kolbe deeply and wished fervently to live for the rest of his life in the friary where Father Kolbe had once lived. His wish was not realized for various reasons though." It was presumably the genuine Marian devotion of Father Kolbe that changed Bishop Urakawa's mind.

Brother Sergiusz, who is in charge of the Lourdes grotto now, said, "It was the most comfortable place for Father Kolbe. He came here to pray almost every day." The Lourdes grotto, whose foundation Father Kolbe had laid, was gradually improved: there are five relief sculptures of the Mysteries of the Rosary now, and trees like camellias, Japanese apricots, cherry trees, azaleas, and maples add the colors of the seasons to the Lourdes grotto. The statue of Our Lady in the grotto has ever since been looking far out over the houses of Nagasaki in silence, with her hands folded in prayer.

CHAPTER 17

The Scent of Holy Virtue in the Soup

What was the scent of holy virtue that Father Kolbe gave off? I tried to see the image of Father Kolbe through the eyes of Brother Kasjan who devoted himself to cooking throughout his life.

The Reason He Became a Cook

Ever since Brother Kasjan had come to Japan in 1932, he consistently worked as a cook for about fifty years — which is rare! He entered the friary in Niepokalanów in Poland when he was twenty-six years old. Unfortunately, there was no receptionist to greet him when he arrived. So Brother Albert, the cook, welcomed him. That sealed his fate.

When he showed the letter of admission to Brother Albert, he was taken to Father Kolbe's office. Fortunately, Father Kolbe was in. As Brother Kasjan had travelled from a small town that is now in the Soviet Union on a

Brother Kasjan worked as a cook 56 years and passed away in 1988.

train for a whole day and a night, he was somewhat tired.

Father Kolbe said gently, "Please rest, you must be tired." Recalling that moment, Brother Kasjan said, "But there was a machine making a loud noise and, moreover, there was no place to rest. So I looked into the kitchen. That was all she wrote. I have been in the kitchen ever since. It's been a long time! Nine months had passed since Niepokalanów was built. There were twenty friars and fourteen novices. My number was thirty-four. Brother Zeno was a novice."

Now in 1982, Brother Kasjan is in good health and lives in the friary in Konagai-machi in Nagasaki Prefecture. Brother Kasjan entered the friary in Niepokalanów in July. Brother Sergiusz entered ten days ahead of him, and Brother Romuald and Brother Grzegorz had entered two months earlier. They became lifelong friends.

At the end of September, all the farm families got together and dug potatoes. Brother Albert went to them every day to ask for potatoes.

In the meantime, Father Kolbe assigned Brother Kasjan to be in charge of the kitchen. He had no experience as a cook. His father was a teacher in an elementary school and his mother did not teach him any cooking skills. He cooked in his own fashion: he kneaded flour, rolled it out and cut it in his own way. After frying it, he mixed it with cabbage and cheese. When he cooked macaroni, Father Kolbe was very pleased because it just happened to be his favorite food.

After Brother Albert came back from asking for potatoes, he was assigned to work in the busy office and never returned to the kitchen. So in the end, Brother Kasjan had to prepare all the meals for the big household.

On the Solemnity of the Ascension of Our Lord Jesus Christ in May, 1930, Brother Kasjan successfully completed his novitiate and made his temporary profession of vows.

"On that day two telegrams reached Niepokalanów: one was from Father Kolbe in Japan, telling that the first issue of *The Knights* had been published. The other was from the friary of Lwów, the death notice of major seminarian Bonifacio."

Seminarian Bonifacio was one of Father Mirochna's senior students and was also acquainted with Father Kolbe. He suffered from tuberculosis but he was offering up his pains for the missionary work in Japan. It must have been Divine Providence that the two telegrams arrived on the same day.

Two years later, in 1932, when Brother Kasjan chanced upon Guardian Father Florian in the garden, Father Florian suddenly made an important announcement to Brother Kasjan: "You have to go to Japan. Father Kolbe asked me to send you there. Please prepare for your departure and arrange for a cook to replace you." "What? To Japan?"

It did not matter whether he wanted to go or not. He was not asked his wish, whether he would like to go. Brother Kasjan left Poland with mixed feelings. At the time of his departure, there were more than one hundred friars and one hundred and thirty minor seminarians in Niepokalanów. Niepokalanów (the city of the Immaculata), whose seed Father Kolbe had sown in the wilderness near the capital Warsaw, grew rapidly and continued working on a large scale.

A Day of Prayer and Work

Daybreak comes first to Himi Pass in Nagasaki City. *Mugenzai no Sono* lies in the direction of Himi Tunnel from the Pass. The friars get up at 5 a.m. They assemble in the chapel in silence. The morning starts with prayer. They spend an hour and a half meditating, participating in Holy Mass, and praying the Rule of the Friars Minor, etc.

Breakfast is very simple. Brother Kasjan boils water and prepares bread and a barley coffee that is called "*kawa*" in Polish. To make it, Brother Kasjan roasts barley with oil in a frying pan until it turns into black powder. Then he boils the powder in water and lets it rest overnight. The upper layer of the water is drunk and the dregs at the bottom are thrown out. The water is cloudy and grey but tastes smooth. They do not eat any cheese, vegetables, or fruit. And they always eat their three meals in silence.

Brother Kasjan had a deep devotion to Saint Joseph.

When Brother Kasjan came to Japan, he had no idea what kind of food he would be serving. Father Kolbe said, "I will give you money so that you can buy necessary items. But I don't need anything for myself." He made it clear he did not want anything special for himself. He emphasized, "It's enough if we eat what makes us healthy. To be delicious is unnecessary. Just be careful about food that has rotted. That's all."

Father Kolbe was the fastest eater. He just ate a little and was done! Following a short rest after the meal, he went to work. He never removed his habit even when he did heavy work in sweat and mud.

Everyone in *Mugenzai no Sono* did his best to publish *The Knights*. The number of the printed copies reached 50,000 with the December 1932 issue. The more the work increased, the more short-handed they were. Brother Kasjan said, "Whenever visitors came to *Mugenzai no Sono*, Father Kolbe served them a meal and

THE SCENT OF HOLY VIRTUE IN THE SOUP

invited them to do a bit of work for the Immaculata. He was convinced that people would receive her blessing if they worked for her. He always spoke to the visitors about the Immaculata."

While the friars were engaged in publishing *The Knights*, Brother Kasjan prepared food in the kitchen. He also washed their clothes and mended their socks when he had spare time. When he came to Nagasaki, the friars were in extremely poor health and they were exhausted. The hefty friars like Brother Romuald and Brother Celestyn collapsed one after another. Brother Grzegorz had a heat rash which suppurated and Father Kolbe suffered from insomnia and stomach ache.

"The first cook was Brother Zeno. As he was busy, he made simple meals. Perhaps that is why Father Kolbe had stomach trouble. He did not eat much. He did not eat Japanese food such as miso soup, seafood products and rice cakes much, because of his stomach problems," said Brother Kasjan.

Once, Brother Romuald went to the Bishop's residence in Oura and looked into the kitchen secretly to get some ideas from what they were cooking. Just as he thought, they cooked Japanese food like *kon'yaku*, fish-paste and sliced raw fish, none of which Father Kolbe liked. But quite admirably, he never said he would not eat them, so he always partook of Japanese food on Fridays, using chopsticks.

Father Kolbe often bought sardines on the way home from Oura after confession. Sardines were very cheap and cost 10 sen per 3 kg. There was almost no meat like beef on the table. In most cases, meals consisted of sardines, soup, and fried barley. At noon the friars prayed the Angelus, examined their consciences, then went into the dining room. While listening to two friars reading in rotation the Holy Bible, *The Imitation of Christ*, or *The Lives of the Saints*, they all ate in silence.

Brother Zeno went to town almost every day. He always came back after lunch and annoyed Brother Kasjan. "Brother Zeno was a busy man. He didn't have any free time. In Poland, he used to shave his face while walking around. He didn't need a mirror. He was a smooth talker and no one could beat him; he was very good at promoting himself! His fault was to oppose the superior, as Father Kolbe wrote. Whenever he went to town, he came back late. When I said, 'I'm trying to clear the table,' he retorted angrily, 'You know nothing. Don't worry. I'll eat whatever there is.' Then he ate only bread. Nevertheless, to my amazement, he was very strong."

As Brother Zeno walked a lot every day, his shoes quickly wore out. When that happened, he put on Father Kolbe's shoes without permission as, quite conveniently, they wore the same size. But Brother Zeno was tricky and did not return them, until he had also worn them out! So we always bought two pairs of shoes at the same time.

The Holiness of Father Kolbe

After lunch the friars visited the Blessed Sacrament together and then rested. When the bell rang, they started working again. Grand silence continued until 3 p.m., and they did not talk at all during the silence. If absolutely necessary, they spoke in a low voice.

After putting the dishes in order, Brother Kasjan took a breath. This was the only time he was able to relax. He prayed alone in the chapel and spent time in meditation. Then he went back to the kitchen again. He cooked the food that Brother Zeno bought on the way back from distributing *The Knights* in town. One day Brother Zeno bought cabbage. Then Brother Grzegorz who was responsible for accounting said, "It's expensive! Why did you buy it? Potatoes are cheaper and good enough." When Brother Zeno bought apples, Brother Grzegorz said they were a luxury and he would not eat them.

Father Kolbe did not compel such a poor life at that time but the friars themselves had a fervent desire for propagation of the Faith in their hearts. Father Kolbe always said, "I want to get souls.

Brothers should work only for the sake of the Immaculata." They all quickly agreed with what Father Kolbe said.

Father Kolbe sometimes asked Brother Kasjan to go with him to the clinic of a Catholic doctor. Brother Kasjan was also responsible for sick friars.

"Shall we go to the hospital together?" Father Kolbe often had strange swellings on his legs, shins, neck, and stomach one after another. After pus came out of a swelling in his neck, it left a hole mark behind. Father Kolbe and Brother Kasjan walked for an hour from Hongouchi to Suwa-shrine. Father Kolbe used a walking stick. When they arrived at the streetcar stop, Father Kolbe suggested to Brother Kasjan, "Let's walk further and save the money for the publication of *The Knights*. In spite of the pain from the swellings, they both walked further into the town of Nagasaki in order to save the mere 3 sen of the street car fare for the propagation work.

Unfortunately, Doctor Fukahori, whom Father Kolbe regularly visited, was not at his clinic. His wife said, "Please wait a minute," and served them something cold to drink. Father Kolbe said, "Let's take a short walk while we wait," and he went out. While Brother Kasjan was keeping step with Father Kolbe, the following memory flashed through his mind: soon after he had arrived at Nagasaki, he was oppressed by a sense of failure. He became pessimistic and thought, "I can't study. I don't have time. Life is hard. I want to go back to Poland." When he confided it to Father Kolbe, his expression immediately turned grim, but he did not say anything — he just remained silent. Both went out of the room without saying a word — then, they walked.

When Brother Kasjan visited Father Kolbe the next time, they walked outside in silence as well. The third time, Father Kolbe stood in the room in silence. Perhaps he was praying. It was the heaviest cross for him to see a friar give up and go home. Brother Kasjan saw a sad countenance in Father Kolbe's eyes at the moment. Unable to bear it, Brother Kasjan ran out of the room. After that, he never mentioned going back to Poland again, no matter how hard his life became.

While listening to what Brother Kasjan told me, I asked myself what is this scent of a saint that surrounds Father Kolbe? Was it his singular devotion to the Immaculata, his sincere personality, or his fervent enthusiasm for propagating the Faith that never stopped trying to win souls? Or was it fraternity or intimacy that came from his profound understanding of human weakness?

"We brothers confided in Father Kolbe as if we were speaking to Father Saint Francis. We often exchanged letters with him in spite of the fact that we were in the same friary. Father Kolbe did not punish us. He used neither sticks nor whips. He imposed no reparation. He always consoled us with tender words. We brothers were all equal before him. He did not discriminate between working friars and priests. He loved all of us as children of Our Lady. He already said at that time that he would gladly offer his very life for the sins of one brother."

Does the scent of holy virtue mean his warm-hearted consideration for the brothers? A close analysis into this leads one not to think so.

I imagine Father Kolbe sipping plain soup. Where is the light of a saint in such a man? When I was thinking of Father Kolbe through the eyes of Brother Kasjan, I hit upon a short phrase: *The Immaculata did it within him!* Father Kolbe, sipping plain soup, lived a life which did not differ from that of ordinary people in appearance. But the one thing in contrast was that he was full of grace and responded to it with total devotion.

His mouth, eyes, behavior, thought — in short, his interior — was filled with the Immaculata, something no other person could see. When we perceive the breath of Our Lady, a soup's aroma may well transform into the scent of holy virtue. From the beginning Brother Kasjan loved and respected Father Kolbe from the bottom of his heart and surely experienced the scent of a saint in his body odor.

After dinner, the friars would visit the Blessed Sacrament and then relax in the evening. This was the time when they could unwind the most. Some friars enjoyed playing chess, speaking in Polish; others played games or musical instruments. Father Kolbe, Brother Grzegorz, and Brother Sergiusz played chess. But Brother Kasjan did not join the relaxing friars. His work did not end yet. He did the laundry alone until late into the night. Of course, this was done with the permission of Father Kolbe. Yet, even after having given the permission, Father Kolbe was worried that Brother Kasjan's chronic kidney disease would return.

After evening prayer, the friars went to sleep in grand silence. After they fell asleep, Brother Kasjan continued to do washing outside the house. Then Father Kolbe, who was supposed to be asleep, appeared in the darkness. He, who had weak lungs, could not possibly help Brother Kasjan with this chore. Instead, he sat beside the wash tub for a long time, just talking about the Immaculata quietly and comforting Brother Kasjan, until he had finished his task.

"Strangely enough, Father Kolbe did not speak of Poland."

Night falls silent in the hills of Nagasaki. The midtown lights flicker in the distance. Even without hearing tales of his distant homeland, Brother Kasjan knew deep in his bones that he was in a foreign country, far from his home.

NOTE: Brother Kasjan passed away on January 5, 1988, at the age of eighty-five.

CHAPTER 18

Winter in the Room of Flame-colored Wooden Walls

During the winter of Father Kolbe's third year in Japan, his room was unheated, as usual. Only the wooden walls, with reddish-brown lacquer, reminded one of a burning flame.

Christmas without Snow

Poland, located in eastern Europe, has severe winters. On November 1st, All Saints' Day in Warsaw, there is almost always snow. Warsaw is at the same latitude as the center of the Sea of Okhotsk which lies far to the north of Hokkaido. In contrast, winters are mild in Nagasaki, located in the southern part of Japan. It almost never snows here before Christmas.

Soon after the long-awaited, small three-story friary was completed in December, 1932, it was Christmas time. It was Father Kolbe's third Christmas in Japan.

That year, the friars planned a special celebration of Christmas, in part because the friary was just newly built. We have a letter that Father Kolbe wrote on that very Christmas Eve. "It is 4:45 p.m. The brothers are decorating a Christmas tree. Unbaptized children will gather to celebrate Christmas at 5 p.m. tomorrow. There is no snow here. Rain washes over the potatoes and Japanese radishes, and brings the mandarin oranges down from the trees." Brother

Romuald, who loved children, invited boys in the neighborhood and held the first Christmas party.

Aijiro Komori, one of the boys, said: "We, children of Hongouchi, picked persimmons and played softball in the autumn. In winter we played marbles, menko, and set a net to catch pale thrushes at Mt. Hiko. Foreign friars were rather exotic, and the ill-mannered boys rushed to them."

There exists a rare picture, taken in the dining room on the second floor of the friary where the decorated Christmas tree was placed. The wall was painted with reddish-brown lacquer and the ceiling beams were exposed. Thirty-one boys gathered there. Girls were not allowed to enter the friary. Two boys who helped Brother Romuald, Kanzo Miyahara and a boarding student named Fusasaburo Yamashita, are also in the picture. Mr. Miyahara is now the president of the Society of Saint Vincent de Paul which engages in relief services for the poor and the sick in Nagasaki City. Yamashita later became a Trappist. For whatever reason, Father Kolbe is not in the picture.

Making use of this old photograph as a clue, I visited the houses

The first Christmas party with thirty-one boys was held in the dining room of the friary.

in the neighborhood and discovered the identity of some of the other boys. One boy is still alive and works as a stone manufacturer. Another died as a sailor in the battle of Okinawa at the end of the Second World War. A sign maker looks like he was in the photo, so I could easily identify him. Although a part of Nagasaki City, Hongouchi was an area where no Catholics lived. Conversion was difficult. Nevertheless, Aijiro Komori, one of the boys, was led to the Catholic faith. It must have been God's Divine Providence.

Propagation of the Faith is a mysterious thing. Even though Father Kolbe had such a great enthusiasm for spreading God's word, few of the residents in the area around *Mugenzai no Sono* converted to Catholicism. He said to the friars: "The aim of the Immaculata, who led us to Japan, is to convert unbaptized people. But conversion itself occurs not by our effort but by the Immaculata. In order to manifest that to everyone, she chose humble instruments like us.

"Please tell the Japanese people about God at first, and then about Our Lady. The Japanese are innocent and good, but they don't know that the Immaculata is the Mediatrix of all Graces. The grace of conversion will not be given without the intercession of Our Lady."

Strangely enough, the neighbors did not convert in spite of his eagerness. The baptism of Aijiro Komori was like a single flower that bloomed in a desert.

About ten years after the picture had been taken, a girl from a Catholic family in Urakami came to *Mugenzai no Sono* to help out. Her name was Harue and she mended the clothes of the friars. "It is quite an ordeal to come here from Urakami every day." Father Donat, who was guardian then, looked for somewhere for her to board and found a place which happened to be Aijiro's home in Hongouchi. Aijiro and Harue became acquainted and eventually got married. Aijiro also was baptized at the time of their marriage. So the Christmas party ten years earlier finally bore fruit!

His parents and brothers are not Catholic. But his three sons and one daughter got married and all his line cherish their Catholic faith. "Father Kolbe and *Mugenzai no Sono* are my foster parents of faith." Sixty-three-year-old Aijiro attends daily Mass, as the friary is close to his house.

Write Down the Words and Actions of Father Kolbe

Father Kolbe's room was just in front of the dining room on the second floor. When the friars moved from the narrow attic to the newly built house, Brother Sergiusz was given the privilege of his own room because he served as the head of the friars. "Fortunately, my room was just next to Father Kolbe's room," Brother Sergiusz said with a smile.

"Father Kolbe had me make a small window in the wall between our rooms. It was 30 cm long and 40 cm wide, and he passed various messages to me through it. It could be opened only from his side. It brought Father Kolbe and me closer to each other. I consider myself very fortunate for having taken care of Father Kolbe. It occurred to me that I should write down his words and actions, as he would surely be a saint in the future. This is the notebook I wrote back then."

Brother Sergiusz showed me an old notebook. On its front cover was written in Polish: "Diary of Brother Sergiusz. No one may read this personal diary."

The diary consists of forty-seven pages, in which Father Kolbe's words and actions from January to April, 1933, are recorded. This is a valuable document that tells of his life in Nagasaki. I asked Brother Sergiusz to translate all of the diary into Japanese. The following is a summary:

> Father Kolbe said, "Please forget me, after I die."
>
> A photographer delivered pictures of Father Kolbe, which Brother Sergiusz received. As there were about ten or so, he

took out some of them without permission in order to keep as souvenirs. He distributed a few to other friars and handed about five pictures to Father Kolbe. "Is this all? There are too few! The photographer promised me more than this. Where are the others?"

Brother Sergiusz returned two of the pictures. "Is this really all? How many pictures do you still have?" "Four — I'll bring them at once!" Hot-blooded Brother Sergiusz shut the door with a bang and went out of the room. He got the pictures back from the friars and returned directly to Father Kolbe.

Father Kolbe then had a heart-to-heart talk with Brother Sergiusz: "Please forget everything about me after I die. I hope you will always remember the Immaculata. If you think about me, it's quite human, but like chasing a mirage. Please always think only about the Immaculata."

Brother Sergiusz did not reply and went back to his room with a sullen attitude. Then the small window opened. "How many pictures do you want?"

"I don't want any."

"I see." The window closed.

But it opened again after a while. "Brother Sergiusz," Father Kolbe called — and handed him one picture. Brother Sergiusz said, "Thank you," in a small voice, and accepted it.

Father Kolbe said, "Strive to become a possession of the Immaculata."

"We have just one month until the feast of Our Lady of Lourdes. We must prepare for the feast. How should we make ready for it?" Father Kolbe asked everyone in Japanese and answered by himself: "May we make progress in becoming possessions of the Immaculata. Beginning now, until the feast of February 11th; then, I hope we will continue to strive to become possessions of the Immaculata all year long. Why should we prepare like this? It is because the Immaculata prepared special blessings for *Mugenzai no Sono* (the friary of the Knights of the Immaculata). As *Mugenzai no Sono* belongs to the Immaculata, Our Lady gives us special blessings. In addition, this year's feast is the 75th anniversary of Our Lady's apparition at Lourdes."

Father Kolbe said, "I feel like blood is rushing to my head."

Brother Sergiusz, the head of the friars, went to Father Kolbe's room and said, "Brother Romuald is seeking permission to continue printing *The Knights* during Vespers." Then Father Kolbe confided to him: "I feel especially ill these days. I have a terrible headache and feel like blood is rushing to my head. During Mass I am in considerable pain. I feel I am becoming gradually weaker. Though I have meals as usual and sleep well at night, I am in poor physical condition. But please don't tell anyone about this. If people in Poland know about this, everyone will be worried. Please keep it to yourself."

Brother Sergiusz suddenly became sad and thought that Father Kolbe might die soon. Father Kolbe might have sensed what Brother Sergiusz was thinking and said to him soothingly, "As this is what the Immaculata is doing, I entrust everything to her and have nothing to worry about."

Father Kolbe said, "Please let me make a small sacrifice."

Shortly past ten o'clock at night, the small window opened and Brother Sergiusz heard Father Kolbe's voice: "Brother, you always loosen the straw of my bed and make it soft. Please do not do that from now on." "Why not? If I don't do that, it won't seem right, Father." "Brother, please let me make this small sacrifice. Even if you do not loosen the straw, it's not bad for the health. Please do not do that anymore," said Father Kolbe imploringly and he shut the small window.

I May Die Tonight

Father Kolbe said, "Never be apart from Our Lady."

One night, after all the friars were asleep, the small window opened, and Father Kolbe called Brother Sergiusz. When he went to Father's room, he was sitting on the bed in his habit, swaying and gasping, while repeatedly calling the name of Our Lady. When Brother Sergiusz came close to him, he seemed to be relieved and said, "Please sit here." He grasped Brother Sergiusz's hand and spoke in a small voice, "I don't know whether I can hold out tonight. I have a rush of blood to my head and my heart seems to be weakening little by little. My dear Brother, if I die tonight, please give these, my last words to the brothers. Never leave the Immaculata. If you forget Our Lady, *Mugenzai no Sono* will perish."

Brother Sergiusz was startled and was about to call the other friars, but Father Kolbe stopped him. "I will tell you how you should deal with the documents. There are letters from the Minister Provincial in the bottom drawer. Please take them to Father Matsukawa at Oura, and burn the copies of the replies that I wrote to him, as well as my personal diary and other writings."

Listening to this, Brother Sergiusz expressed a bit of dissatisfaction, saying "Do you think that I want to do this? I can never bring myself to burn everything, including your diary and writings!" "My dear brother, you can do that. Our Lady will make it possible for you to do as I told you now. There are spiritual letters from brothers in Niepokalanów in the drawer over there. You must not read them. Please burn them as soon as possible, too." The serious look in his eyes made Brother Sergiusz believe Father Kolbe would die that very night. Looking back on that day, he said, "Father Kolbe talked only about the Immaculata in his agony. 'Our enterprise will prosper, if we become perfect instruments of Our Lady and make an effort in that way. If I should be called to Heaven now, *Mugenzai no Sono* in Japan will develop successfully, following Our Lady. We don't have to worry.' I think this is what Father Kolbe wanted to say."

After a while Father Kolbe regained his composure and said, "Our Lady seems not to have called me yet," and encouraged Brother Sergiusz to get some sleep. "When I went back to my room, it was 1 a.m. On the other side of the small window, Father Kolbe finally seemed to be sleeping comfortably."

There was nothing like a fire to warm Father Kolbe's room. Only the wooden walls with their reddish-brown lacquer gave the impression of a burning flame.

Father Kolbe said, "Now is the time to make known the Immaculata and to love her."

"Today is the last of the eight days after the feast of Our Lady's Apparition at Lourdes. For a long time going all the way back to the Middle Ages, our Franciscan order worked to make the Immaculate Conception a dogma of the Church. We can regard the period from the age of Saint Francis to the middle of the 19th century when the dogma was finally proclaimed, as the first part of the history. The second part is the period since then and it's the time to spread devotion to the Immaculata.

"The workers of the first period were Saint Francis, Saint Bonaventure, the Franciscan theologian, Duns Scotus, and others. In order to prove that their claims were true, the Immaculata herself appeared in Lourdes and said, 'I am the Immaculate Conception.' The first part ends with this. But may we rest complacently now? No, we must take up the important tasks of the second part. We have to bring everyone to God by making the Immaculata known all over the world and by getting all mankind to love her. This is the aim of *Mugenzai no Sono*."

When I translated the summary of Father Kolbe's words in Sergiusz's old notebook, I felt like I had touched the very source of his thought. It was confidence in the Immaculata that ran throughout Father Kolbe's entire life. His thought did not well up all of a sudden. We can find its roots in the Order of Friars Minor Conventual.

I felt very deeply how strange this thing called a document is. It is all there in the simple notes that Brother Sergiusz took.

Appropriate to the late medieval age, Saint Francis of Assisi called himself "a Knight of Jesus Christ." Now, seven hundred years later, Father Kolbe has raised the banner of "the Knights of the Immaculata." Father Kolbe's heart is to be found in the course of the life of Saint Francis — this thought filled me with an indescribable sense of satisfaction.

CHAPTER 19

Discord Among the Friars

*Another priest came here with the zeal
for propagating the Faith. But it was unfortunate for him
to have encountered Father Kolbe.*

Father Konstanty

A small graduation ceremony was carried out at the Oura Seminary in Nagasaki in March, 1932, for nine diocesan seminarians who were promoted to theological studies. Father Kolbe wrote in his letter to Poland at that time: "Philosophy final examinations

Nine seminarians graduated from Oura Seminary (in the back row of the photo).

took place the other day. Of my philosophy students five will go to Tokyo, two to Rome, two to France and one departed to Heaven because of typhus. Finally, I am no longer tied to the seminary."

There was an epidemic of typhus the year before and seminarian Hirayama died of it. One of the seminarians who went to Rome was Father Banri Nakashima and one who went to Paris was Father Shiro Iwanaga.

These former seminarians appeared as witnesses in the film about Father Kolbe, "The Miracle of Love" that the Daughters of Saint Paul recently produced. After seeing his students off, Father Kolbe resigned his post as a professor of the seminary. Seminarians Mirochna and Aleksy, who had studied with the diocesan seminarians, came to study theology under the guidance of Father Kolbe. But it was not acceptable that only Father Kolbe would teach them. Therefore, twenty-seven-year-old Father Konstanty was sent to Nagasaki. This academic young priest studied in the Master's Course at a university in Warsaw and had a strong build. He arrived at Nagasaki with three other friars including Brother Kasjan who was going to work as a cook.

Father Kolbe taught Dogmatic Theology and Ethics, whereas Father Konstanty taught Biblical Theology and Ecclesiastical History. Father Kolbe was fond of saying, "The priests who work at *Mugenzai no Sono* should receive a special formation appropriate for the purpose of the Knights of the Immaculata through the minor and major seminary." For that reason, he wanted at all costs to have a comprehensive theology program, but the number of teachers was insufficient and they did not have their own buildings or facilities. In fact, what they had was more akin to a home school. However, the classes continued. This theology course at *Mugenzai no Sono* was authorized by Bishop Hayasaka and two major seminarians from the diocese also came to receive instruction.

Father Konstanty was a young priest with a zeal for the propagation of the Faith. Father Kolbe, ten years older than he, had high hopes for him. But his hopes were soon dashed and a rift between them developed. Father Kolbe was blessed with a lot of working brothers but not with priests. Father Metody, one of the first priests to come to Japan, returned to Poland after only six months. Now Father Konstanty also began to show signs of persistent hostility toward Father Kolbe.

Father Kolbe wrote frankly: "Since Father Konstanty entered our Order from the Diocesan Seminary, and he was ordained a priest only recently, I was not surprised at his thoughts. I talked with him repeatedly but in vain. Now he is my biggest cross."

Diverse men, diverse minds. If one tries to promote a project, opponents will surely arise. I suppose Father Konstanty was an ordinary priest without malice. I cannot help thinking that it was unfortunate for him to have met Father Kolbe. This young academic priest may have felt 'abnormality' around Father Kolbe and may have become antagonistic instinctively. The reason why he opposed Father Kolbe seems to have been threefold:

- The first point was that Father Kolbe's emphasis on Marian devotion seemed too excessive to Father Konstanty, who was a commonsensical teacher. Father Kolbe referred to Our Lady in everything. He lived with Our Lady day in and day out. This seemed abnormal to Father Konstanty.

  Father Kolbe had published an article in *The Knights* in Poland (*Rycerz*). It was entitled "For the Birthday of *Mamusia* in Heaven." *Mamusia*, which means mother, is a childish expression like "mommy." In opposition, Father Konstanty wrote an article entitled: "Is it Right to Refer to Our Lady Like This?" I don't know whether he thought Our Lady was in competition with her Son, but he had this article published in a magazine of the Society of the Sacred Heart of Jesus in Poland. It may seem a trifling matter, but it was a serious issue for the two priests involved.

- The second point was Father Kolbe's life of holy poverty. As he lived in extreme poverty, Father Konstanty worried he might even found a new religious order. In terms of discipline, labor, and poverty, the situation of *Mugenzai no Sono* was far different from that of the other Conventual Franciscan friars. Therefore, the leadership of Father Kolbe seemed even like an aberration to Father Konstanty. So he sent a report to the Minister General of the Order in Rome and complained that a dangerous person was trying to leave the Order and found a new one! The Minister General is said to have believed the report.

- The third point was the method of propagation only through *The Knights*. Father Kolbe regarded mass communication as the best way of propagation and concentrated all his energy on publishing the magazine. He cut the living costs and applied them to the publication of *The Knights*. But publication required too much funding for the facilities, materials, and other operating expenses. Besides, the results of the propagation were not available in hard numbers in spite of their sacrifices in publishing *The Knights*. Father Konstanty wondered whether the magazine had any effect in converting the Japanese people and he wanted the spreading of the Faith to center on preaching the Gospel.

He Bit the Head of the Marian Statue

There is no more painful thing than living in the same house with one's adversary. Even in convents past and present there are surely small conflicts deriving from the incompatibility of temperaments or a difference of opinions. But how did Father Kolbe behave toward his opponent?

Father Kolbe wrote: "Father Konstanty is unable to grasp the ideal of Niepokalanów. According to him the mission of our Order was fulfilled with the proclamation of the dogma of the Immaculata, and now we only need to celebrate the feast. He worries about the tight bond between *Mugenzai no Sono* and Niepokalanów. Nor can he understand that the Mother of God is the Mediatrix of All Graces."

On the contrary, Father Konstanty said, "Father Kolbe, you claim Our Lady is the Mediatrix of All Graces, but no one knows how this dogma may change in the future."

Father Kolbe asked, "Why do you think so?"

"That's what is written in the theological books and famous theologians also say that."

"In which books is it written? Please bring them."

Father Konstanty came back holding many theological books and said, "Please look at this part."

"Okay, but now please read what is said next."

The answer was there! Father Konstanty was driven into a corner. Unable to contain himself any longer, Father Kolbe said, "Please correct your statement officially in the presence of the other friars. Otherwise, they will waver in their faith."

"But he did not want to correct his statement," said Father Mirochna, who was a seminarian at the time.

Although Father Kolbe emphasized devotion to Mary as the Mediatrix of All Graces, that feast day disappeared from the liturgical calendar after the Second Vatican Council.

It does not mean that Our Lady ceased to be the Mediatrix of All Graces. In *Lumen Gentium, the Dogmatic Constitution on the Church of the Second Vatican Council*, it is written: "the Blessed Virgin is invoked by the Church under the titles of Advocate, Auxiliatrix, Adjutrix, and Mediatrix. This, however, is to be so understood that it neither takes away from, nor adds anything to, the dignity and efficaciousness of Christ the one Mediator." We can see that Father Kolbe's insistence was never wrong.

The objection of Father Konstanty continued. In the summer of the same year Father Kolbe wrote: "I was indirectly informed that

Father Konstanty wrote to you, Most Reverend Father Provincial, saying that my health is quite poor. But you don't have to worry. I feel even better than before I left for India. I rather worry about him. He has no appetite and cannot sleep. He also complains that the nerves in his back and his head ache. A doctor says he is suffering from a nervous breakdown. The injections the doctor gives him seem ineffective.

"Father Konstanty is a big cross for me. Until now I have never been faced with a cross like this. Whatever makes the friars happy and gives them pleasure, either saddens him, bores him, or gets him agitated. What I am most worried about is that his influence is becoming evident among the friars. He speaks in such a way that their devotion to Our Lady will be lessened."

One day, seminarian Mirochna was studying in his room. There was a table near the window, on which a small statue of the Immaculata was placed. He sometimes took a rest, gazed at it and offered ejaculatory prayers. Father Konstanty happened to pass by at that moment. He talked to Mirochna through the window and said with persistence, "It's not good to put too much emphasis on Marian devotion like Father Kolbe does." The seminarian would not give ear to him. Then, the priest got angry, grabbed the statue of Our Lady and bit its head!

"What are you doing, Father?" cried Mirochna in astonishment! "It's a sacrilege...." What a terrible thing! He bit not the heel of Our Lady as the devil did, but of all things, the head of Our Lady! "Father, please stop it!"

Mirochna took the statue away from him. Then he informed Father Kolbe of this incident. His response was serene: "Father Konstanty is a good man. He is devout and earnest. He opens his mind honestly. He behaved in such a way just because he has been suffering from a nervous breakdown and from insufficient spiritual preparation."

There exists a defense written by Father Kolbe in response to the report Father Konstanty sent to Rome.

1. It is claimed that some Japanese people threw away *The Knights* we distributed on the street without reading it. As for this, it is customary in Japan for people to throw away magazines after reading them. I myself found the portrait of Japan's Emperor and Empress, who are revered almost as gods here, among the garbage.
2. Then there is the matter of the returned eight hundred copies, from the six thousand copies that we sent to Osaka for publicity. He may claim we wasted the postage fees on those books. But since the rate of returned books is only fourteen percent, we consider that successful enough.
3. A priest of a monastic order who has been in Japan for thirty years said that the content of *The Knights* was not suitable for the Japanese people. For that matter, we should believe the Japanese who have converted. In truth, that priest does not read *The Knights*.
4. Father Konstanty claims that *Mugenzai no Sono* should be no different from the other friaries of our Order, which do not have a special purpose. But I can never change the purpose of Niepokalanów. I am prepared to appeal to the Holy See. Changing the purpose would violate the intention of our benefactors and would be a major problem for the future of our Order.

Twelve Disciples Remained

A loud voice was just heard from Father Kolbe's room on the second floor. It was the voice of Father Konstanty. Brother Kasjan came close to the door anxiously. Previously, Father Kolbe and Father Konstanty had argued in the dining room. The issue was always the same. Each time, Father Kolbe would pray so that he could calm down. The Provincial had also warned him not to argue in front of the friars. Suddenly, Father Konstanty burst out of the room, saying, "I'll leave!" Father Kolbe noticed Brother Kasjan and asked, "Did you want something?" "No, not really. I was just worried about you..." "Thank you," Father Kolbe said in a small voice. "He's a very good man but he doesn't understand what I'm trying to tell him." Father Kolbe looked very sad.

Father Kolbe was different from other ordinary people in that he did not shut out his opponents, no matter how greatly they disturbed him. It is quite normal to exclude those who stand in one's way, but Father Kolbe did not ask the Provincial to return Father Konstanty to Poland. He just endured the situation. Meanwhile, it was decided that Father Kolbe would go back to Poland in April, 1933, in order to participate in the Provincial Chapter. Of course, Father Konstanty would be his deputy while he was away.

"What will happen in my absence?" Father Kolbe felt depressed. We can see his great anxiety from the following entry that Brother Sergiusz made in his diary.

"In the evening, I took a walk with Father Kolbe near the ground on which a new chapel will be built. Then Father Kolbe told me what we should do during his absence: 'Father Konstanty may change the state of *Mugenzai no Sono*. If such a thing does happen, you shall talk together with other friars and choose the best way to deal with it. Today he told me very clearly that he hated the Knights of the Immaculata.'

"I was surprised and asked how he had replied to Father Konstanty. 'I said nothing but just smiled at him,' Father Kolbe said with a solitary look."

Finally, the morning of his departure came. Father Kolbe looked around the dining room and said, "When I go to the Provincial Chapter, twelve friars will remain here. You are just like the Twelve Apostles. Who is John?" Someone said, "Brother Henryk is John." He was a tailor. "Who is Peter?" "Brother Sergiusz!" came the swift response from seminarian Mirochna. Everyone agreed that Brother

Sergiusz's character was similar to that of Peter.

Father Kolbe left from Dejima wharf in Nagasaki, on a ferry boat from Japan to China. He wrote a letter to the friars who came to see him off: "While watching you become smaller and smaller in my sight, all that the Immaculata has accomplished during these three years occurred to me. When I left from this port three years ago, two brothers came to see me off, but this time I can tell the Provincial Chapter that there are twelve apostles. And the Immaculata herself has attracted a lot of people."

To which of Our Lord's apostles did Father Konstanty correspond? After Father Kolbe had left, Father Konstanty felt liberated and promptly started a reform according to his own plan. However, there were also good things that happened.

Brother Sergiusz said, "I meditated for eight days before the ceremony of solemn vows. This was the first 'meditation without labor' since I entered the Knights of the Immaculata. Only then could I take time every day to write in my spiritual diary. It is because Father Konstanty was the superior then.

"When Father Kolbe was in Poland, I made my solemn vows with Brother Kasjan on July 2nd. Father Konstanty was always opposed to Father Kolbe's way. Father Kolbe made us work even during our retreats, because we had a lot of work to complete. On the other hand, Father Konstanty told us not to work during the retreat. He was very strict but I was pleased with that. I could meditate peacefully for the first time. Such a busy man like Brother Kasjan did not have to work!

"Father Konstanty? He was not a bad person at all. At that time, every priest in the Polish Province was against Father Kolbe. Father Konstanty was no different from the others."

CHAPTER 20

The Cobble-Stone Streets of Rome

While I was writing this manuscript, I had the chance to visit Rome. There I visited the places associated with Father Kolbe.

On the Way Home

Entrusting *Mugenzai no Sono* to the Immaculata, Guardian Father Kolbe left Nagasaki on a steamboat for Poland. The purpose of this trip was to participate in the Provincial Chapter in May, 1933. On his way home, he stopped in Rome. At first he set out for the Headquarters of the Order of Friars Minor Conventual near Piazza Venezia. He met Minister General Father Orlini there and made a status report on *Mugenzai no Sono*. He felt this was necessary because Father Konstanty had often sent his opposing views from Nagasaki to the Minister General. But according to a note by Father Kolbe, the situation seemed to have changed for the better: "Reverend Father Minister General agreed to all and told me to write down everything I want in a letter."

Father Kolbe must have been relieved. He esteemed holy obedience above all, so he could probably unburden his heart before the Superior. It was the Jubilee Year. With a light heart, he went through the Holy Door of Saint Peter's Basilica in the Jubilee Year and obtained the plenary indulgence he had always hoped for.

The Jubilee Year is usually celebrated every twenty-five years. As it had been celebrated in 1925, the next Jubilee Year should have been 1950. But 1933 was declared a Jubilee Year because it was the 1900th anniversary of the death of Jesus Christ, since he had been crucified at the age of thirty-three. It had never happened since the first Pope Saint Peter, that a Jubilee Year was declared twice by the same pope, so this became the main topic of conversation on the streets of Rome.

I can easily imagine Father Kolbe walking quickly with light steps in Saint Peter's Square, the tail of his habit fluttering in the wind. My imagination was aided by the fact that I myself had the chance to go to Rome and stand in Saint Peter's Square when I was writing this manuscript. I arrived in Rome in November, 1981, after I had made a pilgrimage to holy sites in Israel for eight days. This pilgrim group of the Nagasaki Diocese in which I participated was guided by the Auxiliary Bishop of Nagasaki, Hisajiro Matsunaga.

The Holy Door was on the observer's left at the entrance to the grand Saint Peter's Basilica. After Father Kolbe arrived in Rome, the beatification ceremony of Gemma Galgani took place there. The new Blessed was an Italian woman who had died thirty years earlier at the age of twenty-five. She often received the grace of mystical visions and ecstasies, and later was given the stigmata. Father Kolbe sent a sacred image of the new Blessed to *Mugenzai no Sono*.

After I visited Saint Peter's Basilica, I headed for the Headquarters of the Order of Friars Minor Conventual where Father Kolbe had most likely stayed. According to the record, the Minister General advised him to remain until the feast of the Ascension to have an audience with the Pope and participate in the ceremony at Saint John Lateran Basilica. Therefore, Father Kolbe decided to interact with the Japanese seminarians at the Pontifical Urban University, take part in the Ascension Thursday Mass, and then depart for Poland.

Seven Years of Study in Rome

Father Kolbe had a deep connection to Rome. I had long hoped to visit sites associated with him if I ever got the chance to visit Rome. He went to Rome for the first time when he began his studies. In the autumn of 1910, the young Father Maximilian arrived from Poland when he was only eighteen. What did he think of the Eternal City? At that time he wrote the following passage in a letter to his mother: "There is great danger in Rome. I heard that women tempt even monks here. I'm worried." Even today it is sometimes said that Japanese tourists walking alone there find it a dangerous city!

The fall season in Rome appeared cold and lonely to me, as the dead leaves of the trees fell on the roofs of cars parked along the side of the street.

Father Nishiyama, Brother Ozaki, and Brother Roman from right to left.

Father Kolbe was ordained a priest after having studied seven years in Rome. Fortunately, my dream came true and I was able to visit the sites associated with Father Kolbe under the guidance of Father Tatsuya Nishiyama, who had lived at the Headquarters of our Order for a long time. Of course, we started from the Headquarters where the Minister General resides even now. The Basilica of the Twelve

Apostles there has a fairly long history: the tombs of the Apostles Saint Philip and Saint James are located in the Basilica. The courtyard, the corridors, and the dining room on the second floor still exist as they were during Father Kolbe's day. The dining room is simple in the Franciscan manner. In front of the Headquarters is the Piazza Santi Apostoli. Father Nishiyama explained, "This is a famous piazza in Rome. The seat of the Province of Rome is also here. The Palazzo Chigi-Odescalchi of Bernini stands just in front of the piazza. Even now proclamations to the citizens of Rome are carried out in this piazza."

But this famous piazza has been converted into a parking lot and people get shoved into the corner. "I hear Father Kolbe studied philosophy at the Pontifical Gregorian University for three years, and theology at the International Seraphic College of our Order for four years. Where is the Gregorian University?" I asked. "It is just behind the piazza." Turning the corner in the back of the piazza, just as he said, there was a narrow alley and a semicircular gate. We found the University in front, going through the gate. "Is this a university? It seems like a government office. Where is its athletic field?" "Athletic field?" Father Nishiyama burst into laughter upon hearing my question and said, "There is no such thing in Roman schools," which made me feel slightly disappointed. The Gregorian University has a long history, having been established in the 16th century. Walking along the University building, we reached the Trevi Fountain which was crowded with tourists.

"Where did Father Kolbe live when he was a student?" "Perhaps he lived at the International Seraphic College at San Teodoro." Father Nishiyama took me there.

We got off the bus and walked on the cobble-stone streets for a while. The main ruins of ancient Rome are found all around here. We can see the circular Colosseum and the Palatine Hill. And also a small church, the Basilica San Teodoro, in the middle of the Roman Forum, where stone pillars are scattered about. The International Seraphic College was along a narrow street, the Via San Teodoro, in front of the Basilica. "Is this the College?" I thought it should be much larger, as it was called "International."

The College was a low, two-story, long, narrow building and its outer wall was made of red clay. It looked like an economy hotel in the countryside. Its lattice-windows struck me as very much a Western-style building. As might be expected, Father Nishiyama said, "It's a hotel now." "Ah, just as I thought," I nodded. There was a memorial room to Father Kolbe on the second floor. The room contained an altar of about twenty-five square meters. The habit Father Kolbe had worn and cuts of his hair were displayed on the wall.

"He was here for seven years." This poor room was nonetheless an important place where Father Kolbe's spirit grew deeply in the Immaculata. It was also in this room where he founded the Knights of the Immaculata. I closed my eyes and prayed. There was neither a sound nor a trace of another person. The room seemed too lonely to be associated with a saint.

We left the building and walked down the cobble-stone streets of Rome looking for a bus. The Tiber River was nearby.

"As the bus follows a roundabout route, it takes much time. But it takes only about fifteen minutes to get to the Gregorian University on foot. Father Kolbe probably walked there." I suddenly imagined young Father Kolbe in his habit walking along the cobble-stone streets, eyes downcast, passing by the ruins of ancient Rome.

The International Seraphic College was moved to another district and to a much nicer building. In the old student list, he was recorded as the 277th student: "Maximilian Kolbe, from Province Galicia. Admitted to the College on October 29, 1910. Ordained as a priest on April 23, 1918. Granted the degree of Doctor of Philosophy at the Gregorian University. On July 22, 1919, he was granted the degree of Doctor of Theology at our College and was graduated. He was an excellent and holy young man."

A Letter to Nagasaki

Staying in Rome on the way to the Provincial Chapter, Father Kolbe wrote a short letter to *Mugenzai no Sono*. It is very interesting because it summarizes how he felt, being away from Nagasaki, and what he was usually thinking about.

Dear Children!

How are you? You are probably waiting for my letter from Niepokalanów which will tell you the results of the Provincial Chapter, but I'm still on the way. [It was foreseen that the Minister Provincial, and possibly the Guardian of *Mugenzai no Sono*, might be changed at this Chapter.] New machines and new workers have been added. I imagine that you are doing well without me and that you are all healthy in body and soul with the help of the Immaculata. Silence, frequent ejaculatory prayers, and ever more fervent love for the Immaculata. [He underscored the word silence with two lines! He always underlined important parts.] The action of this love is manifested in the fulfillment of her will, that is, holy obedience. Please make mutual concessions in things you don't like, in order to attain peace, and also for the health of your body.

Let us pray that she will give us blessings and we can be her good instruments, and that she may act in and through us at her discretion. If we are against her will, I hope she will use her force without consideration for the freedom of our will and lead us according to her will by all means.

I have never seen such a fervent love for the Immaculata. One can feel the pulse of Father Kolbe's heart in this short statement. There is no worldly anxiety in this letter he wrote from Rome, such as whether the enterprise is going well in his absence, or whether there are troubles. He entrusts everything to the Immaculata and hopes that each of us will be her perfect instrument spiritually and that she will freely act in and through us every day. I believe this to be his only life-long wish. At the end of this letter, he added in Romanized Japanese: "Sincere greetings to Brother Marian (Sato) and Brother Amaki. How are you?" His tenderness overflows on these pages.

Facing the Trevi Fountain, a resting place for tourists, if we go up the alley on the right side, we get to the Basilica of Sant'Andrea delle Fratte. This is a famous church where Ratisbonne, a famous Jewish lawyer, was converted to Catholicism by the grace of the Miraculous Medal. And this is also the church where Father Kolbe celebrated his first Mass. On his third visit to Rome, following the completion of his studies there, Father Kolbe presumably visited this unforgettable church and renewed his devotion to the Immaculata and to the grace of her Miraculous Medal.

Incidentally, he was ordained a priest in another church of Sant'Andrea, the Basilica Sant'Andrea della Valle on the Vittorio Emanuele II Street. On the altar of this church is hung a big sacred painting of Saint Andrew being martyred, bound to the X-shaped cross.

Fifty or sixty meters away from the church where Father Kolbe celebrated his first Mass is the former building of Sacred Congregation for the Propagation of the Faith (*Propaganda Fide*). Father Nishiyama emphasized the existence of this old building and said, "I suppose Father Kolbe must have visited this building many times on his way to Japan for missionary work."

In front of the building there is a small square, and a statue of the Immaculate Conception stands on a high column. Piazza di Spagna (the Spanish Steps) is located close nearby. There are many luxury souvenir shops where one can speak Japanese around here. We noticed a young Japanese couple standing idly by there, with a map.

Father Kolbe was granted an audience with Pope Pius XI; in more recent times, our forty-two pilgrims from the Nagasaki Diocese had an audience with Pope John Paul II, thanks to Father Nishiyama who arranged the audience.

When the Pope's visit to Japan was determined in February, 1981, Father Nishiyama was appointed as his Japanese tutor. He was suddenly summoned by the Pope. When he timidly went to the Apostolic Palace, he was guided not to the audience hall but to the Pope's dining room, a sanctuary, a place where the general public is not allowed.

Of course, Father Nishiyama went there in his Conventual Franciscan black habit. Getting a glimpse of this habit, Pope John Paul II said, "It is the same habit Father Kolbe wore," and he seemed to have friendly feelings to Father Nishiyama from the beginning. Thinking now was the time, Father Nishiyama emphasized, "I am from the friary of Nagasaki that Father Kolbe built. I graduated from the minor seminary Father Kolbe founded and finished my novitiate there." Hearing this, the Pope was pleased all the more and said, "Today is December 3rd, the feast day of Francis Xavier. I start learning Japanese today."

Francis Xavier is the pioneer of the Faith who proclaimed the Word of God in Asia. It was an appropriate day to start learning an Asian language. As the Pope was very busy, he did not have much time to learn a new language, so he had special training every day in Japanese while having his meals. "Thanks to his busy schedule, I could enjoy eating meals with the Pope every day," Father Nishiyama said with satisfaction. Although the Pope received only two and a half months of training, his Japanese was excellent and he seemed to win over the hearts of many people in Japan. The Pope may still have been enjoying a kind of afterglow from his visit to Japan when we had the audience with him. As soon as he saw our pilgrim group, he said aloud, "kami ni kansha" ("Thanks be to God!" in Japanese)!

When I met the Pope, I think I said, "I came from the friary of Blessed Kolbe in Nagasaki." Presumably, hearing the name of

Brother Ozaki was granted a special audience with Pope John Paul II. (1981)

Blessed Kolbe, he suddenly called out, "Father Nishiyama, Father Nishiyama!" in Italian. When Father Nishiyama approached from the corner, the Pope said to me, "You have to become like Blessed Kolbe."

I felt a lump in my throat when I heard this! I owe it totally to Father Kolbe that I was granted a special audience with the Pope. His hands were soft and communicated to me the warmth of Christ.

When Father Kolbe visited Rome in 1933, he probably experienced the glowing warmth of the Vicar of Christ during his audience.

Father Kolbe stayed in Rome for three weeks. After having participated in the liturgy in the Lateran Basilica as he had planned, he left for Poland and arrived at the good old friary of Niepokalanów on June 13th.

NOTE: The Sacred Congregation for the Propagation of the Faith has been renamed the Congregation for the Evangelization of Peoples.
Father Kolbe was born at Zdunska Wola in Poland on January 8, 1894. He entered the Minor Seminary of the Conventual Franciscans when he was thirteen. Five years later, he went to study in Rome.

CHAPTER 21

The Sound of Army Boots in the Distance

In 1933, the year of the birth of Prince Akihito [the current Emperor Emeritus of Japan], Brother Maciej came to Nagasaki.

The Conversion of a Spy

In 1933, the sound of army boots seemed to resound everywhere and the times were about to change drastically. In those days, Japan's military was vigilant against Westerners, especially regarding as its greatest enemy the Soviet Union which had overthrown Czarist Russia, calling it "Red" and hating it. Poland bordered this Socialist country and had long and strong ties to Russia.

The changing tide of the times eventually reached the friars of *Mugenzai no Sono*.

Mr. Shigeo Yoshino was a detective of the Nagasaki Police Department.

As the friars of *Mugenzai no Sono* were from a neighboring country of the Soviet Union, Mr. Yoshino, working undercover, joined the friary as an assistant in the printing room and lived with the friars in order to carry out secret surveillance on the Polish friars.

"He was engaged in the work of *The Knights* with us, wrote addresses and also picked out types," said Brother Romuald. Much to Mr. Yoshino's surprise, the friars' life was completely transparent! Their life was just oriented to seeking God and there was nothing

A police detective came to spy on the friars and then converted.

to hide. As they lived in holy poverty, their entire life was completely visible. There was no secret room or safe to store money. "Maria" was their open password as the friars replied with "Maria" when they were addressed with "Maria." They had no ambition except to spread devotion to the Immaculata. Mr. Yoshino gave up and joined in.

"Having been touched by Father Kolbe's love and personality, Mr. Yoshino reformed, opened his mind to Father Kolbe and studied the Catechism. Finally, he was baptized," said Brother Romuald. Then he showed me a dark photo, saying, "This is the picture taken in commemoration of his baptism." It was taken in the dining room on the second floor and Mr. Yoshino is sitting straight up in the center, surrounded by the friars. He certainly looked like a police detective. Next to him sat Father Konstanty. Father Kolbe was not in this picture because he had gone back to Poland.

"It was Father Aijiro Yamaguchi (later Archbishop) of Nakamachi Church who baptized him with the Christian name of John the Baptist," said Brother Romuald.

This entire account sounded too good to be true! Did it really happen? Did a police detective really live in the friary as a spy, then convert and get baptized? It seemed to me like a piece of fiction!

There was the following entry in Father Kolbe's diary in March, 1933: "An unbaptized young man named Yoshino received a copy of *The Knights* in a streetcar, and later came to us. He started to work for us *gratis* and seemed to be at peace here. He has understood the Faith and will be baptized in the near future, although his family is against it."

Was the person who went so far as to inform Father Kolbe of his family's objection really a police spy? I waited for a chance to validate the story I had heard. In 1980, the chance presented itself on the 50th anniversary of the arrival of the Knights of the Immaculata in Nagasaki. The staff of a video project from Tokyo became interested in the photo of Mr. Yoshino's baptism and requested an interview with the friars.

Father Mirochna, Brother Romuald, Brother Sergiusz, and Brother Grzegorz were those who knew the details of the event best. When they gathered, I asked them once again to confirm the story.

"Did a detective really come to spy on you and then convert?"

"I remember him well. Mr. Yoshino was a spy," said Brother Romuald at first. "He took his meals with us, worked together with us, and said he would like to be a friar. At first, we didn't know he was a spy. But later he confided it to us. He told us he had been sent by the police — that he had wronged us and that he was very sorry for it."

"How long had he been here?"

"About three months. We should not confuse Mr. Yoshino with Mr. Yoshida, who worked here for a long time. Mr. Yoshino just stayed here for a short time. He repented from the bottom of his heart and said that he knew well what he had done. I don't know what became of him."

Mr. Yoshida is the man I mentioned in the case of a theft.

"Another detective from the Nagasaki Police came here later on in order to thank us for having looked after Mr. Yoshino," added Brother Sergiusz. But it was still not clear whether Mr. Yoshino was a professional detective, or someone the police had suggested to spy on the friars and report back to them when he went out at times. Brother Sergiusz said, "I think he was a detective."

Father Mirochna followed, "In those days the police had doubts about foreigners. They thought we might be financially supported by the Russian Government. They asked frequently when and from where our funds had come when Father Kolbe was the Guardian of the friary. Their manner of investigation was so bad that I got angry once: 'You are too much. We haven't come here for business or politics.' Later on, after the war had started, their behavior became much worse."

Brother Grzegorz said, "Antonio Yoshida was also secretly connected with the police. Another military policeman came and asked us to accept himself in the friary. You talked with him, Father Mirochna?" Then Brother Grzegorz looked into his eyes. "Although you say so, I cannot remember the man," Father Mirochna replied, knitting his brow.

In the end, the friars probably did not blame or interrogate Mr. Yoshino, who confided a serious secret that he was a police spy. They did not hate him just because he was a police informer. They embraced Mr. Yoshino as a neighbor and let the incident pass. It seems that is why they did not remember him so well. His later life remains unknown.

You Are a Spy

While I was reading Father Kolbe's letters from that time, I came across the following passage and I thought it was a serious matter. The letter was written to the Polish Embassy in Tokyo.

We need a certificate of permission to take photographs

here. The reason is that Nagasaki is a restricted military zone. The regulation is especially severe for foreigners and we have to show identification cards. Recently there was trouble about this matter. One friar took a photo for *The Knights* in Poland without knowing the regulation. As he didn't have a certificate of permission, he was suspected of being a spy and he had to appear in court. It was confirmed that he didn't have any intention of spying, but he had to pay 30 yen, because he had no certificate of permission. The newspapers and magazines reported, out of curiosity, that we are either engaged in a money-making business or we are spies. Therefore, I hope you will kindly issue identification cards to us.

This was a serious case for *Mugenzai no Sono*. It was Brother Seweryn who took the photo. He was among the first friars who came to Asia, and he had a camera.

In Nagasaki were the world-famous Mitsubishi Shipyard and the Mitsubishi Arms Factory. The Anti-Aircraft Artillery was deployed at the top of Mt. Inasa. But for the friars, the customs and the scenery of Japan were very interesting. It was quite natural that they took pictures and wished to send them to their homeland. Actually, Father Kolbe had left many photographs behind.

It is not clear which pictures became an issue. Brother Sergiusz remembers the events this way: "After having taken pictures, Brother Seweryn went to the headquarters of the restricted military zone to get permission. He was unable to obtain permission, as he had taken pictures of the prohibited zone. They said that he was a spy and told him to submit the negatives of the pictures. He was severely reproved, under suspicion of intent to sell the pictures to a foreign country.

"After that, a plainclothes policeman came to *Mugenzai no Sono* to conduct an interrogation. Father Kolbe was back in Poland but Father Konstanty was there. He became angry with the policeman's arrogant attitude."

Father Konstanty was a young, strongly built, big man with a beard. His surly attitude provoked the policeman. "Where is the priest with the spectacles?" "He is in Poland for a meeting." "He was gentle but this one is impudent," the policeman spit out and furiously remarked, "We will expel the one who took the pictures as a spy!"

The event was promptly reported to Father Kolbe who sent a telegram to the friary at once. "As soon as I return, I will take responsibility and settle the matter." Fortunately, the bishop intervened and the police became convinced by the testimony of one Japanese priest that Brother Seweryn was not a spy. The matter was settled but the fine of 30 yen was a severe loss to the friary.

There is only one photograph of *Mugenzai no Sono* from which the mountain behind (Mt. Hiko) was cut off with scissors. On the reverse side, we see a red faded seal stamped: "Censored by the Headquarters of the Restricted Military Zone Nagasaki." This was probably the first picture taken following this photography incident.

Brother Maciej Comes to Japan

Whenever I mention a friar distributing copies of *The Knights* at the Oura Cathedral or at the Peace Park, many recall "the big foreigner."

His name was Maciej Janiec.

Brother Maciej came to Japan in May, 1933, when Father Kolbe was back in Poland for the Provincial Chapter.

Brother Maciej was born in 1902, the second of nine sons in a farming village in southern Poland which was some two hours by carriage from the old capital of Kraków. He grew up helping with the farm work, raising cattle and horses. At one point he joined the army, but then came to learn of Niepokalanów by reading *The Knights*. He entered the friary when he was already twenty-eight. The day of his entry was the Feast of the Apparition of Our Lady

Brother Maciej distributed The Knights *at Oura Cathedral.*

of Lourdes, France. He still remembers that Father Kolbe made a speech about it. Two weeks later, Father Kolbe and his group left for Asia.

Brother Maciej assisted with the cooking and printing at the friary in Poland. One day the Guardian suddenly asked him, "How would you like to go to Japan?" He answered promptly, "I would." He crossed the Indian Ocean by steamship with three other fellow friars and landed in Nagasaki. It was a long voyage that lasted thirty-eight days.

Brother Maciej wore a full chestnut-brown beard and, at thirty-one years, was the oldest of the four. Brother Norbert was twenty-seven. He worked in sewing and cooking for only one year and then returned home. Brother Iwo was twenty-six. He was in charge of laundry; however, he became ill and after five years went back to Poland. He still lives in the friary in Warsaw today (in 1982). Brother Jordan was twenty-six. He was responsible for office work for five years before returning home.

Only Brother Maciej hung in there. He seemed slow and sluggish with his big body, but he chugged right along like a locomotive. He had neither an academic career nor any special skill but religious life just came naturally to him. He lived with Father Kolbe for only three years.

"I didn't live long with Father Kolbe; I didn't talk with him nor did I quarrel with him. I don't remember him very well. Whether sitting or speaking, his body and legs were often shaking. I went to confession to Father Kolbe in his room. I didn't visit his room to speak with him on any other occasion, nor did I get any letters from him."

Right after his arrival in Nagasaki, Brother Maciej worked in the kitchen, the laundry, and the bakery. Later he kept two cows and milked them to provide nourishment to the friars. Just before the end of the Second World War, he was forcibly detained at Mt. Aso in Kumamoto Prefecture by the Special Higher Police, but he was released without incident.

After the war he kept cows quietly and baked special, large bread. From about 1955 he went to Oura Cathedral for propagation and distributed *The Knights*. As milk and bread became more available, he stopped keeping cows and baking bread. Since about 1965, he has devoted himself exclusively to distributing *The Knights* at Oura Cathedral.

He gets up at five-thirty every day. After finishing the Liturgy of the Hours, he goes to distribute *The Knights* by streetcar and stands on the street corner until evening. He goes out in his black habit even on rainy days or extremely hot days and talks to people, without hesitation, in his limited Japanese. He is a person whose ruddy face overflows with tenderness.

"Father Kolbe started *The Knights*. Brother Zeno handed it out. Now I'll give it to you. Do you want to read it? You'll have the blessings of Our Lady." He does not talk much but he gets right to the point. Having been talked to by this simple friar and given a copy of *The Knights*, many were led to the Church. Brother Maciej is the friar who dispenses the blessings of Our Lady.

The big, foreign friar standing on the stone-paved street by the Oura Cathedral, which is full of Christian history, has become a famous sight in Nagasaki and he was often covered in TV programs and magazines.

When asked about his age, Brother Maciej, being naive, answers proudly, "Eighty!" More recently, he always adds, "Japan's Emperor is one year older than I." Then he explains, "I came to Japan in 1933, the very year Prince Akihito [the current Emperor Emeritus] was born."

At that time, the Emperor was Hirohito who is called the Emperor of Turbulent Times. From the casual comment of Brother Maciej that Emperor Hirohito was almost the same age as he, I recollected that the times around 1933 showed signs of the forthcoming turbulent age when Japan plunged into war. In 1931, the Manchurian Incident occurred; in 1932, Prime Minister Inukai was shot to death by military officers. In 1933, Hitler's Regime took power in Germany.

Brother Maciej came to Japan when political unrest was in the air. Coincidently, he heard that the following military song was passed down from older soldiers to younger ones in the local military regiment in Nagasaki. Its title was "Fond Memories of Poland."

1. Sunshine on the first and second day,
we have rain and wind on the third, fourth and fifth day.
Ice forms this evening.
Frost is white this morning.

2. Having crossed Germany,
I asked, "where am I?"
So sorry to hear!
There in the past was Poland, a country once so dear.

3. The prosperous must decline.

> I know the axiom in my mind.
> A land devastated to such extremes.
> Unimaginable even in dreams.

It's surprising that the former situation of Poland was sung by Japanese soldiers. Even the old man who taught me the song had no idea when it was written or why it was sung.

"When I was born, Poland no longer existed," murmured Brother Maciej. Crooning the song repeatedly, I could not help but feel that the sorrows of his country are still going on even fifty years after his arrival in Japan.

NOTE: Brother Maciej was called home to Heaven in Nagasaki on August 30, 1996, when he was ninety-four.

CHAPTER 22

Summer in the Homeland

Father Kolbe was about to win the chess game. He had just one move left. But he lost because of the advice of an outsider. Father Kolbe stared at the outsider with disappointment.

Peeping through the Keyhole

When some friars got together and spoke of Father Kolbe among themselves, they all agreed that one day he would become a saint.

"So," Brother Sergiusz said, "everyone knows that one should not peep into another person's room. But I was curious about how a saint behaves when he is alone, so I peeped into his room through the keyhole." As luck would have it, Brother Sergiusz's room was next to Father Kolbe's room, and because he was also the head of the friars, he often went into Father Kolbe's room to talk with him; at times, he would peek in before entering. Once Father Kolbe was kneeling on the floor, gazing at the statue of the Immaculata. It was placed just at the level of his eyes. This height had a meaning. He recommended the friars to do likewise: "If you put the statue at eye-level, you can gaze at it without effort. If you put it too high, it will be hard for you to look at it. So, please position it so that you can gaze at it easily."

Brother Sergiusz continued to look into the room, holding his breath. Father Kolbe stood up after a while and kissed the foot of the statue, surely out of profound love for his Mamusia (mommy) in Heaven.

"When I peered into the room, I could clearly see his entire body profile."

On another occasion, he was walking around his small room, praying the Rosary with his hand tucked under the capuche (cape of the habit).

"On yet another occasion, he was sitting in his chair, writing something. Then he stopped to gaze at the statue of Our Lady. He appeared to be dedicating the subject of his writing to Our Lady, perhaps praying something like 'Maria, as this matter is yours, I leave it to your will.'"

I asked Brother Sergiusz: "You said that you had been talking with the other friars about how Father Kolbe would become a saint. When did that happen?"

"Just after Father Kolbe had come to Japan."

"Why did you think that he would become a saint?"

"Because he never got angry; he was always tender, and he lived with a smile, even when he had a lot of troubles! Oh yes, there is one thing I'll never forget."

One day, when Brother Sergiusz was in Father Kolbe's room as usual, Brother Seweryn suddenly rushed in, without knocking on the door. He started shouting, angrily confronting Father Kolbe!

"Manuscripts are always late! We can't spread God's word publishing *The Knights* like this. There is always too much work. I can't keep up with it. Stop publishing such a magazine!" His fierce manner made Brother Sergiusz shrink back and hide himself behind Father Kolbe. Brother Seweryn was one of the friars who had first come to Japan; however, before setting foot in Japan, he got off the ship at Shanghai and prepared for the publication of *The Knights* in the Chinese version. It was not successful, but fortunately his skill was useful in Nagasaki as he had learned Chinese characters.

He was in charge of selecting types, but with only one or two years of experience, this European friar had to exert enormous effort to select Japanese types. In addition, manuscripts were always submitted late. Father Kolbe also had difficulty in collecting Japanese manuscripts. Brother Seweryn's grievance swelled up and finally exploded!

He continued yelling. Father Kolbe sat there, totally serene and gazed at the statue of the Immaculata. Every complaint eventually comes to an end. When Brother Seweryn paused in his complaining, Father Kolbe turned to the raging friar and gently addressed him: "My dear dziecko (child), is that all?"

Brother Sergiusz reproduced the scene: "Father Kolbe looked at Brother Seweryn, willing to talk to him if he ended his tirade. What do you think happened then?" Brother Serigusz got down on his knees in an exaggerated manner. The blood was flushing into his face.

"Brother Seweryn knelt down in this manner at the foot of Father Kolbe and began to weep, 'I'm sorry. I'm sorry.' He glanced at Father Kolbe's eyes, which showed no hatred, but only loving warmth. Although Father Kolbe said nothing, Brother Seweryn suddenly changed his attitude and left the room in tears."

"What did Father Kolbe do then?"

"He told me to take a seat. Then he continued our interrupted conversation with composure. He said nothing to me about Brother Seweryn."

"It is amazing how he replied with such deep love for his brother. Then you friars perceived this to be the sign of a saint. Was there another sign?" "Yes, his profound devotion to the Immaculata. Everything for the Immaculata; he depended only on the Immaculata. He used to say, 'Our work and propagation through publication are really things that the Immaculata does.' That is what made him different from others. Witnessing his deep trust in and ardor for the Immaculata, we thought he would surely become a saint."

Sacrifice is the Act of Love

The friars revered Father Kolbe, who was different from other superiors, more than they did their own fathers. For them, *Mugenzai no Sono* without Father Kolbe was a vacuum! Brother Sergiusz, who took care of Father Kolbe, was especially lonely. In the middle of the night, he had often heard Father Kolbe snoring or breathing. But it was completely quiet now. He felt unbearably lonely as he could not feel the presence of the saint.

In May, 1933, before Father Kolbe departed from Nagasaki, he left the following message: "At the next Provincial Chapter, the Provincial will resign and a new Provincial will be appointed. Then the Guardian of Niepokalanów and also that of *Mugenzai no Sono* will be appointed. Once it is decided, I will let you know their names by telegraph." Brother Sergiusz parted from Father Kolbe at the big gate of the friary. Perhaps he was merely reluctant to take his leave, but he called Brother Sergiusz over and said to him, "You actually look like Saint Peter. You have a strong nature, but yet, you are somehow nervous. However, the Immaculata has a special plan for you. She loves you. Please be sure of it." Then he whispered, "Of all the friars, I especially wish you well and put my hopes in you."

Brother Sergiusz was pleased that Father Kolbe had confided in him. In reply, he firmly declared: "Father, with the help of the Immaculata, I will never quit the friary. I will love Our Lady throughout my life."

This was his farewell to Father Kolbe. As someone had to stay back to look after the friary, Brother Sergiusz could not go to the Dejima wharf to see Father Kolbe off. Then, two days later, he received Father Kolbe's letter from Shanghai.

> As I have but little time, I write you briefly. When I left Nagasaki, all my brothers wanted to come to the steamboat to see me off, but we needed someone to look after the friary.

I am pleased with the sacrifice of Brother Peter (i.e., Brother Sergiusz) who voluntarily stayed behind and played this role. Dear brothers, sacrifice is an act of love. Love without sacrifice is not genuine love. Jesus is the perfect model of this. Christ taught us about love and died on the Cross because of love. We shall sacrifice small things every day in order to show our love to the Immaculata.

You must not despair even if you unfortunately commit a mortal sin and repeat the same sin. Precisely then you have to throw yourself on the mercy of Our Lady, call her name, beg for forgiveness, and continue your work with a peaceful mind after going to confession. It is sad to commit a sin, but if you know your weakness or faults and fight against them, you will please Our Lady more than you saddened her because of your sin.

Did Father Kolbe also have inner conflict? As he was rough by nature and also very sharp, he sometimes had to hold back his feelings against the lack of understanding of those around him.

After supper there was break time. The friars enjoyed recreation in the evening. Father Kolbe was good at playing chess. He did not go easy on opponents in order to please them, but he played to win!

Brother Sergiusz talked about it: "When he was playing chess one evening, I was watching the game from the side. Then Father Kolbe's opponent didn't see the next move with which he could beat Father Kolbe. As he was about to miss the winning move, I swiftly showed it to him before Father Kolbe's turn. The brother won. Father Kolbe, who lost the game, said nothing but he looked at me with a penetrating stare."

He didn't express it in words but it was a sharp, condemning look as if to say, 'Why did you show him?' "He didn't have a tender look on his face as usual. I could see explicitly that he was trying to control his displeasure. I can't forget that look even now."

Father Kolbe was good at playing chess.

But I digress. The Provincial Chapter was held at the friary of Kraków in southern Poland in the middle of July. The Minister General of the Order in Rome also attended. At first, board members were selected and then the discussion was concentrated on the spirit of Niepokalanów and the management of *Mugenzai no Sono*.

Father Anzelm Kubit, Father Kolbe's former classmate, was elected Provincial and Father Florian was elected Guardian of Niepokalanów again. The problem was the Guardian of *Mugenzai no Sono*. Father Kolbe resigned and Father Kornel, the former Provincial, was appointed Guardian of *Mugenzai no Sono*.

Father Kolbe was ordered to return to Nagasaki, teach the theological course at the seminary and take responsibility for publishing and editing *The Knights*. He was also appointed as worldwide director of the Knights of the Immaculata. In any case, he would return to Nagasaki. A telegram was sent.

> Guardian of the friary of Nagasaki, Kornel. (This was written in Polish.) Maximilian comes back. (This was written in Japanese.)

Maximilian was Father Kolbe's religious name. The friars rejoiced to know that Father Kolbe would come back. But something unexpected happened and the telegram caused a stir at *Mugenzai no Sono*! Father Konstanty, who had been waiting for a chance to return home to Poland, interpreted this telegram to mean that he should go back home. Then he started the procedures for departure.

"It means that Father Kolbe will come back, not that you should go back."

He would not listen to the others and said: "No, the telegram tells me to go home." In spite of leaving the friars speechless with astonishment, Father Konsanty went back to Poland without permission. The friars in Nagasaki were without a priest for more than two months.

Baptism on a Diplomat's Deathbed

From the time of Father Kolbe's arrival in Japan in 1930 until the Provincial Chapter in 1933, fifteen brothers had come to Japan. Four other seminarians were added but only two priests were sent to Japan. Of the two, Father Metody went home after only half a month and Father Konstanty left after a year and three months. Father Kolbe was blessed with many fellow brothers but only a few priests cooperated with him. There were priests who appreciated his propagation through publication in Poland but not one among them dared to go to Asia. Therefore, Father Kornel, the former Provincial, decided to go to Japan as there was no other choice. He was Father Kolbe's strong supporter and had been guiding Father Kolbe since he had made his plan to go to Japan. As the Superior, he also had given Father Kolbe permission to settle in Nagasaki and had promoted the development of Niepokalanów. He was born in March, 1890, and was four years older than Father Kolbe.

The day of their departure was approaching.

On the 3rd of August, Father Kolbe went to the Japanese Legation in Warsaw on business. The Minister posted in Poland was

Hiroyuki Kawai. As Father Kolbe had heard by chance that the minister's wife was a devout Catholic, he brought her a statue of the Immaculata as a present. Fortunately, Mrs. Kawai was in the Legation and he could meet her after he finished with his business.

Mrs. Kawai was very pleased with the statue and promised him: "I will invite you to our cottage." It was located in the suburbs of Warsaw. Mr. and Mrs. Kawai had two daughters, one ten years old and the other six years old. They passed their days at the cottage during the summer. When Father Kolbe visited on the promised date, the statue of the Immaculata was placed in an alcove with beautiful flowers.

"Where is your husband?"

Time passed, and Minister Kawai did not appear. Subsequently, Father Kolbe was told that Minister Kawai had been suffering from lung disease and was now seriously ill. He was not Catholic. Father Kolbe decided to visit him on his sickbed before departing for Japan.

Along with Mrs. Kawai and the Minister's mother, Father Kolbe visited the sanatorium where Minister Kawai was hospitalized. As Father Kolbe himself had suffered from lung disease, he could see at a glance that Minister Kawai was in serious condition. He was thin as a rail and seemed barely alive. Fortunately, he was in good spirits that day, and talked with Father Kolbe about religion.

Minister Kawai was baptized on his death bed.

The Minister said calmly, "When I was in France, I heard about the apparition of the Immaculata, the Virgin Mary and the miracles. Actually, I went to

Lourdes and found myself enveloped in the religious atmosphere there but I was not moved to lead a religious life. I also read the biography of Christ in French, but it also did not make me convert to Catholicism."

That day Father Kolbe gave Minister Kawai a Miraculous Medal of Our Lady through his wife and left the sickroom, praying to Our Lady. Through his many experiences, Father Kolbe firmly believed that the Immaculata would definitely give blessings to those who piously wear the Miraculous Medal. He thought it would be the most excellent present for the Minister.

Minister Kawai's last hour came on August 14th. Those at his bedside prayed to Our Lady, and then Minister Kawai told Father Kolbe he wanted to be baptized. He wished to be given the name of Saint Francis of Assisi as his baptismal name. After he was baptized by Monsignor Marmaggi, the Apostolic Nuncio in Warsaw, Minister Kawai said over and over again, "Why didn't I become Catholic much earlier? There is so much peace and joy," and then he passed away. It was the grace of the Miraculous Medal.

After the funeral, the Minister's mother and a domestic servant were also baptized. His two daughters received First Communion from Monsignor Marmaggi. By that time, Father Kolbe and Father Kornel had already left Poland, visited Rome and Assisi, and were on the steamship, *Conte Rosso,* which had departed from Venice for Japan.

It was the end of summer, 1933.

CHAPTER 23

Father Kolbe's Letters to His Mother

Father Kolbe's life started with a letter to his mother and ended with a letter to her. Only those who love their mother and love God can truly love others.

Donate Salary to Japan

Father Kolbe's mother, Maria Dabrowska, was working as an office worker at a convent and led a long life of poverty and service to others. She had reached her sixty-third year. She lived in Kraków, a big city in southern Poland, made famous by an old castle from the Middle Ages when the Kingdom of Poland had prospered. After the Provincial Chapter ended, Father Kolbe headed for Kraków by

Father Kolbe's fervent love for Our Lady came from his own mother, Maria Dabrowska.

train in order to see his mother on his way back to Asia.

At Christmas time the year before, a letter had arrived in Nagasaki from his mother. An 'oplatki' (Christmas wafer) was enclosed with her Christmas greeting. An oplatki is a piece of thin white bread, which people share with one another and eat with joy on Christmas Eve, this being the Polish custom.

Having received this present filled with the love of his dear mother, he responded to her: "Dearest Mother! Today is the Feast of our Heavenly Mother. I am very glad to receive a letter with the oplatki from my earthly mother on this Feast Day. You are the reflection of the Heavenly Mother, just as the Heavenly Mother is the perfect reflection of God's Beauty and Goodness.

"You ask that I see you, if I return to Poland. But we shall entrust our rendezvous to the Immaculata, because we belong to her completely."

Now Father Kolbe left Niepokalanów and headed for the town where his mother lived. He had not seen her for three years. He deeply loved his mother who had led a hard life. Julius, his father, had been dead for twenty years.

His father was a hot-blooded man. When Poland was deprived of its independence, he fought as a leader of an underground volunteer corps against Russia, but he was caught and sent to the gallows. Father Kolbe's eldest brother, Franciszek, did not live near his mother. She lived alone at the Felician Sisters' convent and she was in charge of shopping, office work, and chores for which the sisters were thankful.

She was a tender mother, but when Father Kolbe was a little boy called Raymond, she was strict with discipline. There hung a whip on the wall in their house. When any of her three sons got into mischief, they were often whipped with it. Raymond was active, quick, and somehow obstinate and his mischief sometimes went too far. But at such times, Raymond did not run and hide but went to his mother, sincerely apologized to her and lay face-down on the desk to be whipped.

After he had been ordained a priest, Father Kolbe came back from Rome and was sent to the friary in Kraków, where he fulfilled his dream of publishing *The Knights*. His mother was at his side and helped him. She visited the office and cooperated by mailing the magazines or distributing them on the street. She was a midwife, good-natured, and good at taking care of others.

Father Kolbe wished to comfort her. He wanted to go to the resort of Zakopane with her for a week or so and take good care of her. But it was an impossible dream, as he had to hurry back to Japan this time. Four years later, after he had left Japan and come back home for good, Father Kolbe was finally able to realize his dream and take her to the resort. His mother must have rejoiced with tears when she met Father Kolbe after such a long interval. She handed him the precious earnings she had received for her work for the sisters. She had saved it all, not spending a penny, so that he could use it for the propagation of the Faith in Japan!

He wrote a letter to Niepokalanów from the train: "My mother gave me an offering of sixty zloty. I beg you to send her some photographs." Sixty zloty corresponds to 120 yen at that time. It was a huge amount of money!

In the same letter he wrote an interesting note: "Soon we will arrive at the border. The Provincial, Father Anzelm, advised me to be careful when using the term 'Mamusia (Mommy),' as there are people who don't like it."

In truth, Father Kolbe's fervent love for Our Lady came from his own mother.

Pigs Feet, His Favorite Dish

Father Kolbe finally returned to Nagasaki. After having completed the long voyage across the Indian Ocean, Father Kolbe and Father Kornel arrived at *Mugenzai no Sono* on October 4th, the Feast of Saint Francis Assisi who had founded the Order. More than ten friars who had waited impatiently for them welcomed the new Guardian with joy.

However, in another sense, difficult days were ahead for Father Kolbe. Father Kolbe was the founder of *Mugenzai no Sono* and had been its Guardian until then. Now he had to step back and be obedient as an 'ordinary' priest. It was surely a hard thing from the human point of view; all the harder, as he was competent and considerate. Father Kolbe would undergo a real test of patience for the next three years because, as a subordinate, he could not control the whole of things as he might wish. But his character shone through. On the basis of his immutable faith, he did not hesitate to devote himself to obedience without reserve.

There is a photo of the dignified Father Kornel wearing a black hat. He was slender, powerful, bearded, and sharp-eyed. Brother Sergiusz talked about the new Guardian as follows: "As the new Guardian, he did not make the least remark at all, but simply looked around the friary, and listened to the frank opinions of the friars."

Several days later, the new Guardian finally opened his mouth after breakfast: "From now on, I will divide the tasks into two parts: Father Kolbe will be responsible for publication of *The Knights* and for your spiritual guidance. I will be respon-

Father Kornel, former Minister Provincial, became a new Guardian of Mugenzai no Sono.

sible for the friary as a whole and especially for the care of your health. I cannot ignore this matter. If things continue as they have been going, you will all soon find yourselves in the cemetery!"

Soon after, the nutritional content of their meals was improved according to Father Kornel's principle. He himself went shopping with Brother Romuald every day. He bought cheap ingredients full of nutrition, for example, pigs feet, pigs ear, or pigs giblets. It was just like the early years of Saint Francis. Brother Kasjan on kitchen duty cooked these ingredients.

The arrival of Father Kornel, who had served as the Minister Provincial, brought a sense of relief to the religious life of the friars. The coloring of their faces was visibly improved thanks to him. "Since Father Kornel's arrival, we started to eat Japanese food every Friday. We ate miso soup, potatoes, or sardines with chopsticks. Father Kolbe often dropped his chopsticks at dinner, as his hands shook. He didn't like *kon'yaku* (devil's tongue jelly) or *kamaboko* (boiled fish paste) that much..." Brother Kasjan shook his head and continued: "But he didn't say that he wouldn't eat them. The Guardian was worried about him and asked me to prepare different food for Father Kolbe. But he wanted to eat the same food as the other friars."

Father Kornel was admirable in that respect. He ate everything! He liked *takuwan* (yellow pickled radish) and *rakkyo* (pickled shallot) very much. He bought a pig's foot for 5 sen. It was boiled in a sauce pan, until its meat was softened and fell apart. Garlic and green onion were mixed in. Then, it was kept in a big bowl until it got cold. This was Father Kornel's favorite food.

When he was invited out by somebody and ate something delicious, he would teach Brother Kasjan about the cuisine. Father Kolbe was totally different. He said nothing about food. If he dared say anything, he just said to Brother Kasjan, "It's enough if we eat healthy things. They don't have to be delicious. But just be careful of food that has spoiled."

The quality of life improved with the food. Father Kornel sought comfort and neatness even in poverty. A little later on, the friars took a short trip to Unzen for the first time. They also started to keep cows and pigs. All the chairs, desks, and shelves were made by the friars themselves. Most of them were simple and rough-hewn. But the chairs in the dining room were varnished and the floor was painted. However, Father Kolbe did not like this. When Brother Romuald was varnishing the chairs, Father Kolbe came along and said, "*Moje dziecko* (my child), what are you doing? Is that really necessary?"

"The Guardian told me to do this."

When he heard that, he looked surprised and responded slightly perplexed: "Oh! Please go on with your work." Nothing was farther from his intention than to oppose the will of the Guardian. On another occasion, the big Brother Romuald was hanging a picture in a frame in the hallway, which he had purchased in town at the request of Father Guardian. It was also a longstanding custom of the Order to hang framed holy pictures.

"When I was putting up the picture of 'the Blessing of Saint Francis of Assisi to Brother Leo' and a commemorative photo of the Provincial Chapter in Poland, Father Kolbe passed by."

"My Brother, what are you doing now?"

"The Guardian told me to hang them."

"I see. Well, in that case, please do so."

Then Father Kolbe stopped and, looking up to the framed pictures, he said: "My Brother, when you buy a frame next time, please choose a cheap one without decoration around it. They just get dirty when dust accumulates on them. And, it will be better for holy poverty."

"Father," Brother Romuald replied, "Plain frames cost more than those with decoration. As the wood used for them is more expensive, these ones are cheaper."

"I see," Father Kolbe said with a puzzled look and went on his way.

Sixty-Two Letters to His Mother

After Father Kolbe had left Poland for Japan following the Provincial Chapter, disturbing and sad news reached his mother: A Japanese ship had sunk and Father Kolbe was believed to have perished! It was true that a Japanese ship had sunk, but it was not the *Conte Rosso* on which he had sailed.

A lot of work was waiting for him in Nagasaki. He made the following entry in his diary: "October 26th. I divided work with Father Kornel. He is Guardian, Rector of the Seminary, Director of Novices, and he is responsible for all of the friars and the whole curriculum. He teaches ethics and liturgy. I am the spiritual leader of the friars and teach dogma, Bible, canon law, and Church history. I also serve as director of the Knights of the Immaculata."

After he had caught up with his work to some extent, Father Kolbe wrote a letter to his mother before Christmas, 1933: "I wish you Merry Christmas with love and now share the oplatki with you. Our Lady successfully led me to *Mugenzai no Sono*. Fortunately, I arrived in Nagasaki, without drowning. I hear that you got the news of a shipwreck with two fatalities from Niepokalanów. It was indeed a Japanese ship!

"Our work is difficult here. There is a huge number of people who are not baptized, about ninety million, while Catholics are just 200,000, i.e., one in 450. But our hope lies in the Immaculata. We need above all grace for the conversion of souls. Therefore, I want to ask you and the Sisters for daily prayers and sacrifice for the Japanese. As for me, I am all right."

After having retired from the post of the Guardian, Father Kolbe's health gradually improved. Previously, he had often strangely trembled or suffered from abdominal pains, but now those symptoms disappeared. In particular, the boils did not appear.

The best medicine for his stomach ache was wine. Whenever he drank it, the pain ceased. Although wine was very expensive in those days, he drank a little as medicine. When friars got ill, he also had them drink wine. He always had a slight fever and he kept a thermometer at hand. His normal temperature rose from 98.9 or 99.1 to 100.4 degrees. But Father Kolbe did not stop working, saying that he would work as long as he could, since he thought he would not live long.

"He used a urinal then," Brother Sergiusz said. "I looked after it as my duty. One morning Father Kolbe did not leave his bedroom. I was very worried and went to see him. He said, 'I bled from my mouth,' and he was taking a rest. He didn't say how much he bled. He tried not to cause us anxiety. I didn't see any blood."

Father Kolbe did not worry about it, saying, "The Immaculata will take care of it. I have confided everything to her."

He wrote another letter to his mother around this time: "I am in the midst of unbaptized people. We have a mountain of work to do. What's important is that seventy million people don't know the Immaculata and Our Lord Jesus. For December, the month of the Immaculata, we will print sixty thousand copies of *The Knights*. It will still reach fewer than one in a thousand, but we don't lose hope. With the help of the Immaculata everything will go better."

He added at the end of both letters: "I am wondering whether to write a letter to Franciszek. May the Immaculata guide him!"

Father Kolbe had studied in the seminary with Franciszek, his eldest brother, who later withdrew from the seminary, got married, and worked in a hospital. His married life was not going well at that time and, according to a rumor, he got divorced. For Father Kolbe, this was painful news about a family member. Subsequently, Franciszek died in Auschwitz during the Second World War.

Father Kolbe's youngest brother Alfons became a priest but he had died suddenly three years before. The only hope for his mother was Father Kolbe who was working in Asia. She loved him very much. As a token of her love, she preserved all the letters she had received from Father Kolbe. A collection of his letters began twenty-five years after his death, and a volume was published at Niepokalanów four years later. The number of his letters amounted amazingly to eight hundred and thirty-nine, sixty-two of which were to his mother.

Father Kolbe's love for his mother revealed itself in these letters. The first letter and the last letter he wrote were addressed to his mother: The first letter was written on October 28, 1912, when he was studying in Rome, the last having been penned in the concentration camp of Auschwitz on June 15, 1941, just two months before his death: "All is well with me. You don't have to worry about me," he continued to reassure his mother to the last.

Reading his collection of letters starting and ending with a letter to his mother, I cannot help but feel that loving one's own mother and loving God are preconditions of true love for others.

His mother, Maria Dabrowska, died in the convent of the Felician Sisters in May 1946, just after the end of the Second World War, and went home to see her holy son.

CHAPTER 24

Leaving Everything to *The Knights*

Even a person of great virtue gets angry when persistently provoked. "Father Kolbe got angry only once."

Let's Learn Chinese Characters

The friars were preparing for their fourth winter in Nagasaki. So far, they had spent their winters in an unheated friary. When Father Kolbe had guests, the best he could do was to serve them hot tea as "an interior heater." But this winter was different. Thanks to Father Kornel, they made a stove themselves and their life became warmer. One of the friars who was good with his hands built a special stove stacked with bricks inside and surrounded by a tinplate. The new Guardian stopped their "work-only life" and brought some comfort to their religious life.

At first, he set up a laundry room. Then he built a hut with a large oven where the friars baked their own bread. The loaves were big, as were the friars themselves! Brother Maciej was in charge of baking.

"The bread was big and round, about 30 cm in diameter and about 15 cm in height. When kneaded and patted, it became round. We placed it on the wooden board like a scoop and slid it into the oven. It was very delicious," said Brother Sergiusz nostalgically.

Several years later, the friars slaughtered a pig in the friary for Easter, which was actually illegal. They did it in the laundry room and put its meat and feet on the dough kneading table. A cat watched for an opportunity to steal them.

A friar kept guard so that they would not be stolen. Then he noticed a crack between the chimney and the roof. In a fluster he stuffed the crack with an old mosquito net at hand. Without knowing about this, Brother Maciej set a fire in the oven. Now this became a serious matter. The mosquito net caught fire in a second and the hut was filled with smoke! In a panic, Brother Maciej shouted something in Polish but the flames only grew higher! It turned out to be a big incident and a fire engine came. Brother Maciej was reproached severely by the police. But "I didn't admit that we had slaughtered a pig." It happened after Father Kolbe had returned to Poland. Later a new bakery hut was built.

Following the bakery, a cow shed was constructed. The friars kept three cows and milked them as a source of nutrition. They drank milk every day and milk-soup was also served. "Milk was a luxury," said Brother Sergiusz. "We fermented milk in summer and made yogurt that the Polish like to eat. It's called *kwaśne mleko* in Polish."

Back one morning when Father Kolbe was still with them and breakfast was almost over, Father Kornel, the Guardian, turned to Father Kolbe and urged him as usual: "Let's study Japanese." Father Kolbe wrote Chinese characters on the blackboard that was hung on the wall in the dining room. He was certainly not proficient at writing Chinese characters. We can see his Japanese handwriting

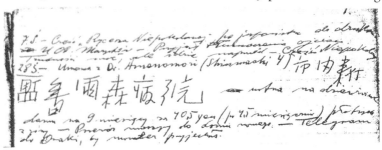

Father Kolbe sometimes wrote Chinese characters in his "Nagasaki Diary."

here and there in his Nagasaki diary, which was mostly written in Polish. "Amenomori Hospital, Shinmachi 4, Nagasaki City," "Toraemon Hirata," "Akira Osawa," etc.

Even though his handwriting was bad, he explained the pronunciation, meanings, and origins of the characters with confidence. He used the textbook written by Rose-Innes, a Protestant scholar. Father Kolbe wrote to him and urged him to convert — here we observe the mind of Father Kolbe who devoted himself to spreading God's word.

"Rose-Innes, who lived in Japan, sent a dictionary to Father Kolbe as a reply," said Brother Grzegorz. The friars gazed at the characters written on the blackboard and transcribed them. They put the memo paper, their daily assignment, into their pockets. They took it out during the break and committed the characters to memory within that day.

Certainly, improvement of the facilities at the friary required funds that had been donated by the readers of *The Knights* in Japan as well as in Poland. Father Kolbe's concern was whether "the funds of Our Lady" might be used up for their daily expenses and would not be available for other needs.

Leisure is what creates culture. One day Brother Bartłomiej hung a beautiful lace curtain in the reception room. When I think of it today, it was not too gorgeous. But Father Kolbe complained to the Guardian and made Brother Bartłomiej remove it. He got rid of it, while murmuring. Presumably, superfluous things did not have any meaning for Father Kolbe who made much of holy poverty. In such an atmosphere, a strange feeling came to exist among the friars ever since Father Kornel had taken up his position as Guardian. It was an air of dissatisfaction about spreading God's word through publication, which was vital to Father Kolbe. Brother Bartłomiej stood out as the strongest opponent. It was not simply because he was told to remove the curtain, but propagation through the magazine seemed futile to him. Father Kornel rather sided with Brother Bartłomiej. The Guardian asked Father Kolbe not to increase the number of copies of *The Knights* for financial reasons. It was a big blow to Father Kolbe but he willingly obeyed his Superior.

Folding Prayer into Pages

Every morning Father Kolbe walked around the printing office where the friars worked. "Don't you have worries? Please tell me if you have any. Thank Our Lady if you have none."

During the daytime, the friars took turns making thirty minute visits to the Blessed Sacrament in the chapel, no matter how busy they were. Father Kolbe was convinced: "Unless we fold our prayer into the pages, the Japanese will not convert."

Brother Romuald was bigger than the average person. Being very tired due to the heavy workload, he used to doze off during prayers. One day, although he knew he should not fall asleep and did his best not to lean on the prie-dieu, he could not beat his fatigue and surrendered himself to slumber.

Just at that moment, Father Kolbe came to visit the Blessed Sacrament and gently provided support to the big Brother Romuald from behind and let him lean on the prie-dieu. Father said, "Please make yourself comfortable." "Then I suddenly woke up. The gentle attitude of Father Kolbe embarrassed me," said Brother Romuald smiling. "He often visited the Blessed Sacrament at that time: twice in the morning and several times in the afternoon, gazing at the tabernacle with eyes aglow! I felt that it was the prayer of a saint."

Looking back on those good old days, Brother Sergiusz said, "As Father Kolbe had retired from the post of Guardian, he had more time to spare, and opportunities to communicate with the brothers increased, which we all welcomed. On Saturdays, he especially allocated a certain period for communication and we enjoyed spiritual conversation with him."

Although the friars had many difficulties, they also had delights.

Those who know love can endure any difficulty or adversity. The spiritual guidance of Father Kolbe brought the young friars close to the Immaculata. Father Kolbe himself was a good example. He always called out "Maria." Or it would be more appropriate to say that he breathed Maria rather than called her.

"For example," explained Brother Romuald, "When Father was looking for something, he spontaneously said, 'Oh, Maria' with a sigh."

I asked Brother Romuald, "Did you always say 'Maria' when you were folding *The Knights*?" "No, it was a spiritual prayer. When we put each sheet of paper into the folding machine, we worked with a prayer intention. Unless we fold our prayer into the pages, the Japanese won't convert. That's it."

When I entered the Knights of the Immaculata at the end of the Second World War, Father Kolbe's spirit was still strong there. When we started to write a letter or a note, we used to start it with Maria.

Father Kolbe often wrote the letter "M" inside a circle with a red pencil. One friar asked him, "Does it mean Maximilian?" "No. It is Maria." Father Kolbe used Maria as his signature. When the friars met each other in the friary, or entered a room, they started their conversation after saying "Maria." The same was true for telephone calls; they spoke the name "Maria" with a gracious European pronunciation.

"When did the custom begin?" I asked Brother Romuald.

"It started the year I entered Niepokalanów. I was already wearing the habit. The evening of the exaltation of Our Lady was held on the Feast of the Immaculate Conception and it was then that we decided it. As Trappists say '*Memento mori* (Remember you must die)', we shall say 'Maria.' Everyone agreed with this proposal. It has been a tradition since the foundation of Niepokalanów. But there was a point to be noted. We should not say Maria many times over to the same brother in the same place…"

"What was your first impression of Father Kolbe?"

"He seemed to be a strict person. But my impression changed when I talked with him. I sensed that he was really different. He was inaccessible at first glance but gentle when one spoke with him. He was such a father!"

"Were you aware of his sense of humor?"

"Yes. When I became sick, Father Kolbe came to my bed and asked, 'Do you want to see what the world has never seen?' Of course, I said 'yes.' Then he took out an egg he had concealed, cracked it open and said, 'The world has never seen what's in this.'"

His humor seems to have been somehow philosophical. One day during a break, Father Kolbe showed a photo to the friars and talked about Bishop Berti. After a while he said, "Let's put it in Berti."

"An envelope is called *koperta* in Polish. He made a pun based on similar pronunciations of Berti and *koperta*." This is what I heard from Brother Romuald.

He Got Angry Only Once

In May, 1932, Brother Bartłomiej arrived in Nagasaki together with Father Konstanty and Brother Kasjan, who was responsible for the cooking. He was twenty years old and in charge of selecting types. He stayed nine years in Nagasaki and was living as a friar in the USA as of 1983, when this book was published. He could not understand that the copies of *The Knights* he made with difficulty were distributed for free. But Father Kolbe's principle was obvious: he wished to distribute the magazine, into which the blessings of Our Lady were folded, to all families in Japan. Individuals as well as families would receive God's grace, if they were united to Our Lady.

Father Kolbe never thought of making a profit. He surrendered himself to God's Providence and devoted himself to God as an instrument of the Immaculata. But Brother Bartłomiej did not have such a firm confidence. One day he saw someone in the market tearing up a copy of *The Knights* to wrap up a fish. He was greatly shocked!

"We should have *The Knights* read more effectively. Will we get good results, if we carry on propagation in this manner?" Soon after the Guardian changed, young friars gradually became dissatisfied and came to oppose Father Kolbe to his face. As Brother Bartłomiej especially objected time after time, even Father Kolbe eventually scolded this young friar severely: "You are always saying this! We publish the magazine not for business but for the propagation of the Faith. This is Our Lady's enterprise. Don't forget it!" He was visibly angry then.

Brother Romuald told me of his unforgettable impression at that time: "Father Kolbe was always gentle but he got angry only this time." Brother Zeno stood by Father Kolbe and distributed copies of *The Knights* efficiently. But one copy per 1,000 people was still too few. In Poland, the number of the copies of *The Knights* increased by some 10,000 every month, whereas the situation was different in the mission field of Japan. Father Kolbe felt dissatisfied but he did not lose hope.

Father Kolbe sent questionnaires to churches around Japan and asked missionaries for advice as to how *The Knights* could permeate the public. His only desire was to publish as many copies of *The Knights* as possible and to make the Immaculata known to as many Japanese as possible.

At that time there was one reader to whom he sent *The Knights* for three years without getting any response. But suddenly that reader sent 5 yen to Father Kolbe!

One copy cost 3 sen and a one year subscription cost 30 sen in those days. 5 yen was almost the amount of a seventeen year subscription.

"I told you so." Father Kolbe reported this event to the friars. Soon after that, the reader started to write to Father Kolbe.

Father Kolbe was filled with hope: "*The Knights* should be distributed to every island in Japan. In addition to *The Knights* which we are currently printing, I want to publish a general magazine for non-Catholics as well as Catholics, *The Knights* for youth and women and also a newspaper."

He laid down a careful plan: "The friars will go to towns and villages to distribute *The Knights*. As Japan is an island country, we will build a ship for Our Lady and spread God's word, sailing on this ship from island to island." He described his future dream this way in the Polish magazine, *Misja katolicka*.

When Father Kolbe and Brother Romuald went to Osaka to purchase paper, they stayed at Tamatsukuri Church and visited the Osaka headquarters of the *Asahi Newspaper*.

In front of the monstrous modern printing machine that came complete with its own veranda, Father Kolbe's eyes glowed in an uncanny way. After he left the newspaper company, he said passionately: "We must use such a machine for the Immaculata. If only the Minister General gives us permission, we will publish a daily newspaper as soon as tomorrow! We have to start at once." Brother Romuald gave him the cold shoulder and said pessimistically, "It is not so simple. We don't have a facility. In addition, we have too few friars. It is impossible!"

"This is not a problem. What's important is whether the Immaculata wishes it or not." Father Kolbe said solemnly. This was his principle.

He did not start with funding, qualifications, and other conditions. The point was the wish of the Immaculata which would be disclosed through the will of the Superior. Once the will of Our Lady was manifested through his obedience, he just moved forward. There was no hesitation in his action.

Before long, Father Kornel came to understand Father Kolbe's true intention and four friars were added in August, 1934. So

Father Kornel gave permission to resume printing *The Knights*. Brother Sergiusz remembers that as many as 63,500 copies of *The Knights* were printed during Father Kolbe's stay in Nagasaki. One copy cost 3 sen, including postage.

In those days, the streetcar fare in Nagasaki City cost 6 sen.

CHAPTER 25

Enduring Chest Pains

A sick and weak Father Kolbe survived sixteen days in the starvation bunker. Such strength of spirit was fostered during his time in Nagasaki.

Was He Really Seriously Ill?

There was no effective medicine for tuberculosis before and during the Second World War. It was regarded as an incurable disease. It is said that Father Kolbe was suffering from a serious case of tuberculosis when he came to Nagasaki to spread God's word. "He was seriously ill. Nevertheless, he worked more than the average person," reflected Father Mirochna, who had lived with Father Kolbe for six years.

Is it true? Could a man suffering from a serious case of tuberculosis take a long trip to Asia, start a printing enterprise, and write countless manuscripts and letters? Such achievements defy common sense. It is just unbelievable! Is there any method to verify the fact more scientifically? While I had this simple question in my mind for a long time, I unexpectedly found an X-ray of Father Kolbe's lungs.

This image was developed on a photographic paper 7.6 cm long x 9.5 cm wide. Some numbers were written at the bottom. As far as I could make out, this photo had been taken on February 7, 1927, three years before Father Kolbe came to Japan. At that time,

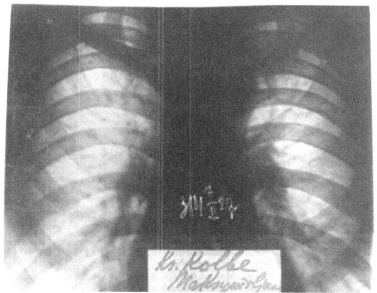

An X-ray of Father Kolbe's lungs was taken in 1927, three years before he came to Japan.

he would have been in the sanatorium of Zakopane located in the mountainous area of southern Poland.

I wanted to show the photo to a specialist to get his diagnosis. So I consulted with an ophthalmologist I knew. He introduced me to Dr. Akira Ashizawa, a Catholic radiologist who worked in the Radiology Department of Mitsubishi Hospital in Nagasaki City.

I had an appointment with Dr. Ashizawa on a hot sunny day in 1972 or 1973. He welcomed me kindly and carefully examined the troubling X-ray.

At first he made a general observation and said, "The lower part is missing." In fact, the part of the lungs next to the diaphragm was not in the image. "But that part is rather unlikely to suffer from tuberculosis. If some lesion ever existed in that part, it would probably have been something other than tuberculosis."

"How is the sharpness of the photo?"

"The image is not clear, since it is not the original negative but rather a copy of it. I can't judge whether it is a reduced print from a larger negative or a close print from a fluorograph."

In any case, from a professional point of view, he admired the excellence of the photo taken in the 1920s. Then he examined it in detail. The apical zone of the left lung is darker than the right one and the rear pleural cavity of the left lung is narrower than the right one. "Judging from these, we may consider that the lesion was from the apical zone to the upper zone of the left lung. This is characteristic of a pulmonary tuberculosis that occurs in general in the apical zone of the lung, especially at the rear."

As a non-professional, I was concerned about the dark shadow in the middle of the left lung.

"Judging from this, if he was suffering from tuberculosis, he must have caught it many years ago. The outer side of the left lung is slightly darker than that of the right lung. I'm not sure but it seems to have something to do with the left rear pleural cavity."

His diagnosis was correct. After Father Kolbe had returned from Rome, he became seriously ill and entered the hospital in August, 1920. It was seven years before this photo was taken. He was hospitalized in the sanatorium in Zakopane and served as its chaplain. But his condition showed little improvement and he sometimes spat blood. The dark part of his left lung seemed to bear the trace of accumulated fluid. The fluid already had disappeared and it seemed that adhesive pleurisy had remained there.

In April, 1921, Father Kolbe left the sanatorium and returned to the friary in Kraków. After that, he sometimes needed a change of air and in October, 1922, he was transferred to the friary in Grodno. In September, 1926, he went into the sanatorium of Zakopane for the second time. In April, 1927, he left the sanatorium and went back to Grodno. There is no other record of his hospitalization.

"There is no abnormality in the heart and the central shading. Judging from this photo, his right lung is almost intact."

"Is it true?" I thought it strange because I heard that three-quarters of both of Father Kolbe's lungs had been affected by tuberculosis.

"Was he not seriously ill?" "If I should diagnose him based only on this photo, I don't think that he was the kind of patient who absolutely had to be hospitalized at once and get strict medical treatment." "How was his condition?" "Well, if it were today, I'd tell him that if he takes his medicine and stays in bed for a while, he will recover."

"Dr. Takashi Nagai examined Father Kolbe and said that he needed complete rest. Dr. Nagai wrote this in his manuscript. Was it an exaggeration?"

"In those days there was no other treatment than having complete rest no matter how far along the illness had progressed. Prescribing complete rest had a different meaning in those days from today when medical care has been highly developed."

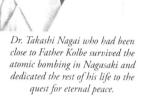

Dr. Takashi Nagai who had been close to Father Kolbe survived the atomic bombing in Nagasaki and dedicated the rest of his life to the quest for eternal peace.

Going out of the hospital, I had mixed feelings: I felt on one hand relieved and on the other hand betrayed. The doctor diagnosed that Father Kolbe was not seriously ill at that time. I left the hospital, a bit puzzled about the diagnosis.

How to Surmount Medical Common Sense

Dr. Yasuo Fukahori argued against the diagnosis with his low but powerful voice: "I examined Father Kolbe many times. He sometimes had a fever of 100 to 102 degrees. Obviously, his condition was bad. Both of his lungs were also bad."

Dr. Fukahori examined Father Kolbe for several years beginning in 1930, when he was a young medical doctor with three or four years' experience. He was working in the pediatric department of

Nagasaki Medical College then. "I took many X-rays of Father Kolbe at the college, but they were all burned because of the atomic bomb and are no longer extant. I remember very well that Father had a high fever and trembled from chills; nevertheless, he continued to work."

"I advised him: 'It is absurd. You should go to the hospital,' but Father Kolbe answered, 'It's okay.' Therefore, I often quarreled with him, as I was concerned that it might be transmitted to other friars. But no one else suffered from tuberculosis. The method of treatment in those days was rest, nutrition, and fresh air. But Father Kolbe had none of these. His food was poor and he didn't rest. As a medical doctor I don't understand how he could survive so long."

Brother Sergiusz had a slightly different opinion. Although he lived next door to Father Kolbe and took care of him, he said, "I scarcely had the impression that Father Kolbe was sick or that he had only one lung. It's true that he was a bit sickly but he didn't seem seriously ill. If he was really so ill, it means that he successfully concealed his poor physical condition."

It might be true that Father Kolbe tried to keep his illness secret. He never complained, but he wrote a letter in May, 1935, saying that his illness had become difficult to bear. It was addressed to Father D'Ambrosio, Vice Minister General of the Order of Friars Minor Conventual in Rome.

> I get fairly weak and don't know when my earthly life will end. So I have a favor to ask of you. Before I breathe my last, I would be happy to see — if the Immaculata so wishes — an indulgence bestowed on the Knights of the Immaculata.

His last, earnest wish is evidenced in these brief sentences.

Dr. Takashi Nagai belonged to the Radiology Department of Nagasaki Medical College and supposedly examined Father Kolbe around this time; he wrote in his essay that it had been in 1935. He graduated from the college in 1932, majored in radiology, and became an assistant there in 1934 when he was twenty-six. He was baptized in July of the same year. When he placed a stethoscope on Father Kolbe's chest, he shouted with astonishment in spite of himself, having heard several kinds of abnormal sounds: "This is serious! Both of your lungs are bad. You need complete rest."

Years later, after Father Kolbe was thrown into the starvation bunker in the Auschwitz concentration camp, he lived longer than the other prisoners. How could he survive so long, with his sick and weak body?

To save the life of one man must not have been the only reason Father Kolbe chose to die in his place. He must have wished to accompany to the end the nine prisoners sentenced to death. Especially since he voluntarily offered to die, how could he breathe his last earlier than the others? Here is the problem. No matter how strong a man's spirit is, the flesh has its own weakness. That's just the reality of man. Father Kolbe took the place of a man on July 29th and was given a lethal injection on August 14th. He endured sixteen days with his fragile body, without drinking or eating. What could make this possible other than spiritual strength? I guess that his strength was fostered not only in the starvation bunker but also in Nagasaki. But where did it come from?

Dr. Nagai wrote:

> It was something inconceivable to medical common sense. I wondered how he could continue spreading God's word with such a fragile body. Then Father Kolbe said, lifting his hand slightly with a smile, "This is the secret." I saw a Rosary shining in his hands.

The Sick are the Treasures of the Friary

There is a saying: Fellow sufferers pity each other. There is also a similar saying in Polish: *Wzajemne współczucie chorobie.* (Mutual compassion for illness.)

Father Kolbe, who experienced illness himself, understood the state of mind and the agony of the sick. So when a friar got ill, Father Kolbe looked after him more cordially than the friar's own father would have. The friars lived far from their own country and their own family members. How could they carry on with their religious life if they did not help each other when they became ill? Father Kolbe cherished the sick as the friary's treasures.

Brother Romuald cannot forget Father Kolbe's tenderness toward the sick. "Father Kolbe said, 'Those who are ill work very hard in the eyes of God while lying on their beds.' He was certainly grateful to God when no one was sick in the friary. But he sometimes worried that the blessings might be fewer at such times."

Brother Romuald sometimes collapsed in spite of his big body. Father Kolbe showed his warm-hearted consideration in his Nagasaki diary: "Brother Romuald suddenly fell down. This was the third time. The cause was that he rode a bicycle too much. But I had another cause for concern about him."

Brother Romuald caught a cold and got a fever of 104 degrees. Then Father Kolbe said, "I'll make you better quickly," and filled the wash tub half-full of cold water. He had the friar with a fever bend low in it, as he splashed water over his back with a towel. Consequently, his entire body cooled down. Father Kolbe wrapped him up with a bed sheet ready for that purpose, had him lie down and covered him with a futon. Then Brother Romuald sweated a lot and the temperature went down to 97 degrees and he felt relieved. "You feel better, don't you?" This was Father Kolbe's method of fighting off a cold.

"But it is dangerous unless we do it carefully. Father Kolbe was like a medical doctor. He knew how to treat patients," Brother Romuald said, in admiration of Father Kolbe.

Brother Kasjan, the cook, was suffering from kidney disease. "Father Kolbe brought Communion to me in my room. When he had guests, he guided them first of all to the sick, saying, 'Sick people have God's blessings. They are the best workers in the friary.'

He always consoled the sick and told them not to worry."

Father Kolbe made Brother Kasjan eat watermelon every day. He said, "We have to endure illness also with obedience. We receive God's blessings then."

In those days there were two Polish seminarians, Mirochna and Aleksy. Mirochna was not energetic all the time and Aleksy was suffering from timidity. Father Kolbe called him "the Lamb of Francisco." As he was timid, it took time for him to confess. When he was the first one to confess, other friars were troubled because they had to wait for a long time.

"Was Our Lady satisfied today?" asked seminarian Aleksy with a sorrowful face.

"Yes, she was," answered Father Kolbe. He always showed his patience to his fellow brothers. "In that respect, Father Kornel sometimes reproached me in strong language," said a friar with a pout. "But Father Kolbe always helped me tenderly."

Brother Grzegorz was troubled by idle thoughts when he was praying. Delusions welled up one after another. He could not prevent his mind from being distracted. One night he knocked on Father Kolbe's door, not knowing what else to do. Father Kolbe was still awake, walking around the room, praying the Rosary.

"*Dziecko* (Child)," said Father gently, and let Brother Grzegorz in his room, welcoming him with a great show of cordiality.

"Father, I can't pray because of idle thoughts welling up."

Then Father Kolbe told him the following fable: "Once there was a knight. He said to a farmer that he would give his horse to the farmer if he could say a Hail Mary once without any distraction. Then the farmer replied that it was very easy because the Hail Mary is a short prayer.

"Soon after the farmer had begun the prayer, he asked the knight: Sir, does the horse have a saddle?"

"See how it is," said Father Kolbe smiling. "We all have many weaknesses. It's difficult for us to say a Hail Mary even once without distraction. Let's entrust everything to Our Lady and please feel at ease."

Brother Grzegorz has not forgotten this conversation with Father Kolbe, even after fifty years.

CAHPTER 26

Boys in the Sea Breeze

In the fifth year of the Knights in Nagasaki, boys from the Goto Islands, which were called the Islands of Faith, entered the friary as candidates. These boys had a future ahead of them in which their dreams might become reality.

Nuzzling a Beard Against the Cheek

The Goto Islands are located in the East China Sea, 100 km from the port of Nagasaki. They are called Goto, "the five islands," because there are actually five main islands in the archipelago, Hisakajima being one of them. As the existence of the site of heroic martyrdom called Royanosako (small prison) suggests, there have been many devout Catholics on this island.

On a spring day in 1936, Yasugoro Nakamura, the fifth son of a farmer, was stopped by a priest after Mass.

"Nakamura, have you thought about entering the friary?" "I haven't studied much and I don't know anything about the friary. It's impossible!" "You can do it; Father Kolbe has come to recruit candidates. There's a farm at the friary. The friars also have a printing machine and they publish magazines. You should think it over."

Yasugoro answered, "Please ask my father and mother. If they say yes, I will go." "It is you who enter the friary, not your father or mother. Think about it." Yasugoro was unexpectedly moved to enter the friary at that moment. His father did not really agree with it, but his mother encouraged him: "If you do your best to the last, you may go. Once you enter the friary, you have to carry it out at any cost."

"I won't pay your travel costs," said his father. Yasugoro was still undecided but he carried firewood to the seashore in order to earn the boat fare. His friend, who was one year younger than he, decided to go to the seminary in Nagasaki. Yasugoro was frequently urged by this younger friend to join him in Nagasaki and in the end he decided to do so.

His father, who had been opposed to his entering the friary, relented at last and bought him a ticket to Nagasaki. He boarded the ship, *Chofuku-maru,* with his father. His mother saw him off at the harbor waving a white towel for a long time.

Once they reached the city of Nagasaki, his father, a country man, felt helpless. So he invited his younger brother, Yasugoro's uncle who lived in Inasa, to go out shopping. They went to the busy street and Yasugoro's father bought clothes for his son and a wicker trunk. His father carried the trunk on his shoulders and went up the slope to the friary. At that time a two-story church with mortar walls had been built in *Mugenzai no Sono.* There was a small tower with a cross on the roof and one could clearly see the church at the foot of Mt. Hiko.

They arrived at the entrance of the friary and pushed down the wooden handle on the door. The bell rang and before long, out came a bearded European friar.

It was Brother Henrico, the first European Yasugoro had ever seen. Yasugoro's uncle said, "I have brought you a candidate." The three visitors were led to a reception room with wooden walls.

After a while Father Kolbe appeared. He mistook Yasugoro's young uncle for the candidate and said with pleasure, "Will you devote yourself to Our Lady? Welcome!"

"No. It's not me. This little boy." "Oh, so he is the one?" The young boy wore a kimono with a splashed pattern. "How old are you?" "Fourteen," the boy answered in a small voice. Father Kolbe nevertheless seemed to be satisfied. He took the boy by the hand, drew him near and nuzzled his beard against the boy's cheek, saying, "You will devote your whole life to Our Lady, won't you?"

The words "your whole life" weighed heavily upon Yasugoro, but his main concern was rather the pain in his cheek. He couldn't very well say "stop it," and was surprised at this Western expression of affection. "Well then, I will receive him as a child of Our Lady," and Father Kolbe accepted the boy who smelled refreshingly of the sea!

Yasugoro parted from his father and uncle then and there. The building in which they were had just been completed in August, 1934. A reception hall, a religious items shop, and an assembly room were located on the first floor; the chapel was on the second floor. This was the third largest building in *Mugenzai no Sono*. There was another door at the end of the dark corridor. The sanctuary was behind the door and no woman was allowed to go there.

It was just about noon and lunch had begun in the dining room. As soon as Yasugoro entered, he felt weak at the knees. More than twenty big Polish friars with ruddy, bearded faces were there and they spoke gibberish! It was a strange sight which he witnessed for the first time. What surprised Yasugoro all the more was that he found among the friars Hideo Hatanaka, a boy from Hisakajima, the same island he came from. He wondered, "Why is he here?" On top of that, he was wearing a habit. He was one year older than Yasugoro and they had often played together at primary school and had swum together. More amazing was that he was speaking the European language!

It was as if Yasugoro had stepped into a cage of wolves. Yet in this very cage he found Hideo and was greatly relieved! Then he was somehow moved to tears and sniffled. Everybody laughed and said that he cried because he was homesick. But he himself told me that he had cried with astonishment at the strange new world he had jumped into.

His Senior Hideo Hatanaka

Even before Yasugoro entered the friary, Father Kolbe had his eye on his "Christian Island."

After the formal church had been erected and the facilities of the friary had been put into place through Father Kornel's efforts, Father Kolbe himself visited Hisakajima in the Goto Islands in October, 1934, in order to recruit candidates.

The first candidate was Hideo Hatanaka, who had been helping his father with net fishing after leaving elementary school. Having heard that a Franciscan priest had come from Nagasaki, Hideo went to see him. This was how he met Father Kolbe.

Father Kolbe made the following entry in his Nagasaki diary: "November 30th, Friday. At the beginning of the retreat of the liturgical year, Hideo Hatanaka came to the friary with his father. Hideo was born in 1920. I accepted this candidate when I said Mass in Eiri."

Father Kolbe's faith and love were planted in the hearts of the Japanese friars.

Hideo, having a small build, was called "Piotr" and was loved by the friars. Piotr is the Polish nickname for Peter. Piotr took the habit and the name of Dominic.

"I worked at the printing office. When I was selecting printing types, Father Kolbe came and greeted me saying 'Maria.' When he found me working alone, he came close to me and hugged my head tightly, saying, 'Let's devote ourselves entirely to Our Lady.' This often happened. As Father Kolbe himself had recruited me, I think he cherished me."

Hideo told me a secret, heartwarming story about Father Kolbe and a dog. It was winter when he entered the friary. One cold night, Father Kolbe heard someone tapping lightly at his door. "Who could it be at this hour?" He opened the door and found a dog at his feet. It must have tapped at his door with its tail. At first sight he knew that it would give birth soon. "Poor thing!" Its paws were trembling slightly. When he patted the dog, it pulled at the hem of his habit repeatedly. "Oh, all right," he took the dog to the printing office. He called Brother Gerard Radziewicz to come.

Brother Gerard, in charge of the printing office, appeared from between the machines and sprinted over to Father Kolbe. He was slim and tall and had a long stride. This twenty-one-year-old friar came with Brother Roman Kwiecień, Brother Mikołaj, and Brother Jacek on August 10, 1934. Five days after their arrival, the consecration of the church was carried out. He did not know Japanese yet. With the pregnant dog between them, Father Kolbe talked with Brother Gerard in Polish.

Brother Gerard, who was fond of animals since his childhood, was just the right person to look after a dog. He spread shreds of paper in a box and put the soon-to-be-mother into it. The dog fell asleep, presumably because she had warmed up. Dominic Hideo Hatanaka stared at how things were going. Before long, quite a few cute little puppies were born. Father Kolbe came to supervise and smiled with gentle eyes behind his glasses.

"Father Kolbe was gentle. But he too was a human being, so I thought he would have at least one fault. I never found one," said Hideo. And during the winter of the following year, a day came that Hideo would remember for the rest of his life.

The friars wore shoes all day long and also came into the room with their shoes on, as was the custom of Europeans. Hideo was not used to wearing shoes and in addition snow must have stuck to the soles of his shoes. Brother Hatanaka missed a step on the stairs going down from the third to the second floor. He slipped down with a loud thud, falling hard and fast.

He stopped just in front of Father Kolbe's room. "What happened?" Father Kolbe ran out of his room. Young Brother Hatanaka was in terrible pain but never let on. "Are you okay?" asked Father Kolbe anxiously. "I am okay," he answered smiling grimly, but in fact he was seriously hurt. Later they found out he had a slipped disc in his back.

A Brother Keeps a Dog

When we read a letter Father Kolbe wrote in those days, we can understand what his intention was regarding the vocations of the Japanese youth.

"Only the Japanese can further the propagation of the Faith in Japan — not we foreigners. The articles in *The Knights* are more effective with the Japanese when they are written by their compatriots, not by us foreigners. For this reason, I believe it is not appropriate to set up a Province with Polish fathers and brothers. We have to be rather the seeds for the formation of Japanese friars according to our spirit of consecration to the Immaculata. Only the Japanese can develop the work in their own country."

But it was no piece of cake to form Japanese candidates in the mission area. The first Japanese friar, Marian Shigeo Sato, who had entered the Order back in the Oura years, quit three years later. The religious life consists of one sacrifice after another. One cannot continue it without daily self-renunciation.

Yasugoro Nakamura was at first assigned to the section of printing types in the printing office. Together with Hideo Hatanaka he engaged himself in returning the types to their places silently all day long. But for Yasugoro who was from a farming family it was quite difficult to handle the printing types. Whenever he put the smallest types in their places, he got a headache from eye strain. The smell of ink and lead was disgusting. The noise of the printing machine made his head feel like it was stuck in a vise. Unable to endure it any longer, he eventually sat down at his desk with his head in his hands. Then Father Kolbe called him, "Maria! Do you have a headache? Are you tired? Please go to bed and rest."

Yasugoro had only known Father Kolbe for a little more than a month. There is a photo of him with Father Kolbe. Hideo Hatanaka is also in it with Yasugoro wearing a kimono with a splashed pattern. In total, there are four Japanese and three Koreans in the photo.

"We did common work called 'pospolita' at that time. The friary was surrounded by bushes. After lunch, all the friars cultivated the land in their habits. As we could not employ workers, we worked hard with shovels, pickaxes, and hammers during recess. I was very much impressed that they not only preached but that they also worked hard themselves."

On the other hand, Dominic Hideo Hatanaka suffered from acute lower back pain and unfortunately left the friary because of it. Though he had been recruited by Father Kolbe himself, his religious life continued only three years. In contrast, Yasugoro Nakamura persevered in his religious life. He was drafted during the war and suffered from lung disease. Nevertheless, he endured all the hardships with his mettle. He said, "I've never thought of leaving the friary." His parents who had encouraged him were already dead by then.

Having served as a catechist and a driver of a kindergarten bus, he presently (1982) works as a receptionist for the Knights of the Immaculata.

Among the friars there are many unique and cheerful ones as one often finds in the Franciscan order. But one can scarcely find anyone as special as Brother Gerard. He was assigned to the printing section by Father Kolbe when he came to Japan in 1934. From then until now (1982), he has been working in the printing section consistently without ever having changed his working place. This is a rare case!

Moreover, he has been engaged in the unpleasant task of waste disposal, distributing newspapers and letters, packaging and transporting items and various repairs. After having devoted himself wholeheartedly to his main printing work, he willingly works tirelessly as a receptionist at night without having a break. He has a very gentle voice. One more unusual thing is that he never returned to Poland.

Brother Gerard was very fond of animals, especially dogs.

"You have vacations. You had many chances to go home such as the Beatification of Father Kolbe or the 50th anniversary of your vows. Why didn't you go back?"

He always answered, "Stop it," which meant I'd better not ask such a thing. He is very fond of animals. Like Saint Francis he loves birds and insects and cherishes all living things. When insects stray into the corridor, he carefully takes them out. Cats and pigeons gather around him spontaneously. He likes dogs best of all — not small dogs but big ones! He has had several generations of German shepherd mutts. He lives with his dogs and speaks to them in Polish. Both of his dogs understand only Polish.

There is even a rumor that the reason he is unwilling to go abroad is that he cannot leave his dogs. What motivated him to keep dogs may have been Father Kolbe's directions to look after the pregnant dog on that cold winter night. Now he is nicknamed "the dog keeper."

NOTE: Bother Gerard died on April 11, 1986, at the age of seventy-three.

CHAPTER 27

Farewell to Japan

He would never again set foot on the soil of Nagasaki. He entrusted his fellow friars and boys to Our Lady, and then departed.

From Poor Poland

Poland, when written in Chinese characters, is the same word for turbulence, ups and downs, in Japanese. As this word suggests, Poland has been full of ups and downs throughout its history. At the time of Father Kolbe's birth, Poland was unfortunately divided among its neighboring countries and ceased to exist as a country. It was just after the First World War that Poland won independence as the People's Republic of Poland. But after that, Poland was invaded by the German army.

In the fall of 1971, I visited Father Kolbe's home country. After having participated in Father Kolbe's beatification ceremony at Saint Peter's Basilica in the Vatican, I visited the sites closely connected with him. I can never forget my first impression of Poland, a country in Eastern Europe: "Just unbelievable that Father Kolbe came all the way to Japan from such a poor country." I don't know whether the poverty was simply the reality of any socialist country or the specific result of the Soviet Union's exploitation. Food and daily necessities were scarce and even the state-run department stores were lacking many items. The attitude of sales clerks was business-like and cold. Horse-drawn carts moved slowly down the streets.

There were few automobiles and only five traffic lights at most, even in a big city. The poverty touched me deeply. How did Father Kolbe and other friars come to leave this poor country and throw themselves into Asia? It seemed to me a reckless adventure. It is not hard to imagine that Poland in the 1930s was even more impoverished than what I saw in 1971.

What Father Kolbe wrote in a letter of May, 1934, seems as if it were meant to take issue with my conclusion. It was addressed to a female student of a commercial school in Tarnów. "In Japan there are sixty-five million pagans. Catholics amount to a little more than one hundred thousand and there are only slightly more than two hundred priests. Here, material wealth is sufficient but what is that compared to spiritual poverty?" Certainly, what Father Kolbe means by spiritual poverty is the scarcity of the Catholic faith in Japan. In contrast, most of the population of Poland was Catholic and the people had an admirably strong faith. "But we do what we can do in order to lead the Japanese to salvation. For example, we print 60,000 copies of *The Knights* every month. It is a small number, but we cannot publish more for the time being. We trust the Immaculata, who sees our humble efforts and will make it possible for us to expand propagation through publication someday. In Japan the publishing business is highly developed. There are many publications in Japan. The Japanese people can be said to be '*rozczytana*.'"

He called the Japanese *rozczytana*, i.e., "reading a lot." We can see from this why he staked the realization of his dream on the publication of *The Knights*.

His argument was clear. He wrote: "The Immaculata is the Mediatrix of All Graces. Every conversion and sanctification is the work of grace. Therefore, the conversion and sanctification of people will be accomplished by their approaching the Immaculata as the Mediatrix of All Graces."

With this in mind, Father Kolbe, as an editor, sent a letter of request to priests all over Japan. "The purpose of publishing *The Knights* is to lead people to the Immaculata, the fountain of conversion and sanctification. I would appreciate it if you would advise me how we should go forward in terms of editorial work, production, or the most effective method of propagation." There is no document at all about how many responses came from the priests, or what kind of concrete advice they might have given him.

Farewell Excursion Cancelled Because of Rain

Everyone is happy to return to one's homeland. As early as March 1936, the year of the Provincial Chapter, Father Kolbe sent the first report to his mother: "Provided that a war doesn't break out, I will leave for Poland by ship in early June. If I have to take the Trans-Siberian Railway, I will leave at the end of June."

During his stay in Japan he went back to Poland three times. Although he attended the Provincial Chapter, which was held every three years in spite of the difficulties, he must have been very pleased to finally return to the country where his mother lived.

In April, 1936, the last year of his stay in Japan, Father Kolbe established the "Hongouchi Seminary" in cooperation with Father Kornel. Its purpose was to form the Japanese friars, and its rector was the twenty-eight year old Father Mirochna, who had just been ordained the previous year. He had been prone to illness when he was young but now his sufferings bore fruit.

"We had a feeling that Father Kolbe would never come back. Father Kolbe entrusted to me the editorship of *The Knights* and the education in the minor seminary. I was very young then. But I was Father Kolbe's pupil; he brought me to Japan and here I became a priest. I did my best out of gratitude for what he had done for me."

Father Mirochna was proficient in Japanese, and he visited Goto and Hirado to recruit boys for the minor seminary. Brother Romuald, whom Father Kolbe assigned as dormitory inspector, said,

"There was a minor seminary in the diocese. The religious orders had none of their own. Father Kolbe founded the first non-diocesan minor seminary. Many people noticed it. There was talk that there might not be any candidates because the boys would go to the diocesan seminary. Yet the first minor seminarians numbered nineteen. That was a large number! People saw our success, and another religious order also established a minor seminary. But we had the largest number of seminarians. I remember the total number reached 118."

Of course, it was after the Second World War when the number reached 118. Seven out of the first nineteen seminarians became priests. I think the percentage was quite high. There are three photos of Father Kolbe with the seminarians, very valuable historical documents.

Father Kolbe was photographed with Polish friars before his return to Poland.

The friars decided to hold the friary's farewell party for Father Kolbe at Mt. Unzen. "It was a luxury in those days to go all the way to Mt. Unzen," Brother Yasugoro Nakamura said, looking back on that time. "All the friars were to go by bus. It would cost a lot. Father Kolbe nevertheless said, 'Let's go.' He knew that this would be the final farewell. He said, 'Let's confide in the Immaculata. If the weather is fine, she wants the excursion. If it rains, she doesn't want it.' It rained heavily on the day, so the Immaculata didn't want it."

If it rains, the Immaculata doesn't want it. That is a very Father Kolbe way of thinking.

On April 5th, Father Kornel left for Poland via the USA. He did not intend to return to Japan again. He had come to Japan in order to help Father Kolbe, but he had no intention to die and be buried in Japan. Anyway, he had served his three-year term. He built the church and founded the minor seminary. He also had contributed to the economic life of the friary. He thought it was enough.

Father Kolbe was to depart for home on May 23rd, a little ahead of schedule. In February, Father Gracjan and another brother came to Nagasaki in place of the two priests.

On the day of departure, the friars and minor seminarians went to see Father Kolbe off at the Dejima wharf. The two young candidates, Yasugoro Nakamura and Hideo Hatanaka, walked down the slope toward the wharf. When they got to the police station of Hotarujaya, a taxi caught up with them. Father Kolbe and Father Gracjan were in it.

Father Kolbe said, "Get in," and to their good fortune, they were able to sit beside him. Yasugoro came into close personal contact with Father Kolbe then.

I looked into the newspapers relating to that time in the Nagasaki Prefectural Library, wondering, "What was the ship Father Kolbe boarded to depart from Nagasaki? I know he arrived in Nagasaki on the *Nagasaki-maru*." May 23rd was a Saturday and the newspaper said that the *Shanghai-maru* of the Japan Mail Steamship Company left for Shanghai at one o'clock that day. I also found an article in the same newspaper stating that Father Kolbe had applied for permission to establish a minor seminary in Hongouchi. "The term of study covers four years. Subjects equivalent to those taught in junior high school will be taught. Its purpose is to let the student attain spiritual peace based on the truth and to form persons with loyalty, patriotism, and integrity of knowledge and virtue." We can easily perceive the spirit of those days here. When I read the newspapers around the date, I saw headlines such as "The Great Reform of Prime Minister Mussolini" and sensed the turbulent atmosphere of an era heading for war.

The City of Nagasaki Seen Through Tears

Father Kolbe presumably left Nagasaki with great reluctance. Three priests, seventeen brothers, and eight candidates from Japan and Korea remained in *Mugenzai no Sono*. In addition, he entrusted

Father Kolbe was looking at Japan from the Shanghai-maru *for a long time.*

nineteen cherubic boys and 63,000 monthly copies of *The Knights* to Father Mirochna.

Brother Sergiusz told me that it was very hard for him to part with Father Kolbe. "Father Kolbe loved Japan and the Japanese people from the bottom of his heart. He said he wanted to die and be buried in Japan, this country of martyrs. He wished to come back again, if possible. But we anticipated that he would not be able to come back, judging from the overall situation. However, as the Provincial Chapter was still ahead, we could not be sure of it. Father Kolbe used to say that the Immaculata would take care of everything."

The *Shanghai-maru* pulled away from the wharf. It gradually sailed away from the city of Nagasaki. Tears blurred his eyes behind his glasses. The idea would have crossed his mind that he could never come back to Japan. We can perceive a part of his feeling in the letter he wrote to *Mugenzai no Sono* from Shanghai. "As I was sailing farther and farther away from the coast, this thought came to my mind: 'Maybe I am looking at this land for the last time in this world.' Then I got moved to tears spontaneously. But children,

Farewell to Mugenzai no Sono — *Niepokalanów in Japan. (1936)*

remember that it is all for the Immaculata. The true Niepokalanów will be only in Heaven."

On May 26th, he transferred to another ship in Shanghai and sailed off again. When he landed in Naples, he learned Father Bede Hess had been selected as Minister General of the Order of Friars Minor Conventual. Then he participated in the Provincial Chapter held in Kraków, Poland, from July 13th to 16th. In this conference, Father Kolbe suggested the establishment of another Niepokalanów in Korea.

At the Chapter, Father Kolbe was appointed Guardian of Niepokalanów in Poland. Many friars in Poland had hoped for this. Father Kolbe would not return to Japan. After this conference he would only live five more years. Soon thereafter, both Japan and Poland were plunged into war.

"We missed Father Kolbe very much," said Brother Sergiusz, shaking his head. "For a while he gave us spiritual guidance through his letters from Poland. It was a great encouragement for our spiritual life. The reason why we loved Father Kolbe was that he loved us all equally and, what is more, very deeply. Whether one was a priest, a brother, Catholic or non-Catholic, he loved one as a brother or sister created by God, without distinction or partiality. His charm lay exactly in this fact.

"Finally, I want to share with you Father Kolbe's unforgettable words. He said, 'When I die, please forget everything about me. Instead, please think about the Immaculata and never forget her even for a moment.'"

Father Kolbe shaved his beard off after he went back to his homeland. He also recommended the friars to shave off their beards upon leaving Nagasaki. Up to then they grew beards after the image of an Asian sage. But in Poland, beards were not so popular and people did not wear beards, with the exception of the Jewish men. It was because they had heard that Asian sages wore beards, so they just imitated them.

Beards had even become a symbol of Father Kolbe. Of course, some friars were against growing beards. Some could not grow a thick beard, and others just regarded them as bothersome or messy.

When they arrived in Nagasaki, they were still weighing the pros and cons of wearing a beard. Therefore, Father Kolbe asked for the Provincial's advice. His answer was: "You should let your beards grow for the time being."

During the six years Father Kolbe was in Nagasaki, four priests, four seminarians, and twenty brothers came to Nagasaki from Poland. As the number of the friars increased, the issue of growing beards was brought up again. Before his return to Poland, Father Kolbe held a conference and put this dispute to rest. He wrote in a letter, "On May 20th, the conference of the friary, carefully considering the current situation in Japan, decided to prohibit growing beards and to require those who grow beards to shave them off entirely, but the elderly may do as they wish." Brother Zeno kept his beard to the end.

Later on, the Polish friars who had remained in Japan came to face various problems during the Second World War: pressure from the military, lack of food, prohibition of publication, closure of the minor seminary, etc. During that time, Father Kolbe died in the Nazi concentration camp of Auschwitz in August, 1941.

In 1943, a postcard came from East Europe to *Mugenzai no Sono* to inform the friars of Father Kolbe's death, but the details of his death were still unknown.

In 1945, following the Second World War, a detailed report that the merciful Father Kolbe went into the starvation bunker in place of a father reached Nagasaki. The friars who remained in Japan were greatly saddened at the news.

Poland was still a country of ups and downs even after the war. Although a Catholic country, Poland had adopted a communist system under the influence of the Soviet Union. Although the political system seemed complicated, the sky at night was just as clear and beautiful as ever!

I was fascinated by the beautiful sky full of stars in this Eastern European country. It was probably due to a clear atmosphere without pollutants. I had never seen so many stars and such big stars! Carrying on Father Kolbe's spirit, Brother Zeno and a dozen friars remained in Japan. It was not until more than twenty-five years later, after the Pacific War had ended, that they could see the stars in the skies of their homeland again.

NOTE: Father Kornel Czupryk passed away in the friary of Radomsko in Poland on June 6, 1988, at the age of ninety-eight.

CHAPTER 28

The Promise of Heaven

My visit to the Lourdes grotto in the hills behind the friary, to which my mother took me, was the turning point in my life.

The Secret on Christmas Night

During a long life, there will be secrets which one cannot tell anyone. In many cases, secrets cover up something dirty. Most secrets are kept to oneself in order to conceal shame.

Father Kolbe also had a secret. But in his case, it was not covering up something dirty in his life, but something sweet. It was during the Christmas season after he had ended his sixth year of missionary publication work in Nagasaki and had returned to Poland that he dared to confide it to his fellow friars. He had returned to Poland in May, 1936, so this means he revealed his secret some seven months later.

At Niepokalanów, a nativity play was put on every year by the friars and minor seminarians on Sunday evenings during the Christmas season to celebrate the birth of Christ. That year, the other friars went to see the play as usual. Before the play started, Father Kolbe said, "If anyone wants to be with me, please remain here in the dining room." A dozen senior priests and friars stayed behind.

Then, Father Kolbe began to open up in an atmosphere reminiscent of Christ's Last Supper. He said that terrible sufferings would come soon; and however the world might change, whatever sufferings might afflict them, they should never forget the Immaculata. Then he said, "Continue to love the Immaculata. My dear children, I am very happy now. Even though we face many difficulties and contradictions in life, we can enjoy great happiness and peace even in this world."

Father Kolbe continued speaking, with love overflowing in his eyes behind his round-shaped glasses. "I want to confide a secret to you. The Immaculata promised me that I would go to Heaven for sure."

At that moment, utterances of surprise and joy filled the room. Of course everyone's attention focused on the promise of Heaven. "Father Kolbe, would you let us know more precisely about that? When and where did you receive this blessing?"

Father Kolbe was tight lipped; but pressed by everyone, he finally spoke up.

"I was granted this special blessing when I was in Nagasaki."

He wouldn't say any more than that. When I heard this story from a Polish friar, I became very interested in knowing when and where in Nagasaki he received this special blessing.

I tried to imagine the grounds and the layout of the friary in the era of Father Kolbe. If Our Lady promised him Heaven, it must have happened when Father Kolbe faced his most difficult time. In other words, the invitation to Heaven cannot be easily separated from "the sufferings through love." We do not look for the consolations of Heaven when we are leading an easy and satisfied life or an affluent life. Well then, when would Father Kolbe have had the hardest time? I asked a few Polish friars what they thought about it deep in their hearts.

To Lourdes in the Hills behind the Friary

Brother Romuald, a veteran friar, said with confidence, "That was when Father Kolbe was in Oura. We had the hardest time in Oura. Those who had gathered for a conference of Catholic publishers tried to stop the publication of *The Knights of the Immaculata*. That was a big problem."

Certainly, there was such slander. As Father Kolbe was totally committed to the missionary work through publication, the aggressive opposition must have broken his heart. But I do not at all believe that he received the special blessing during the Oura period, which was when they had just arrived. The hard times must have come later.

I suppose it was the time when Father Kolbe opened the Garden of the Immaculata (*Mugenzai no Sono*) at Hongouchi. At that time friars, including a young priest, left Nagasaki for home, and seminarians betrayed him. He was in such a terrible shock that he was laid up in bed for several days. This was the time of his greatest hardships. His room, which is now housed in the Kolbe Museum in Nagasaki, is where I believe he received the promise of Heaven.

In this simple room which is permeated with the fragrance of Father Kolbe, we can perceive the faint breath of the Queen of Heaven. Brother Sergiusz has a different view: the promise of Heaven is, so to speak, God's invitation to Himself. When do people become aware of such an invitation?

It is when they reflect in their solitude.

When people come into contact with solitude as a real existence that runs deep throughout their life, they discover God. The Lourdes grotto in the hills behind the friary, suffused with solitude, is the best place for being absorbed in prayer. Father Kolbe went there every day. He prayed to the Immaculata in solitude and contemplated God. This was the nearest place to Heaven for him. He left all his troubles and worries in the friary and talked to Mary intimately, without being disturbed by anyone.

Brother Sergiusz witnessed these things and he says, "I think Father Kolbe received the promise of Heaven at the Lourdes grotto."

The Lourdes grotto that Father Kolbe built in Nagasaki offers a quiet place for prayer today.

Well, he may be right. Father Kolbe and the Immaculata may have been united firmly in this place in the quiet hills behind the friary where no human voice could be heard. Father Kolbe built the Lourdes grotto in Nagasaki and modeled it after Lourdes in France, the famous Marian pilgrimage site known for its miraculous healing water. The grotto remains a legacy from Father Kolbe who deeply loved Japan and the Japanese people.

Instead of a Postscript

During the Pacific War, I lived with my mother in Nagasaki. I visited the Lourdes grotto in the friary of the Knights of the Immaculata accompanied by this devout woman, who was a descendant of the hidden Catholics of Urakami. This visit became a turning point in my life. As it was wartime and I was lonely with no one else at home but my mother, I often visited the friary by myself.

As a boy in 1943, I thought the lives of the Polish friars seemed strange. When I look back on those days, the spirit of Father Kolbe still seems to have remained there. Here are some of my memories of that time.

Brother Ozaki's mother often visited the Lourdes grotto with her son.

At first the Franciscan habits struck me as odd. They were somewhat different from the soutanes which the diocesan priests wore. The Franciscans wore white cords around their waists and hooded capes over their shoulders.

The Polish people were big! Although they spoke halting Japanese, they talked in a friendly way and they were very tender-hearted. As I hardly went out during the war, they became my main companions. I was struck by their total devotion to Mary. They displayed beautifully the statue of the Immaculata in the church and in every room as well, and put great importance on the religious life. The friars' demeanor when they prayed together was also wonderful! The altar was decorated with many flowers and people sang many beautiful hymns at Benediction, in spite of the wartime.

These Polish friars had just published a magazine in Japanese. Now the publication was banned and there were old, blue copies of the magazine lying around. They seemed not to have much money for daily life. They neither drank alcohol nor smoked cigarettes. Their house was humble and all the desks, chairs, and shelves were handmade.

The friars worked silently by themselves. They came all the way from Poland to Japan. I found a kind of tenacious toughness in them. Leaving the future to divine providence, they extended a hand to people in trouble. These Westerners had a zeal that most Japanese lacked.

Blue eyes dazzled me as a boy. In those days there were no homes around the friary. I would climb the hill to visit them, all the while feeling that the dwelling of these foreign friars was far from the dust and dirt of the town below.

Soon I became accustomed to visiting the friary of the Knights of the Immaculata. I started sweeping out the Lourdes grotto by myself and helping the friars make religious statues, and I even stayed overnight with them once in a while. When we approached the reception desk of the friary, Brother Zeno would welcome us and call my mother "elder sister."

Perhaps my mother seemed very young to Brother Zeno, despite the fact that her life was full of struggles after my father died of a disease during my elementary school days.

It was Father Mirochna who was especially kind to my mother and me. He once said to us, "In the time of Father Kolbe this place was called the Garden of the Immaculata (*Mugenzai no Sono*). But Japanese people felt uneasy with this name. Some interpreted *Mugenzai no Sono* as the garden of 'infinite sins (*mugenzai*).' So we call it the Knights of the Immaculata to avoid misunderstanding."

One evening, as I climbed up the hill to visit the Lourdes grotto, I heard friars and minor seminarians singing a Marian litany in Latin in front of the statue of the Blessed Virgin Mary. I was fascinated with its melody. I was strangely attracted to the song and thought, "I want to sing the Latin hymn like the minor seminarians do." When I confided this to Father Mirochna, he extended his arms and gladly accepted my offer: "Of course you can! Come to us. We are waiting for you."

I talked it over with my mother and she gave me her permission: "I am a widow and you are my only child. But if you want to go to the Blessed Virgin Mary, I will offer you to her." But my relatives opposed my proposal. They questioned whether it was God's will to leave my own mother and go to the seminary or whether living in a family was not more important?

I was not willing to ignore their opposition and enter the seminary. I felt very sorry for Father Mirochna, because I had promised him that I would go. As it pained me to see him face-to-face thereafter, I seldom visited the friary.

After that, I started working in the arsenal in Urakami. In the summer of 1945, I was a hot-blooded youth of seventeen. After work one day, I was going to have to fight with one mechanic who worked with me. This was an inevitable fight, since I could not possibly get along with him.

Then the atomic bomb exploded!

So much for my anticipated fight! Having entirely forgotten it, I ran about trying to escape from the horrific destruction. Fortunately, I was not injured, so I was able to make my way out of the arsenal and wandered about aimlessly.

I stepped over the dead and dying. "Please help me! Take me to the hospital, please." Many people stretched out their hands to me in desperation! I brushed their hands off and continued to wander about on the devastated land in a daze.

I had no way of helping others. It was all I could do to stay alive myself. When I ran toward the hills, I came across the mechanic boy with whom I promised to fight. He was seriously wounded in the stomach and lay in agony. "You deserve it!" I looked down on him with such disdain. Whenever I reflect on my attitude then, my heart aches.

After I had wandered about the atomic wasteland for two months, I finally joined the Knights of the Immaculata. The motive for my joining was that I was greatly shocked by the atomic bomb on one hand, and I remembered the promise I had made to Father Mirochna on the other. I could not enter the Knights of the Immaculata while my mother was alive. I was now free to do so, because she had been called to Heaven. As if they had a mind of their own, my feet just took me up the hilly road to the friary.

Autumn rain fell softly that day. Without an umbrella I got soaked to the skin and knocked on the door of the Knights of the Immaculata. Brother Zeno came out and asked, "Where is your elder sister?"

"She died in the atomic blast," I answered.

"What a pitiful boy!" Brother Zeno said, as he wiped my face.

That is how I joined the Knights of the Immaculata, and then I heard the story of Father Kolbe.

Father Kolbe was thrown into a starvation bunker in the concentration camp of Auschwitz and offered his life for a family man!

Father Kolbe who truly lived love!

Whenever I heard his story, I was struck by the difference between his greatness and what I was. Father Kolbe was forty-seven and I was still seventeen. But thirty years' difference in age was not the problem. I had run about in the atomic wasteland in order to preserve my own life. Though he experienced the war as I did, he gave up his precious life for a total stranger.

I came to admire Father Kolbe totally. After I became a member of the Knights of the Immaculata, I went to the minor seminary which Father Kolbe had founded.

More than ten friars who had lived with Father Kolbe were still alive. I became interested in his life when I was in the seminary, and I wrote down their memories one after another. During these interviews my image of Father Kolbe became more and more vivid.

After I had graduated from the minor seminary, I started seminarian training, as I wanted to be a priest. But in this most important period, I contracted tuberculosis and was forced to spend a long time recuperating. After that, I became a friar. Meanwhile, the one-story, wooden printing office, the three-story friary, the church, and the baking room were all torn down, and new buildings were put up in their place.

Time flies! When I first learned about Father Kolbe, I was seventeen years old. Now without having noticed it, I have lived longer than he did.

When summer arrives each year, my heart aches as usual.

What was terrible in my atomic bombing experience was not its destructive power, but the misery I witnessed as children deserted their parents, and elder siblings their younger ones, and they all just ran away. The uninjured such as myself regarded the symptoms of atomic-bomb sickness as infectious and left those affected, even our own parents, behind in the dark trenches in the mountains, in order to protect ourselves. We thought that we would lose our hair, have diarrhea, and our gums would bleed if we did not isolate ourselves from them.

It is quite true that we had no other option in the atomic wasteland since there were no medical doctors, but it was nevertheless a cruel way to behave. I still hear them cry:

"Don't desert us!"

"Please love us!"

What was terrible for me was that the entire Urakami neighborhood fell into such a miserable state. If another atomic bomb should be dropped and I found myself again in the atomic wasteland, would I flee again? Would I turn my back on injured people, desert friends, and look down coldly on my fellow worker whom I was supposed to fight?

I cannot say for certain.

But now that I know of Father Kolbe's life in Nagasaki and of his entire life of love, maybe — just maybe — I would plant my feet there and not abandon them.

Afterword

It was December 13, 2018, when I visited Friar Tomei Ozaki at the Saint Kolbe Memorial Museum, which is located beside the Friary of the Knights of the Immaculata (formerly called *Mugenzai no Sono*) in Nagasaki City. I was invited by him and we had a heart-to-heart talk about Father Kolbe. He showed me many documents he himself had collected during his lifelong inquiry into Father Kolbe's life. In the reception room where the portrait of Father Kolbe was hung, he spoke passionately about the need for a good study of Father Kolbe. He hoped that through such a study many people would become better acquainted with Father Kolbe. After the meeting, Friar Ozaki's remarks weighed heavily on my heart.

Father Kolbe is my beloved saint. I have been familiar with him for a long time, because my grandmother was a subscriber to *The Knights of the Immaculata*. I have often visited Saint Kolbe Chapel in Hongouchi Church, situated in the Friary of the Knights of the Immaculata.

There is another reason that I could not but take Friar Ozaki's suggestion seriously. The morning of December 13th, when I talked with him, it was still the evening of December 12th, the Feast of Our Lady of Guadalupe, in Mexico. Our Lady of Guadalupe is very important to Nagasaki Junshin Catholic University where I work, because Bishop Hayasaka, who had accepted Father Kolbe in Nagasaki Diocese, entrusted the image of Our Lady of Guadalupe to the sisters who run our university, back when Father Kolbe was still in Nagasaki.

After thinking the matter over, I decided to translate Friar Ozaki's "Father Kolbe in Nagasaki" into English, hoping that through this English translation Friar Ozaki's book, which vividly illustrates Father Kolbe's life in Nagasaki, will reach more readers in the English-speaking world.

I would not have accomplished this translation with my limited abilities if Professor Kevin Doak of Georgetown University had not offered me his help. He is not only one of the most famous Japanologists in the USA, but also the English translator of *Miracles*, a novel about Father Kolbe written by the famous Japanese writer, Ayako Sono. I would like to express my heart-felt thanks to this most reliable collaborator and supervisor of this project.

I also thank Father Masatoshi Yamaguchi OFM Conv., the editor-in-chief of *The Knights of Immaculata*, still published in Nagasaki, who kindly provided us with invaluable old photographs of Father Kolbe and the Polish friars.

I also want to express my sincere gratitude to Mrs. Therese Doak, who read the whole translation through and gave me many important suggestions for improvement.

May I finally offer sincere thanks to all the people involved in the Academy of the Immaculate who decided to publish this book, edited and printed it, and proofread my manuscripts.

ON THE FEAST OF OUR LADY OF GUADALUPE, 2020, NAGASAKI
Shinichiro Araki
NAGASAKI JUNSHIN CATHOLIC UNIVERSITY

Introduction of Author, Translator, and Supervisor

Author

Tomei Ozaki (real name: Koichi Tagawa) was a friar of the Order of Friars Minor Conventual (OFM Conv.). He was born in North Korea in 1928. His family came back to Nagasaki in 1941. He was in the atomic blast in Nagasaki on August 9, 1945, and two months later he was accepted into the friary of the Knights of the Immaculata founded by Father Maximilian Kolbe. He was the chief editor of *The Knights of the Immaculata* and then worked as the director of the Saint Kolbe Museum in Nagasaki. He was the author of several books. *Father Kolbe in Nagasaki* and *Love of Sacrifice* that deals with Father Kolbe's sacrifice, are his major works.

He passed away on April 15, 2021.

Translator

Shinichiro Araki is a professor of Education at Nagasaki Junshin Catholic University in Japan. He is also director of the University's Institute of Christian Culture. He translated Jacques Maritain's *Education at the Crossroads* into Japanese. He also translated into German the Japanese version of the biography of the Servant of God Takashi Nagai, a Japanese Catholic doctor who was close to Father Kolbe and survived the atomic bombing.

Supervisor

Kevin M Doak holds the Nippon Foundation Endowed Chair in Japanese Studies at Georgetown University, Washington, D.C. He has written widely on modern Japanese literature, culture, and thought, and has extensive experience supervising translations from Japanese, especially for the Japan Library Series of the Japan Publishing Industry Foundation for Culture. Among his own English translations are Sono Ayako's monograph on Maximilian Kolbe, *Miracles* (MerwinAsia, 2016) and, with J. Scott Matthews, Akutagawa Ryūnosuke's "The Man from the West," *Monumenta Nipponica* (2011).

Academy of the Immaculate

The Academy of the Immaculate, founded in 1992, is inspired by and based on a project of St. Maximilian Kolbe (never realized by the Saint because of his death by martyrdom at the age of 47, August 14, 1941). Among its goals, the Academy seeks to promote, at every level, the study of the Mystery of the Immaculate Conception and the universal maternal mediation of the Virgin Mother of God, and to sponsor publications and dissemination of the fruits of this research in every way possible.

The Academy of the Immaculate is a non-profit religious-charitable organization of the Roman Catholic Church, a 501(c)(3), incorporated under the laws of the Commonwealth of Massachusetts, with its central office at Our Lady's Chapel, POB 3003, New Bedford, MA 02741.

Special rates are available with a 25% to 60% discount depending on the number of books plus postage. For ordering books and further information on rates to book stores, schools, and parishes contact:

Academy of the Immaculate
P.O. Box 3003, New Bedford, MA 02741
Phone (888)90.MARIA [888.90.62742]
E-mail academy@marymediatrix.com.

Quotations on bulk rates by the box, shipped directly from the printery, contact:

Franciscans of the Immaculate
P.O. Box 3003, New Bedford, MA 02741
(508)996-8274
E-mail: fi-academy@marymediatrix.com.

Facebook.com/*AcademyoftheImmaculate*
Online shopping: *AcademyoftheImmaculate.com*

Made in the USA
Las Vegas, NV
28 November 2022